THE VIETNAM WAR

THE VIETNAM WAR

An International History in Documents

Edited by
MARK ATWOOD LAWRENCE

New York Oxford
OXFORD UNIVERSITY PRESS

Oxford University Press is a department of the University of Oxford.
It furthers the University's objective of excellence in research,
scholarship, and education by publishing worldwide.

Oxford   New York
Auckland   Cape Town   Dar es Salaam   Hong Kong   Karachi
Kuala Lumpur   Madrid   Melbourne   Mexico City   Nairobi
New Delhi   Shanghai   Taipei   Toronto

With offices in
Argentina   Austria   Brazil   Chile   Czech Republic   France   Greece
Guatemala   Hungary   Italy   Japan   Poland   Portugal   Singapore
South Korea   Switzerland   Thailand   Turkey   Ukraine   Vietnam

For titles covered by Section 112 of the US Higher Education
Opportunity Act, please visit www.oup.com/us/he for the latest
information about pricing and alternate formats.

Published in the United States of America by Oxford University Press
198 Madison Avenue, New York, NY 10016
http://www.oup.com

Library of Congress Cataloging-in-Publication Data
The Vietnam War : an international history in documents / edited by Mark Atwood Lawrence.
    pages cm
  Includes index.
  ISBN 978-0-19-992440-0
1. Vietnam War, 1961–1975--Sources. 2. Vietnam War, 1961–1975--United States--Sources.
I. Lawrence, Mark Atwood, editor.
  DS557.4.V575 2014
  959.704'3--dc23
                                                        2013046092

Printing number: 9 8 7 6 5 4 3 2 1

Printed in the United States of America
on acid-free paper

CONTENTS

ABOUT THE EDITOR

MARK ATWOOD LAWRENCE is Associate Professor of History and Distinguished Fellow at the Robert S. Strauss Center for International Security and Law at the University of Texas at Austin. He earned his BA in history from Stanford University in 1988 and his MA, also from Stanford, in 1989. He then worked for two and a half years as a correspondent for the Associated Press in Brussels and Strasbourg. In 1992, he returned to graduate school as a doctoral student at Yale University, where he earned his PhD in history in 1998. Lawrence held a John M. Olin postdoctoral fellowship in international security studies in 1998–1999 and taught as a lecturer in the Yale Department of History in 1998–1999 and 1999–2000. He was appointed Assistant Professor of history at UT-Austin in 2000. There, he teaches a range of courses in international history and the history of U.S. foreign relations. In 2005, he was awarded the President's Associates' Award for Teaching Excellence. Lawrence is author of *Assuming the Burden: Europe and the American Commitment to War in Vietnam* (University of California Press, 2005), which won two awards from the American Historical Association: the Paul Birdsall Prize for European military and strategic history and the George Louis Beer Prize for European international history. His second book is *The Vietnam War: A Concise International History* (Oxford University Press, 2005), which was selected by the History Book Club and the Military History Book Club. Lawrence is also co-editor (with Fredrik Logevall of Cornell University) of *The First Vietnam War: Colonial Conflict and Cold War Crisis*, a volume of essays about the French war in Indochina (Harvard University Press, 2007), and of *The New York Times' Twentieth Century in Review: The Vietnam War* (Fitzroy-Dearborn, 2002), a collection of *Times* reporting related to the Vietnam conflict. He is currently at work on a study of U.S. policymaking regarding the developing world in the 1960s. In the 2011–2012 academic year, he was the Stanley Kaplan Visiting Professor of American Foreign Relations at Williams College.

PREFACE

ON JANUARY 9, 2007, Senator Edward M. Kennedy stepped to the podium at the National Press Club in Washington, D.C., and assessed America's ongoing war in Iraq in words certain to grab the nation's attention. "Iraq," Kennedy declared, "is George Bush's Vietnam." The speech came amid ferocious debate in Washington and across the country about the Bush administration's plan to resolve the war in Iraq, a grueling and bloody affair despite nearly four years of fighting, not by drawing down U.S. troops but through a "surge" in the number of American combat troops in the region. The Massachusetts Democrat insisted that George W. Bush, just like Lyndon Johnson four decades earlier, was responding to frustration by doubling down on a failed enterprise. "In Vietnam," Kennedy said, "the White House grew increasingly obsessed with victory, and increasingly divorced from the will of the people and rational policy." In the end, he added, more than 58,000 American died in a quest for unachievable objectives.

A few months later, President Bush responded in kind as he sought to convince Americans to support his escalatory policy in Iraq despite the difficulties that had befallen U.S. troops up to that point. In Vietnam, just as in Iraq, Bush asserted, "people argued that the real problem was America's presence and that if we would just withdraw, the killing would end." In fact, said Bush, the problem in Vietnam was that weak-willed Americans prevented U.S. troops from using sufficient force and demanded their withdrawal before they could achieve goals that were within reach. The result was nothing less than catastrophe: "One unmistakable legacy of Vietnam," Bush concluded, "is that the price of America's withdrawal was paid by millions of innocent citizens whose agonies would add to our vocabulary new terms like 'boat people,' 're-education camps,' and 'killing fields.'"

This debate—featured in Chapter 10 of this book—demonstrates the intensity of the controversies that still swirl around the Vietnam War several decades after it ended. Why did U.S. leaders escalate American involvement and keep fighting despite the problems they encountered? Would the war have been winnable in any meaningful sense if Americans had made different decisions about how to wage it?

Did U.S. leaders snatch defeat from the jaws of victory by withdrawing American troops in the early 1970s? Scholars and other commentators will likely continue to debate these questions for many years to come.

The dueling speeches from 2007 also underscore the remarkable relevance of the Vietnam War for American politics and foreign policy in the twenty-first century. Both Kennedy and Bush understood that the war could be a powerful rhetorical device to mobilize Americans by tapping into strongly held views about the reasons for America's defeat. They recognized as well that the war remained a widely acknowledged point of comparison in the United States for thinking about whether and how to mount military interventions abroad. For some Americans, the main lesson of the lost war is that the United States should be extremely cautious about undertaking military commitments in distant, culturally alien places. For others, the key takeaway is that the United States, once it decides to intervene overseas, must fight with maximum force and see its commitments through to the end. Policymakers will no doubt continue to invoke contrasting lessons of the war far into the future.

The Vietnam War remains, then, both contentious and consequential—a subject of great interest for scholars but also a matter of enduring significance in politics and policymaking. Studying the war is both a fascinating intellectual undertaking and an exercise in civic responsibility. Yet exploring the history of the war is no simple task, clouded as that history is by generations of polemics and persistent uncertainty about the motives and objectives of leaders on all sides. And then there is the problem of sheer scale. According to one recent estimate, more than 30,000 books have been published about the war, a number that will no doubt grow to even more staggering heights as authors gain access to new sources and open new lines of inquiry. A great deal of this work is— and surely will be—of exceedingly high quality, the result of prodigious research and sharp insight. Still, newcomers to the history of the war, and perhaps even readers with a good deal of background, may be forgiven for feeling overwhelmed.

This book is inspired by a belief that one useful way to study the war is to explore the original documentary record, the raw material of history. Examining the memoranda, speeches, reminiscences, manifestos, cartoons, photographs, and other kinds of material produced in the past carries myriad benefits. Such documents bring history alive by conveying the passions and controversies that surrounded the war as it was unfolding, giving readers a visceral as well as intellectual connection to the past. Reading original material also enables us to glimpse history without the filter of latter-day judgments, no small consideration given the tendency of politicians and polemicists to manipulate the history of the war for partisan benefit. Viewing the past with fresh eyes helps us not only to understand the past but also to evaluate claims about the past made in the present. In the best case, reading documents enables us to think for ourselves and form our own judgments.

The following ten chapters collect sixty-seven primary-source documents stretching from the early days of Vietnamese nationalism and communism at the start of the twentieth century to debates over the lessons and legacies of the war in the early twenty-first. I divide this material into ten chapters that conform to the way in which historians have usually narrated the war. That is, the breaking points between chapters correspond to moments generally recognized as the major watersheds. These moments include, for example, the Geneva peace settlement of 1954, the introduction of American combat troops in 1965, and the Tet Offensive in 1968. By following this approach, I do not mean to suggest that there is no other reasonable way to carve up the war into distinct periods; rather, my intention is to make it easy for readers to use this book alongside any of the widely available texts focused on the American war in Vietnam, including—but certainly not limited to—my own *The Vietnam War: A Concise International History*, published by Oxford University Press.

Despite the simplicity of the book's basic structure, compiling this collection involved tremendous challenges. Most daunting was the simple question of what to include. In part, the problem was sheer abundance of possibilities. The amount of primary material connected to the history of the Vietnam War boggles the mind, making the number of books on the subject seem quaint by comparison. On the American side alone, the mass of documentation is stunning. Taking into account the perspectives of other nations makes the problem infinitely greater, not least because archives in China, Russia, Eastern Europe, and Vietnam have partially opened their doors to historians in recent years. The challenge of this book also lay in defining the central goals of the collection. Should the book concentrate on particular aspects of the war or cover a broad array of themes and topics? Should it focus on the American experience or encompass other national perspectives as well? Should it include a relatively large number of extensively edited documents, or should it collect a smaller number of documents subjected to relatively little cutting? Different answers would yield very different books.

In the end, I followed five basic principles in selecting material to include. These principles sit at the heart of the book and differentiate it from other document collections, many of them superb, that have been published over the years. First, as the subtitle makes clear, the book includes material not just from the United States but also from other countries that were deeply involved in the war, including especially North and South Vietnam. To be sure, half of the book consists of documents reflecting American points of view. This emphasis flows from my belief that most readers of this book will come to the subject interested mainly in the U.S. experience in Indochina. Yet, like many scholars of the war, I am equally convinced that a full understanding of the war depends on viewing it as an episode in world history rather than simply U.S. history. The war, after all, reflected the most important global currents of the twentieth century: the breakdown of colonial empires, the rise of nationalism in the developing world, the tension between tradition and modernity, and the clash between communism and free-market capitalism as systems for organizing life in newly independent societies. Even readers interested narrowly in the U.S. dimension must acknowledge, I believe, that evaluating the U.S. role depends on appreciating the larger international context within which Americans took an interest in Vietnam and ultimately went to war.

For these reasons, the book includes numerous documents from Vietnam and a handful from China, Europe, and elsewhere. Items reflecting South Vietnamese experiences deserve special mention since this sort of material has often been missing from collections of primary sources on the war. My hope is that this book both reflects and contributes to a trend among scholars in recent years to set aside old caricatures of South Vietnam as a mere puppet of the United States and think seriously about the country in whose name the United States went to war.

Second, the collection sets the American war in Vietnam in a broad chronological frame. Unquestionably, I was tempted to focus on the period from 1959 to 1975, the years in which the United States was most heavily involved in Indochina. But there is much to be learned by viewing this period within the longer flow of time. Examining the roots of Vietnamese nationalism and communism in the early years of the century helps explain why a powerful insurgency emerged in the 1940s and 1950s. Similarly, attention to the colonial war between Vietnamese revolutionaries and France between 1946 and 1954 illuminates the process by which fighting in Indochina emerged as an international crisis and lays out the immediate background of the new war that broke out in the late 1950s. Exploring attempts to extract lessons from the war and cope with its legacies in the years since 1975, moreover, demonstrates the enduring importance of the controversies that the conflict generated.

Third, this book blends well-known documents—what one might call "classics" that have been published repeatedly and subjected to extensive analysis—with more obscure materials. My goal in taking this approach is to provide relatively fresh documents that may help open new lines of discussion and illuminate experiences that have received little attention, while also providing landmark documents of indisputable importance. It would have been easy to fill the entire collection with classics. My determination to mix different kinds of documents entailed exceptionally difficult decisions about which well-known items to omit and which to include. One strategy was to exclude treaties, pieces of legislation, and relatively straightforward declarations of policy, items that lend themselves to paraphrase in the chapter introductions, provide relatively little grist for discussion, and are widely available on reliable websites. Following this logic, the book does not include, for example, items such as the 1954 Geneva Accords, the Gulf of Tonkin Resolution of 1964, North Vietnamese Prime Minister Pham Van Dong's declaration of Hanoi's negotiating position in 1965, or the Paris peace agreement of 1973.

Readers may also wonder about the lack of documents connected to some of the most controversial and perplexing moments of the war—the Eisenhower administration's decision not to intervene to save the French war effort in 1954, the failure to hold all-Vietnamese elections in 1956, and the U.S. decision to send combat troops to South Vietnam in 1965, for instance. These lacunae suggest something fascinating and revealing about the war, especially its conduct by the United States. Some of the most pivotal decisions did not result from focused, thorough deliberations in meetings or exchanges of memoranda accessible in the documentary record. Rather, key decisions sometimes resulted from simple inertia or failures to take dispositive action. These moments, crucial though they are, are thus difficult to capture in a book of this sort.

Some of the less familiar documents in this book reflect the attitudes and opinions of "ordinary" people caught up in the war in one way or another—soldiers, low-ranking officials, and refugees. While I have no doubt that these kinds of documents are extremely valuable, enabling readers to delve beneath the level of policy deliberations to appreciate the war as lived experience, they demand a special kind of scrutiny because they are mostly reminiscences written or recorded years after the events that they chronicle. Readers should ask how these materials might distort the past by filtering it through later biases and the vagaries of memory.

Fourth, I have tried to strike a balance between providing documents in their full length and trimming them in the interest of including more items in a book of manageable length. Excerpting always carries the risk of altering meaning, and I want to make abundantly clear that I have at least trimmed, and sometimes extensively cut, every document in this collection. Selections drawn from books obviously entail the most extensive cutting and the most serious risks of removing passages from context. But memoranda, speeches, manifestos, and the like— many of which run several thousand words—also had to be trimmed in order to produce a book containing a critical mass of documents. I have worked hard to preserve the original meaning of each document, but I rest easier knowing that readers wishing to see an item in its entirety can follow the footnote to locate the original.

Finally, I have been guided in selecting documents for this book by what I regard as the four most persistent and important questions that have driven scholarly inquiry into the war for many years. By no means does the collection pretend to provide answers to these questions. Rather, I hope that the materials I have selected suggest at least some basic lines of approach. The questions are the following:

▪ *Why was Vietnam the site of political turbulence and violence in the twentieth century?* Disagreement over this question runs back at least to the 1940s, when Westerners first tried to make sense of the revolutionary movement that laid claim to power in Vietnam at the end of the Second World War. Many government officials in France and the United States dwelled on the communist character of Ho Chi Minh and other anticolonial leaders, fearing that a revolutionary victory would mean a major advance for the international communist movement and a serious defeat for the West in the Cold War. Yet other officials, like many historians in later years, argued that the Vietnamese communists succeeded only insofar as they were able to harness nationalist sentiments that ran far back in Vietnamese history. Above all, in this view, French colonialism in the late nineteenth and early twentieth century created profound grievances among many ordinary Vietnamese and generated fierce anticolonialism that remained the core of the revolutionary movement thereafter. These conflicting ways of understanding political unrest in Vietnam assumed notable importance during the heaviest years of American embroilment. Supporters of the American war viewed intervention as crucial to stopping communist aggression, while opponents argued that the United States was waging war against a fundamentally nationalist movement fighting for Vietnam's unity and independence. Some of the documents in this book, especially in the first three chapters, provide insight into the roles of nationalism and communism in the Vietnamese revolution and the ways in which the two political programs were related and intertwined.

▪ *Why did U.S. leaders decide to commit American power and prestige to Vietnam?* Before the Second World War, most Westerners generally regarded Vietnam as an obscure backwater, a remote corner of the French empire with little political or economic significance to any nation other than France. But the outbreak of fighting in Vietnam in 1946 and the acceleration of Cold War tensions around the same time transformed the country into a major focus of international attention. Many documents in this book, especially in Chapters 2 through 6, offer insight into the range of strategic, economic, and political motives that led Americans to view Indochina as a vital front in the Cold War struggle—so vital by 1965 that U.S. leaders decided to fight a major war there and kept fighting for eight years thereafter despite persistent frustration and setbacks.

▪ *Why did South Vietnam and the United States fail to achieve their goal of a stable and secure South Vietnamese state between 1954 and 1975?* From the start of their struggles against foreign powers during the 1940s, Vietnamese revolutionaries faced adversaries possessing vast military superiority. Yet the revolutionaries defeated first France and then the United States. Explaining this outcome has stirred bitter disagreement for decades. Some commentators insist that South Vietnam and the United States could have prevailed in the war if only they had fought it in different ways. The most common argument in this vein suggests that irresolute political leaders prevented the U.S. military from using sufficient force to achieve American objectives. Other commentators contend that South Vietnam failed because of profound political flaws that no amount of American force could have overcome. Documents throughout the book but especially in Chapters 5 through 9 shed light on these debates.

▪ *What were the long-term lessons and legacies of the Vietnam War?* The war left a trail of devastation and suffering in Indochina and, on a much smaller scale, in the United States. But it had an impact of one sort of another virtually everywhere—in

Southeast Asia more generally, among American allies, and in the communist bloc. All of these arenas deserve careful attention. Chapter 10 touches on the aftermath of the war in Vietnam but concentrates on the debate over the war's lessons as it has unfolded in the United States.

Reasonable people can disagree about which documents would best help us think about these questions. I hope I have made choices that generate discussion of themes that remain important many years after the fighting ended. But the most satisfying outcome of all would be readers using this book as a starting point for further inquiry.

Assembling this collection has constantly reminded me how fortunate I am to have such a generous group of friends and colleagues who share my interest in the Vietnam War. For suggestions and advice about documents, I extremely grateful to Pierre Asselin, Claude Berube, Tim Borstelmann, Bob Brigham, Laura Calkins, Mary Terrell Cargill, Charles Keith, Kyle Longley, Fred Logevall, David Marr, Lien-Hang Nguyen, Jon Persoff, Andrew Preston, Sandra Scanlon, and Truong Buu Lam. Jeffrey Schlosberg, the archivist of the National Press Club in Washington, D.C., provided generous help with two especially elusive documents. I would be remiss if I did not single out Chris Goscha for a special word of thanks. As with other endeavors of mine, Chris was an invaluable source of advice not only about documents but also about the conceptualization of this project. My thanks go as well to Helen Pho, an outstanding young scholar of the Vietnam War who helped me in innumerable ways.

For support while I was working on this collection, I wish to thank the Institute for Historical Studies in the Department of History at the University of Texas at Austin, the College of Liberal Arts at UT-Austin, and the Stanley Kaplan Program in American Foreign Policy at Williams College. Most of all, my thanks go to the director of the Kaplan Program, James McAllister, with whom I had the pleasure of co-teaching a course on the Vietnam War when I was first thinking about this book.

At Oxford University Press, I am extremely grateful to Charles Cavaliere, who proposed this project and did more than anyone to move it to the finish line. Throughout the process, Charles provided the perfect combination of enthusiasm, support, and patience. I am also indebted to several others who helped with the final stages, especially Martin Baldessari, Pamela Hanley, Michelle Koufopoulos, Lynn Luecken, and Wendy Walker. For their valuable feedback on the initial proposal for this book, I wish to thank Pam Pennock, Christopher A. Huff, Andrew L. Johns, Allan M. Winkler, Marko Maunula, David E. Hamilton, Nancy Gabin, Vivien Sandlund, Geoffrey Jacques, and others who opted to remain anonymous.

As with all of my work, this book owes much to my parents, who encouraged my passion for history long ago. My wife, Steph Osbakken, provided not only invaluable love and encouragement but also, crucially, long windows of time when I could escape upstairs to get the project finished. From downstairs, meanwhile, came the chirping and hollering of the incomparable Maya and Bryn—the most pleasant and inspiring music imaginable.

Jon Persoff did not live to see this book come to fruition. But I have no doubt he would have heartily approved of my efforts. I have met few people with so deep a passion for the study of the Vietnam War in general and so much enthusiasm for exploring original sources in particular. He had no idea, I fear, how much I appreciated his conversation and friendship over the all-too-brief years. This book is dedicated to Jon.

LIST OF MAPS

LIST OF ACRONYMS

AID	U.S. Agency for International Development
ARVN	Army of the Republic of Vietnam
CCP	Chinese Communist Party
DMZ	Demilitarized Zone
GVN	Government of (South) Vietnam
MACV	Military Assistance Command, Vietnam
NATO	North Atlantic Treaty Organization
NLF	National Liberation Front
NSC	National Security Council
NVA	North Vietnamese Army
NVN	North Vietnam
POW	Prisoner of War
SEATO	Southeast Asia Treaty Organization
SVN	South Vietnam
UN	United Nations
USSR	Union of Soviet Socialist Republics
VC	Vietcong
VN	Vietnam

Southeast Asia in the era of the First Indochina War

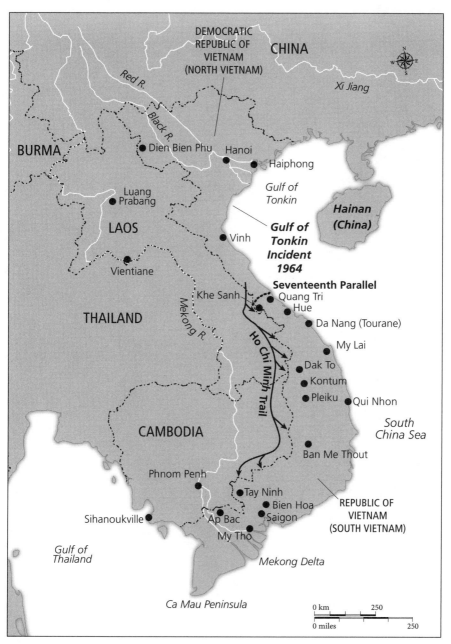

Vietnam, Laos, and Cambodia, with major sites of the war from 1961 to 1975

THE VIETNAM WAR

1
VIETNAMESE NATIONALISM AND COMMUNISM

THE IMPOSITION OF FRENCH imperial rule in the late nineteenth century marked a breaking point in Vietnamese history, generating the basic social and political tensions that shaped the nation's life for many decades. To be sure, it is too simple to draw a direct line from the grievances stirred by French domination to the conflicts of the 1950s and 1960s. Yet a full understanding of events in Vietnam during the mid-twentieth century requires looking back to the colonial era.

French motives for colonizing Indochina—Vietnam along with neighboring Cambodia and Laos—were the same ones that led other European nations to conquer distant territories in the 1880s and 1890s. The French government sought to enhance its standing among the great powers, while industrialists hoped that control over Indochina would ensure access to natural resources and markets. Moralizers, meanwhile, spoke of their desire to Christianize and "civilize" the local populations.

The effects of French colonialism in Vietnam were profound. The concentration of land and wealth in French hands spelled the end of the country's relatively egal-itarian system of subsistence agriculture. Vast numbers of Vietnamese peasants found themselves vulnerable to the forces of global markets and the demands of distant landlords and tax-collectors. In the political realm, French control dele-gitimized traditional sources of authority such as the village councils that had en-sured a degree of local autonomy and the Confucian bureaucrats who had helped knit the country together as a political unit.

Foreign domination generated a powerful sense of discontent from which emerged a nationalist movement determined to restore Vietnamese independence and vitality. At first, the nationalists made little headway, largely because they failed to extend their appeal beyond a small circle of urban elites into the countryside, where the vast majority of the Vietnamese population lived.

Only with the rise of Ho Chi Minh's more radical movement after 1920 did Vietnamese nationalism gain traction. The catalyzing event for Ho Chi Minh was the peace conference that ended the First World War. When the great powers refused to consider independence for colonial territories, Ho Chi Minh gave up on Western liberalism and embraced Leninism, especially its confidence in the revolutionary potential of peasants, as the political philosophy most likely to help achieve his goals. The charismatic and ruthless Ho dedicated himself throughout the 1920s and 1930s to organizing a revolutionary movement that would harness broad social discontent.

Ho Chi Minh and his collaborators formed new organizations and won adherents to their vision. Communist ideas suffused mounting anticolonial agitation, creating the potent blend of communism and nationalism that would characterize the Vietnamese revolution thereafter. Still, the movement stood little chance of achieving its goals if not for the outbreak of the Second World War. Japanese occupation of Vietnam weakened French authority and opened unprecedented possibilities for the revolutionaries. Ho and other nationalists established a broad patriotic front known as the Viet Minh and waged guerrilla war against both the French and Japanese.

When Japan suddenly surrendered in August 1945, a popular insurrection demanding independence and social renewal—the August Revolution—opened the way for the Viet Minh, with Ho's communists in the lead, to claim power. The insurrection culminated on September 2, when Ho Chi Minh declared the establishment of a new nation, the Democratic Republic of Vietnam.

DOCUMENT 1.1

A Vision of Vietnamese Renewal
Phan Boi Chau, *The New Vietnam*, 1907

By the first decade of the twentieth century, a nationalist movement was beginning to take root in Vietnam. One of the most influential voices was that of Phan Boi Chau, born in 1867 to a family of intellectuals from central Vietnam. Phan read the Confucian classics in preparation for a career as a mandarin, a venerated position that combined the functions of civil servant and judge. As France extended its colonial rule over Vietnam in the 1880s and 1890s, however, he changed course and devoted himself to the anticolonial cause. Like other Vietnamese nationalists around the turn of the century, Phan drew inspiration from foreign countries, especially Japan, and believed that the surest path to Vietnamese independence lay in emulating the most modern nations. He founded the Vietnam Modernization Association in 1904 and, after relocating to Japan, began writing anticolonial books and pamphlets that were smuggled into Vietnam. The following excerpt comes from Phan Boi Chau's *The New Vietnam* [Tan Viet Nam], published in 1907. Phan was arrested by French authorities in 1925 and sentenced to life in prison. However, a popular outcry forced the colonial government to release him, and he lived the final years of his life in Hue under French surveillance.

The French stole our country. They gagged our mouths. They tied up our limbs. They blinded our eyes. They plugged our ears. The publication of books and newspapers, the deliberations, the meetings no matter whether during daytime or night, no matter how many or how few participants, no matter whether young or old people, the French strictly forbade them all. We still have to obey their order, even when, in anger, they demanded that we look at our fathers as our enemies. When it pleases them to require us to respect a dog as a king, we still have to acquiesce to their request. Even the king and the mandarins, the rich and the talented people, would not dare go one step away from their houses without asking for special permission from the French. If your taxes are not paid in full to the French, you are regarded as burglars in your own homes. Here are French dogs, French horses, French women, servants of the French: all are free to insult whomever they choose to insult. Seeing them next to our people, it is like paradise on their side and hell on ours. Such iniquity, such inequality, where in the world can one find a more unjust situation? Are we going to sit back and relax instead of rising up to ring the bell of freedom? One who never loses never wins either; we should be determined to break this vicious cycle of oppression.

After modernization we shall wield power in our country. We shall keep our own way of life. Civilization will reign through liberty everywhere. Newspapers will appear on sidewalks, and new books abound. Petitions and lawsuits, verbal and written polemics, will flourish. Domestic and foreign affairs will be discussed in every detail. Writers will be encouraged to create. Every hidden feeling of the rickshaw puller or of the horse attendant, or the mother-widow or the lone orphan, will reach the leaders' ears. Then the people of our country will be drunk with happiness, a happiness as immense as the ocean, the limits of which the eyes cannot fathom, or as high as the sky the contours of which the arms are unable to grasp. Such freedom, how pleasant that will be! . . .

After modernization, first, we have to get rid of all the wretched old practices that have existed through many dynasties. Second, we shall reform all the inhumane institutions set up by the French. Taxes, corvées, head taxes—none of these will remain after independence. All taxes will be decided upon by [a national legislature]. Taxes on this or that commodity have to be agreed upon by our people, and the proceeds must be spent on useful enterprises for the public good. The government can only start implementing its tax policies after the people have given their consent. Our people will not pay even one piaster or one grain of rice, if it is not out of their own will and with enthusiasm . . .

After modernization both the royal court and the society will devote all their efforts to education, moral as well as physical. We shall learn from Japan, China, Europe; we shall learn everything. Day care centers, kindergartens, primary and secondary schools, universities, will be created everywhere, from the cities to the countryside. Right after modernization we shall invite teachers from Japan, Europe, and America. After a while some of the teachers will still be foreigners, but some of them will be recruited from among our own people. Then, after complete modernization, our own people will know more than the people from Europe or America, so that we won't have to invite any foreigner anymore. How to establish schools, how to organize the curricula, how to teach, how to find jobs for our graduates—everything will be copied from the good model of Japan and Europe. We shall study philosophy, literature, history, politics, economics, military science, geometry. We shall study industry, commerce, agriculture, home economics, medicine, forestry . . .

From the Chinese Han, Tang, Yuan, and Ming Dynasties to the French today, the skill of being slave has rather been well fine-tuned by our people. Why is that so? Because none of us has the desire for progress, the longing for adventure; because all of us bask in our stupidity and our weakness, finding that the best way to deal with the world is to indulge ourselves in good food and in sex plays. Our garden and our kitchen represent for us the wide universe. Other people can defecate on our head; still we stand there idle and console ourselves by saying, "I only want my peace." Foreigners may swallow our race and yet we meekly say, "I shall wait for my time." Alas, in this competitive world, where people's dispositions are as poisonous as snakes, where vultures pursue sparrows, the otter swimming after the fish, where can we find someone like the Buddha? If you don't want to progress, people will kill you. Who will care about you if you do not have the sense of adventure?

Even under these circumstances, is our country really incapable of rising up? Please, my dear compatriots, open your eyes in order to wash out the shame inflicted onto our mountains and rivers. All other people behave like heroes; why are we so cowardly and weak-hearted? Other people are all in commanding positions; why are we satisfied with being merely slaves? If all of us have one mind, then we can reach independence. If our desire for progress is firm, our longing for adventure strong, then we shall be able to capture lions and tigers with our bare hands, to catch whales and sharks in the vast ocean. If the strength of one man is not sufficient, then we shall have the strength of ten men. If the strength of ten men is still not enough, then we shall have the strength of one hundred, one thousand, ten thousand men so as to accomplish the task. If everybody in the country is brave to that extent, then the French will not know a single day of peace. This is the first pleasant situation resulting from modernization.

DOCUMENT 1.2

An Appeal to the World Powers
Note by Ho Chi Minh to U.S. Secretary of State Robert Lansing
at the Versailles Peace Conference, June 18, 1919

For anticolonial leaders around the world, the end of the First World War seemed to herald the breakup of colonial empires and the dawn of a new era of national self-rule. U.S. President Woodrow Wilson had repeatedly invoked the principle of self-determination as a key war aim in 1917 and 1918. Eager to encourage Wilson and other powerful world leaders to turn rhetoric into reality, expatriate nationalists living in Europe sought to contact representatives of the victorious powers who gathered at Versailles, outside Paris, in 1919 to draft peace agreements and design the postwar international order. Perhaps the most famous of these nationalists was Nguyen Ai Quoc ("Nguyen the Patriot"), who later embraced another pseudonym, Ho Chi Minh. He sent the following declaration to U.S. Secretary of State Robert Lansing, who accompanied Wilson to the peace conference. One of Wilson's advisers wrote a brief reply acknowledging receipt of the document and a second note promising to share it with the president, but the correspondence went no further.

Since the Allies' victory, all subject peoples are trembling with hope before the prospect of an era of law and justice that ought to open for them by virtue of the formal and solemn commitments undertaken before the whole world by the various Entente powers during the fight of Civilization against Barbarism.

While waiting for the principle of national self-determination to pass from ideal to reality through effective recognition of the sacred right of all people to determine their own destiny, the people of the one-time Empire of Annam, today French Indochina, present to the Noble Governments of the Entente in general and to the honorable French Government in particular the following humble demands:

1. A general amnesty for all indigenous political prisoners.
2. Reform of Indochinese justice by extending to the native population the same legal guarantees enjoyed by Europeans, and the total suppression of the special courts which are instruments of terrorization and repression of the most responsible part of the Annamite population.
3. Freedom of the press and speech.
4. Freedom of association and assembly.
5. Freedom to emigrate and to travel abroad.
6. Freedom of education and the creation in every province of technical and professional schools for the native population.
7. Replacement of rule by decree with rule of law.
8. Creation of permanent positions for elected members of the native population to serve in the French parliament to keep it informed of indigenous demands.

DOCUMENT 1.3
Founding a Unified Communist Party
Speech by Ho Chi Minh at a Meeting of Vietnamese Communists, Hong Kong, February 18, 1930

Disappointed by the failure of the Western powers to grant independence to Vietnam and other colonies after the First World War, Ho Chi Minh turned to communism. It would be V. I. Lenin's radical vision of anticolonial revolution that would inspire the most powerful strand of Vietnamese nationalism over the decades to come. Radicalism gained particular appeal around 1930, when the global economic depression stirred new activism among communists around the world and led Moscow to push for tighter organization of the communist movement. So powerfully did radical winds blow that Ho Chi Minh, well known for his ideological eclecticism, fell out of favor for a time. But Ho nevertheless took a major role when communist leaders gathered in Hong Kong in February 1930 to establish the Vietnamese Communist Party (renamed the Indochinese Communist Party later that year), which knit together various rival groups into a single organization. Ho delivered the following speech on February 18, 1930.

Workers, peasants, soldiers, youth and school students!
Oppressed and exploited fellow-countrymen!
Sisters and brothers! Comrades!

Imperialist contradictions were the cause of the 1914–1918 World War. After this horrible slaughter, the world was divided into two camps: one is the revolutionary camp which includes the oppressed colonial peoples and the exploited working class throughout the world. Its vanguard is the Soviet Union. The other is the counter-revolutionary camp of international capitalism and imperialism, whose general staff is the League of Nations.

That war resulted in untold loss of life and property for the peoples. French imperialism was the hardest hit. Therefore, in order to restore the forces of capitalism in France, the French imperialists have resorted to every perfidious scheme to intensify capitalist exploitation in Indochina. They have built new factories to exploit the workers by paying them starvation wages. They have plundered the peasants' land to establish plantations and drive them to destitution. They have levied new heavy taxes. They have forced our people to buy government bonds. In short, they have driven our people to utter misery. They have increased their military forces, firstly to strangle the Vietnamese revolution; secondly to prepare for a new imperialist war in the Pacific aimed at conquering new colonies; thirdly to suppress the Chinese revolution; and fourthly to attack the Soviet Union because she helps the oppressed nations and the exploited working class to wage revolution.

World War Two will break out. When it does the French imperialists will certainly drive our people to an even more horrible slaughter. If we let them prepare for this war, oppose the Chinese revolution and attack the Soviet Union, if we allow them to stifle the Vietnamese revolution, this is tantamount to letting them wipe our race off the surface of the earth and drown our nation in the Pacific.

However, the French imperialists' barbarous oppression and ruthless exploitation have awakened our compatriots, who have all realized that revolution is the only road to survival and that without it they will die a slow death. This is why the revolutionary movement has grown stronger with each passing day: the workers refuse to work, the peasants demand land, the students go on strike, the traders stop doing business. Everywhere the masses have risen to oppose the French imperialists.

The revolution has made the French imperialists tremble with fear. On the one hand, they use the feudalists and comprador bourgeoisie to oppress and exploit our people. On the other, they terrorize, arrest, jail, deport and kill a great number of Vietnamese revolutionaries. If the French imperialists think that they can suppress the Vietnamese revolution by means of terror, they are grossly mistaken. For one thing, the Vietnamese revolution is not isolated but enjoys the assistance of the world proletariat in general and that of the French working class in particular. Secondly, it is precisely at the very time when the French imperialists are frenziedly carrying out terrorist acts that the Vietnamese Communists, formerly working separately, have united into a single party, the Indochinese Communist Party, to lead the revolutionary struggle of our entire people.

Workers, peasants, soldiers, youth, school students!
Oppressed and exploited fellow-countrymen!

The Indochinese Communist Party has been founded. It is the Party of the working class. It will help the proletariat lead the revolution waged for the sake of all oppressed and exploited people. From now on we must join the Party, help it and follow it in order to implement the following slogans:

1. To overthrow French imperialism and Vietnamese feudalism and reactionary bourgeoisie;
2. To make Indochina completely independent;
3. To establish a worker-peasant-soldier government;
4. To confiscate the banks and other enterprises belonging to the imperialists and put them under the control of the worker-peasant-soldier government;
5. To confiscate all the plantations and property belonging to the imperialists and the Vietnamese reactionary bourgeoisie and distribute them to the poor peasants;
6. To implement the 8-hour working day;
7. To abolish the forced buying of government bonds, the poll-tax and all unjust taxes hitting the poor;
8. To bring democratic freedoms to the masses;
9. To dispense education to all the people;
10. To realize equality between man and woman.

DOCUMENT 1.4

The Complexity of Political Loyalties
Reflections by Duong Van Mai Elliott on the Life of Her Father, a Vietnamese Official under French Rule, 1924–1937

Among the most profound changes wrought by French colonialism in Vietnam was to upend the traditional system of governance. Under the Vietnamese emperors, the territory had been administered by mandarins, civil servants deeply versed in Confucian classics who cultivated an aura of wisdom, honor, and selflessness. The French colonial regime left the mandarin system in place, though subordination to foreign control undermined the power and dignity of the institution. In 1999, the American writer Duong Van Mai Elliott published a family memoir in which she recounts the experiences of her father, Duong Thieu Chi, a highly educated Vietnamese elite who first served the colonial administration as a specialist in finance and then, in 1929, became a mandarin. In the following selection, Duong Van Mai Elliott recalls the effects of French colonialism and the complicated political tensions that operated within Vietnamese society before the Second World War.

M y father received his first appointment in September 1924 as a *commis* trainee, fourth class, in the Finance Bureau in Hanoi, with a respectable salary of 100 piasters per month. He and my mother immediately moved into the city and rented a house. When he got his first month's pay, my father went out and bought a "dress for success" wardrobe: two pairs of shoes, a brand-new umbrella, and a couple of Western suits. He purchased a rickshaw with rubber wheels, and hired a puller to take him back and forth from his office. My father now began his career as a bureaucrat, with an uneventful daily routine that people referred to as "leaving home with an umbrella in the morning, and coming home with it at night." My parents settled into a comfortable lifestyle, complete with a staff of servants and a cook . . .

My father's job was typical of the government positions available to the Vietnamese. Higher level jobs were monopolized by the French. The Vietnamese elite was, of course, unhappy with being kept bottled up in lower positions, but it was a take-it-or-leave-it situation. Except for the government, there was no other viable outlet for employment. The finance office, headed by a Frenchman, had about five sections, each staffed with four or five clerks. My father quickly mastered the paperwork routine that he found so boring that he would take as many days off as he could get away with, often sending his rickshaw driver to the office with a note saying he was sick. Yet he still managed to impress his French boss with his efficiency.

The years my father spent as a bureaucrat—from 1924 to 1929—were a period of dramatic economic expansion. Encouraged by the promise of stability, cheap labor, economic privileges, and tax shelters, French capitalists, newly recovered from World War I, invested heavily in the country. They put their money mainly into enterprises that would produce raw materials for export, such as coal and rubber. By 1924, the investment had triggered a boom that benefited mostly French firms. The expansion, however, came from the sweat of many. Almost a third of the capital was poured into rubber plantations in Cochinchina, which imported thousands of laborers from Tonkin and Annam to tend the trees and gather the sap. The laborers were destitute peasants who were dragooned into these plantations. Once there, they found concentration camp-like conditions. However, they were bound by contracts, and if they tried to escape and were caught, would be viciously punished.

Housing was crude and built in muddy and swampy areas. Food was inadequate and water was contaminated; malaria was rampant. The back-breaking work began in the early morning hours, and did not stop until after nightfall, most of it performed in the blistering heat or in the drenching downpour of the monsoon season. Under these terrible conditions, it was not surprising that many laborers died. Their plight horrified their countrymen and came to symbolize the degradation of colonialism. It also shattered the myth of the *mission civilisatrice*. Even when I was growing up three decades later, I still heard stories of their terrible suffering, long after the inhuman practices had stopped.

The year after my father started his job at the finance office, opposition to the French became more militant and more structured. Before, nationalist leaders had placed their faith in modern education to free their countrymen or their hope in French reforms. There were no organized political movements. When they saw how their faith in reforms had been misplaced, the new generation of leaders turned to armed resistance and political organization to achieve their aims. The most revolutionary and effective of these leaders was Ho Chi Minh. Ho had left the country in 1911, disillusioned by the failure of previous generations of activists to end colonialism and determined to find a new answer. He drifted to America and to England, but found no sympathetic ears or programs of action that he thought would bring a solution. He finally settled in Paris in 1919. At first he tried to appeal to the French government and other Western powers to help Vietnam. But after he was given the cold shoulder everywhere, a frustrated Ho concluded that the Vietnamese would have to win their freedom back themselves, not by pleading but by violence . . .

Communist agents began infiltrating Vietnam from China and by 1930 they had built up enough support to foment labor strikes and peasant demonstrations. In September, the communists launched their boldest protests in Nghe An and Ha Tinh, two of the poorest provinces in Annam. Peasants in several districts revolted and seized power. They formed "red villages," distributed the land they had seized, and ran these districts for three months. In their revolutionary zeal, they also attacked landlords, well-to-do families, and educated people. These attacks scared the middle class and, for the first time, gave them a frightening glimpse of what life would be like for them under communism. Accordingly, they threw their support behind French efforts to suppress this movement and restore order. The repression was brutal and effective. Thousands were arrested and deported to penal colonies, including practically the entire leadership of the Communist Party. By the end of 1931, it looked like this party was finished.

Mandarins whose districts were embroiled in protest marches got into trouble with the French, who held them responsible for the breakdown in public order.

A friend of my father's lost his job in the aftermath of a demonstration in his district. He was dismissed from office for one year, and although he was reinstated later, the incident left a black mark in his dossier, and his career suffered. This period of disturbances made life difficult for the mandarins. If the communist red flag with the hammer and sickle was raised in a village, the local mandarin would be summoned by the *résident* and given a dressing-down. If communist leaflets were disseminated in his territory, the mandarin would be given a warning. Furthermore, the French security police would arrive to investigate and question him, and quite likely the province *résident* would begin to suspect his loyalty, competence, or both. Whenever an incident took place in a province, all the mandarins would receive a confidential memo telling them what had happened and ordering them to increase their vigilance.

It was at this time of political ferment that my father decided to switch from being a finance bureaucrat to being a mandarin. He was well regarded and well paid, but he felt restless in a job that he found devoid of challenge and social prestige. Looking back on his family tradition, he thought that unless he could become a mandarin, he would never measure up to his grandfather and father. Although radicals were condemning the mandarin system as obsolete, my father—and other men who shared his traditional background—continued to yearn to join its ranks. He decided to try his chances in the highly competitive exam that the French held each year to select just a handful of mandarins, and succeeded. The Finance Office tried to retain him with a big promotion and a substantial raise, but he turned them down and left Hanoi for the remote district of Hat Tri, in Phu Tho Province, to assume his new position . . .

With the upsurge in violent protests, maintenance of political security was a much bigger responsibility for my father as a mandarin than it had been for my grandfather. Despite their no-holds-barred suppression of the 1930 uprisings, the French were afraid that they had not wiped out the troublemakers. When my father arrived in Phu Tho, mandarins in the province had received orders to heighten their vigilance, and had been told in no uncertain terms that they would be held responsible for any protest or anti-French activities in their territories. To keep track of outsiders who might try to infiltrate the province to disseminate propaganda and recruit sympathizers, each village chief had to maintain a list of strangers who passed through. Once in a while, the mandarins would conduct a surprise night patrol in the village to see whether the watchmen were making their rounds and whether any suspect activities were taking place. Or they would drop in unannounced to check whether the village chief had kept his register up-to-date. In addition, each district magistrate had to maintain a top secret list of any political suspects in his territory, which he kept locked in his desk drawer.

With the communists busily trying to convert peasants, the mandarins had to compete with them to win the allegiance of the people. They could no longer remain as distant authority figures who governed by wisdom and virtue. To force the magistrates to meet the people and forge closer ties with them, the French province *résident* required each mandarin to make weekly visits to the villages in his territory, in addition to the surprise inspection tours. My father could choose his own villages to visit, but after each trip, he had to file a report to the *résident* . . .

After slightly more than a year in Hat Tri, my father was promoted to Cam Khe, a larger district, also located in Phu Tho Province. The promotion was both good and bad. Of all the districts in the province, Cam Khe was the most difficult to run. The people were more stubborn than those in Hat Tri, and their village chiefs were not at all reticent about lodging complaints against their magistrate with the French *résident*. Another headache for my father was the presence of a French plantation that formed a world unto itself, and was outside his authority. Although they were living and working on Vietnamese soil, Europeans and their properties could be dealt with only by the French officials themselves. The original owner had obtained his property when the colonial authorities were making land concessions to settlers, in the belief that the string of plantations would form a barrier against the infiltration of armed bands into the unpacified delta. By the end of the nineteenth century, large French concessions dotted the midlands, growing cash crops like coffee, jute, tobacco, and tea. Most of the owners lived not on the plantations, but in Hanoi, and paid only an occasional visit . . .

As Western influence grew in Vietnam, those who could afford it began to copy the leisure life-style of the French, taking up dancing, going to nightclubs, and spending time at weekend retreats in the mountains or on the beach. Some went further, smoking opium and entering into liaisons with the hostesses they met in the dance halls. At one point, a cousin of my father's—whom we called Uncle Governor Mau—decided to build a cabin on the beach near Hai Hau, asking my father and several of his friends to contribute twenty piasters each for the construction. When the cabin was completed, Governor Mau held a housewarming party—a boisterous one, as he was a playboy and an opium addict. He had invited young women to keep his male guests company and to dance with them to Western music from a gramophone. None of the wives were asked to attend. There were also card games and opium smoking for those who could not get through the evening without it. Fortunately, my father was never attracted to this drug, preferring Vietnamese tobacco smoked through a water pipe. Governor Mau was the type of mandarin that was giving the whole system a bad name. He did not do anything that would hurt someone—such as arresting innocent people to extort money from their families—but according to rumors he was greedy and took a lot of bribes. In leading a dissolute lifestyle, my uncle had plenty of company within the elite. Their display of excess amidst the general poverty of the population provoked a number of journalists and novelists into condemning their hedonism as insensitive, if not immoral . . .

In his various posts, my father had never had to confront the communists, yet he knew where he stood with them. He understood that, as part of the colonial regime they vowed to destroy, he—like other mandarins—was guilty by association and a target in their eyes. Through the grapevine, he had heard stories of communist intimidation and retaliation, so he knew that he would have to be careful if he ever had to deal with them.

He had also heard of the "red villages" in Annam and of the attacks there against middle-class people like himself, and realized that he would be denied a role, if not eliminated, in the society envisioned by the communists. Yet he also sympathized with them because he understood that they were fundamentally patriots who wanted to drive out the French. For the rest of his career in the colonial government, my father would feel torn between sympathy for the cause of national independence and repugnance for the violent social revolution advocated by the communists.

Among the mandarins, some shared my father's sympathy for the nationalistic side of the communists, while most simply hated and feared them at the same time. A few, however, had no qualms about suppressing them. Among the most notorious in this regard were two mandarins related to my family by marriage: Cung Dinh Van and Vi Van Dinh. Cung Dinh Van was a county magistrate in Son Tay Province who became infamous for his arrest and torture of communist suspects. His favorite interrogation technique was to wire his victims to the batteries of his car, and then start the engine to electrocute them and make them confess. An aunt of mine who had married in his clan was visiting his household one day when she heard the screams of agony of one of his victims. After the Viet Minh came to power, the communists got their revenge and Cung Dinh Van was executed . . .

In 1937, my father's ambivalence toward the communists made him turn down his promotion to magistrate of Xuan Truong, the largest county in Nam Dinh Province, because he had heard rumors that it was a hotbed of communist activities. As a matter of fact, Xuan Truong was the native area of a man known under his assumed name of Truong Chinh, who would later become a hard-liner in the politburo of the Communist Party. My father did not want to be put in a position where he would have to help the French suppress the communists and their sympathizers in Xuan Truong, fearing that it would bring retaliation against him and his family, but also believing that it would be repugnant for him to denounce his own patriotic countrymen to the colonialists for arrest, imprisonment, torture, and even execution.

DOCUMENT 1.5

Americans Weigh the Future of Indochina
Draft Memorandum by George H. Blakeslee, "United States Policy with
Regard to the Future of Indochina," April 1945

As the Second World War in the Pacific drew to a close, it was clear that the United States would play the dominant role in reshaping the political and economic order in the Far East. But what exactly Washington would do about French, British, and Dutch colonialism in Southeast Asia remained an open question. In 1942 and 1943, President Franklin Roosevelt had repeatedly voiced his disgust for French colonialism in Indochina and insisted that the territory must be placed under an international trusteeship after the war to prepare it for eventual independence. However, the president's position never became official policy; in fact, other U.S. officials assured French leaders that the territory would be returned to France. The issue remained clouded in uncertainty in the spring of 1945 as firm decisions about the postwar status of Japanese-occupied territories grew more urgent. In the following memorandum, George H. Blakeslee, an expert in Far Eastern affairs who played a leading role in the State Department's postwar planning, takes stock of the various options for Indochina.

There are three possible solutions for the problem of the disposition of Indochina. It may be restored to France, with or without conditions; it may be granted independence; or it may be placed under an international trusteeship.

RESTORATION TO FRANCE

Considerations in favor of Restoration . . .

If France is to be denied her former position in Indochina she will be to that extent weakened as a world power. It will probably be necessary for the United States to take the lead in any move by which France will be denied her former position in Indochina. If the United States, especially in view of its many unequivocal statements favoring the restoration of the French overseas territories, is the spearhead for partial dismemberment of the French Empire, French resentment will be such as to impose a very serious strain upon our relations and thus tend to defeat basic elements underlying our policy towards France. A disgruntled, psychologically sick and sovereign-conscious France will not augur well for post-war collaboration in Europe and in the world as a whole.

If it is to be the active policy of the United States to seek and insist upon the adoption of measures by which the peoples of dependent areas are to be lifted from their present social condition and are to be given in time opportunity for full self-determination, we should consider whether that aim can best be accomplished in the case of Indochina through cooperation with the French or through denial of any role to France, and operate through an international trusteeship. In reaching that decision we must determine whether it is of more interest to us and the world as a whole to have a strong, friendly, cooperative France, or have a resentful France plus having on our hands a social and administrative problem of the first magnitude . . .

To remedy the more outstanding weaknesses of the French administration of Indochina the United Nations in the Far Eastern area might insist that France be permitted to return to Indochina only after giving commitments to carry out the following reforms:

1. Tariff autonomy for Indochina.
2. The establishment and development of local and central representative institutions; the extension of the franchise as rapidly as possible.

3. Access on equal terms to all occupations and professions by Indo-Chinese; adequate educational and training facilities for all elements of the population.
4. Abolition of compulsory labor and effective supervision of labor contracts.
5. The development of local industries and a more balanced economy.

The chief considerations against placing [these] conditions on France are that such conditions would constitute a discrimination against France and, in view of the national sensitiveness of the French and their devotion to their colonial empire, would probably cause long-continued resentment against the United States, which might embarrass this Government in achieving all of the objectives of its global policies . . .

INDEPENDENCE FOR INDOCHINA

Over 17 million of the 24 million inhabitants of Indochina are Annamites. The Annamites are one of the most highly civilized peoples in southeastern Asia, and it would seem reasonable to suppose that, after a preparatory period, they would prove to be politically not less capable than the Thai, who have successfully governed Thailand for centuries, or than the Burmese who, before the war, had achieved the substance of self-government though not the title.

A nationalist movement of some proportions exists in Indochina. Although the French never favored the growth of an indigenous nationalism, the liberal principles of French political thought inevitably produced a desire for political liberty among educated native people. More particularly, the development of native consciousness may be traced to grievances against the French rulers. Among these might be listed the contrast between the native standard of living and that of resident Europeans, discrimination in wage levels and in social and professional opportunities, the high cost of living which largely nullified the economic advantages produced by the French regime, inequality before the law, alleged abuses of its privileges by the Roman Catholic Church, unfilled promises of political liberties beyond the limited advisory councils in each colony, failure to train natives for progressive participation in administration, and the thwarted ambitions of the native intelligentsia.

However, a preparatory period for independence is necessary. At the present, the elements necessary for the early establishment of an independent Indochina are lacking. The French policy of permitting only restricted native participation in government has allowed no opportunity for the development of a trained and experienced body of natives capable of assuming full responsibility for the direction of governmental affairs. The nationalist movement has been weakened by factional strife and by the lack of a solid organization, and has left the great mass of the people unaffected. The antagonism of the Annamites toward the Khmers and Laotians and toward the resident Chinese also limits the possibilities of early native unity.

AN INTERNATIONAL TRUSTEESHIP

There are two considerations which might appear to favor an international trusteeship for Indochina: the interest of the natives and the interests of the United States.

The failure of France to provide adequately for the welfare of the native population might justify placing Indochina under the control of an international administration, which would follow certain prescribed standards designed to develop the basis for eventual independence and for a rising standard of living among the native population . . .

The interests of the United States are opposed to imperialism and favor the progressive development, economically and politically, of dependent peoples until they are prepared for and are granted independence. The peoples in the Far East have had a vigorous and emotional opposition to western imperialism and this opposition appears to have increased in strength as a result of Japanese promises and propaganda during the present war. It is to the interest of the United States to dissociate itself in every feasible way from the imperialism of the European powers in the Far East. If the United States should participate in the restoration of France in Indochina, with no conditions or provisions looking to the betterment of native conditions and to the development of the people toward independence, it might well weaken the traditional confidence of Eastern peoples in the United States. If Indochina were a problem by itself the solution would appear to be the termination of French rule in Indochina and the establishment of an international trusteeship.

A trusteeship might be created by the projected international organization to function within the framework of the plan for international trusteeships which has been approved by the [State] Department. Or, two or more of the leading powers might set up a trusteeship. The trustee powers would necessarily assume, in the name of the people concerned, all rights and responsibilities of sovereignty including security for the peoples, conduct of foreign relations, financial solvency of the administration, and responsibility and power for all acts of government— executive, legislative and judicial . . .

The perplexing fact, however, is that France is not the only imperialist power in the Far East. Great Britain and the Netherlands also claim the return of colonies which are now under Japanese military occupation. Each of the colonial powers should give commitments to adopt measures of colonial administration, with some degree of international responsibility, which will further the development of their dependent peoples, along the path toward autonomy or independence.

The problem for the United States is whether it will be advisable, especially in view of the effect on United States global policies, to make demands on France in regard to Indochina when similar demands are not made on Great Britain and the Netherlands in regard to their Pacific and Far Eastern colonies.

A Brief Collaboration

Photograph of Viet Minh Leaders and Members of the U.S. "Deer Mission,"
September 1945

While Americans became increasingly concerned with Vietnam's political
status after the war, they also saw the territory as strategically important for
the closing stages of the fight against Japan. U.S. commanders contemplated
an invasion of nearby southeastern China and, in any case, wanted to harass
Japanese forces in the area. Agents of the U.S. Office of Strategic Services, the
forerunner of the Central Intelligence Agency, had been in touch with the
Viet Minh since 1942, but rapidly changing circumstances in 1945 led U.S.
leaders to seek closer collaboration. In July, a seven-man team of OSS officers, code-named Deer Mission, parachuted into northern Vietnam hoping
to train Viet Minh guerrillas to carry out sabotage raids against Japanese
installations and collect intelligence. Over the next few weeks, the U.S. officers
worked with Viet Minh fighters and discussed politics with Ho Chi Minh, Vo
Nguyen Giap, and other Viet Minh leaders. Several members of the Deer Mission formed positive impressions of the Viet Minh and later regretted that
Washington had not chosen to support the Democratic Republic of Vietnam.
The brief collaboration came to a sudden end when Japan abruptly surrendered in mid-August. The photograph above was taken at a farewell gathering just before the OSS team returned to China. Among the individuals in the
photograph are Ho Chi Minh (standing, third from left) and Vo Nguyen Giap
(with hat and necktie). The two Viet Minh leaders are flanking Deer Mission
commander Major Allison Kent Thomas.

DOCUMENT 1.7
Vietnam's Declaration of Independence
Speech by Ho Chi Minh, Ba Dinh Square, Hanoi, September 2, 1945

Vietnam's August Revolution culminated when Ho Chi Minh climbed a makeshift platform in Hanoi's Ba Dinh Square and declared the independence of a new country, the Democratic Republic of Vietnam. "Fellow countrymen, can you hear me well enough?" Ho Chi Minh asked the crowd of perhaps four hundred thousand after reading the first paragraph. The throng roared "yes!" As the following speech suggests, Ho Chi Minh addressed his words not only to his compatriots but also to foreign governments, including that of the United States.

"All men are created equal. They are endowed by their Creator with certain inalienable rights; among these are Life, Liberty, and the pursuit of Happiness."

This immortal statement was made in the Declaration of Independence of the United States of America in 1776. In a broader sense, this means: All the peoples on the earth are equal from birth, all the peoples have a right to live, to be happy and free.

The Declaration of the French Revolution made in 1791 on the Rights of Man and the Citizen also states: "All men are born free and with equal rights, and must always remain free and have equal rights."

Those are undeniable truths.

Nevertheless, for more than eighty years, the French imperialists, abusing the standard of Liberty, Equality, and Fraternity, have violated our Fatherland and oppressed our fellow citizens. They have acted contrary to the ideals of humanity and justice. In the field of politics, they have deprived our people of every democratic liberty. They have enforced inhuman laws; they have set up three distinct political regimes in the North, the Center, and the South of Vietnam in order to wreck our national unity and prevent our people from being united.

They have built more prisons than schools. They have mercilessly slain our patriots; they have drowned our uprisings in rivers of blood.

They have fettered public opinion; they have practised obscurantism against our people.

To weaken our race they have forced us to use opium and alcohol. In the field of economics, they have fleeced us to the backbone, impoverished our people, and devastated our land.

They have robbed us of our rice fields, our mines, our forests, and our raw materials. They have monopolized the issuing of bank notes and the export trade. They have invented numerous unjustifiable taxes and reduced our people, especially our peasantry, to a state of extreme poverty.

They have hampered the prosperity of our national bourgeoisie; they have mercilessly exploited our workers.

In the autumn of 1940, when the Japanese Fascists violated Indochina's territory to establish new bases in their fight against the Allies, the French imperialists went down on their bended knees and handed over our country to them.

Thus, from that date, our people were subjected to the double yoke of the French and the Japanese. Their sufferings and miseries increased. The result was that from the end of last year to the beginning of this year, from Quang Tri province to the North of Vietnam, more than two million of our fellow citizens died from starvation. On March 9, the French troops were disarmed by the Japanese. The French colonialists either fled or surrendered showing that not only were they incapable of "protecting" us, but that, in the span of five years, they had twice sold our country to the Japanese.

On several occasions before March 9, the Vietminh League urged the French to ally themselves with it against the Japanese. Instead of agreeing to this proposal, the French colonialists so intensified their terrorist activities against the Vietminh members that before fleeing they massacred a great number of our political prisoners detained at Yen Bay and Caobang.

Notwithstanding all this, our fellow citizens have always manifested toward the French a tolerant and humane attitude. Even after the Japanese putsch of March 1945, the Vietminh League helped many Frenchmen to cross the frontier, rescued some of them from Japanese jails, and protected French lives and property.

From the autumn of 1940, our country had in fact ceased to be a French colony and had become a Japanese possession.

After the Japanese had surrendered to the Allies, our whole people rose to regain our national sovereignty and to found the Democratic Republic of Vietnam. The truth is that we have wrested our independence from the Japanese and not from the French.

The French have fled, the Japanese have capitulated, Emperor Bao Dai has abdicated. Our people have broken the chains which for nearly a century have fettered them and have won independence for the Fatherland. Our people at the same time have overthrown the monarchic regime that has reigned supreme for dozens of centuries. In its place has been established the present Democratic Republic.

For these reasons, we, members of the Provisional Government, representing the whole Vietnamese people, declare that from now on we break off all relations of a colonial character with France; we repeal all the international obligations that France has so far subscribed to on behalf of Vietnam and we abolish all the special rights the French have unlawfully acquired in our Fatherland.

The whole Vietnamese people, animated by a common purpose, are determined to fight to the bitter end against any attempt by the French colonialists to reconquer their country.

We are convinced that the Allied nations, which at Tehran and San Francisco have acknowledged the principles of self-determination and equality of nations, will not refuse to acknowledge the independence of Vietnam.

A people who have courageously opposed French domination for more than eight years, a people who have fought side by side with the Allies against the Fascists during these last years, such a people must be free and independent.

For these reasons, we, members of the Provisional Government of the Democratic Republic of Vietnam, solemnly declare to the world that Vietnam has the right to be a free and independent country—and in fact is so already. The entire Vietnamese people are determined to mobilize all their physical and mental strength, to sacrifice their lives and property in order to safeguard their independence and liberty.

2

COLONIAL WAR
AND COLD WAR CRISIS

DESPITE HO CHI MINH'S soaring rhetoric, the Democratic Republic of Vietnam (DRV) faced an uncertain future. The new country confronted an economic crisis resulting from five years of occupation and war. Meanwhile, the French government made clear that it intended to reestablish colonial rule in Indochina, and the new regime in Hanoi had few friends abroad to help preserve its independence.

For a time, DRV and French leaders promised to work toward a negotiated compromise: Vietnamese autonomy within a revamped French empire. But the two sides edged closer to war during 1946, and fighting between Viet Minh and French troops erupted in December.

The French enjoyed vast military advantages and nearly captured DRV leaders in the fall of 1947. But the Viet Minh had strengths of its own, not least an effective guerrilla strategy that husbanded resources and inflicted steady losses on French forces. Meanwhile, the DRV extended its political influence, especially in rural areas distant from French strongpoints.

At first, foreign countries mostly steered clear of the conflict. The United States, torn between its anticolonial traditions and its eagerness to rebuild France into a major power, adopted a neutral position, while the Soviet Union and China focused on more urgent priorities. The escalation of the Cold War in 1949 and 1950, however, led all three powers to become embroiled in Vietnam, transforming a colonial conflict of limited significance into a major war with implications for the global balance of power.

U.S. leaders viewed the DRV, with its strong communist coloration, as part of an expansionistic communist movement directed from Moscow, a view that became especially persuasive after Mao Zedong's forces triumphed in China's long-running civil war in October 1949. Fearing a communist takeover of Southeast Asia, the Truman administration backed the French war effort and recognized a French-sponsored Vietnamese regime led by former emperor Bao Dai, which Paris officials hoped might drain support from Ho Chi Minh and gradually gain legitimacy as the government of an independent state within the French empire. Meanwhile, the Soviet and Chinese governments recognized the DRV, and China began sending military aid.

Foreign intervention increased the level of violence but did not bring decisive battlefield results for either side. Only in the political realm did the balance start to tilt. While the authoritarian DRV remained resolute, a weary French public began to turn against what increasingly seemed a debasing "dirty war" that senselessly drained the nation's resources.

U.S. leaders, fearing a communist takeover, opposed negotiations and insisted that the French redouble their commitment to the war. In 1953, the Eisenhower administration increased U.S. military assistance, bringing the U.S. contribution to nearly two-thirds the total cost of the French war, and Paris promised bold political and military initiatives. Yet victory remained elusive. Under mounting political pressure, the French government agreed in October 1953 to hold talks to end the war.

As the two sides prepared for negotiations scheduled to open in May in Geneva, they maneuvered for military advantages that they hoped might bolster their bargaining positions. French plans focused on the construction of a huge base at Dien Bien Phu in a remote valley of northwestern Vietnam. The goal was to lure DRV forces into a major battle and score a sweeping victory. Instead, DRV forces steadily rolled back French defenses during a two-month siege. The Viet Minh victory on May 7 made clear that the French colonial era in Indochina was over.

DOCUMENT 2.1
People's War
Manifesto by Revolutionary Leader Truong Chinh, September 1947

How could the Vietnamese possibly challenge a sophisticated European army that enjoyed huge advantages of weaponry, mobility, organization, and experience? The question weighed on revolutionary leaders in the early stages of the war against France. Their answers followed the thinking of Mao Zedong, the Chinese revolutionary leader and military theorist who was waging his own insurgent struggle across the border. Mao postulated that peasant guerrillas could prevail by waging "people's wars" that emphasized guerrilla tactics and political organizing. In this excerpt from a 1947 book, Truong Chinh, a top communist theoretician and the second-ranking DRV leader behind Ho Chi Minh, similarly calls for a war of attrition that would enable revolutionary armies to build their strength over the long term.

M any people think that resistance consists only in sending troops to the front [to] fight the enemy. In fact, to take up arms and kill the enemy represents only one aspect of the problem. The resistance of our people must be carried out in every field: military, economic, political and cultural.

In the military field, how must we fight?

Resistance in the military field means using every measure, every stratagem, to maintain and develop our own forces, while destroying those of the enemy. It means using force to drive the invader out of the country.

The guiding principle of the strategy of our whole resistance must be to prolong the war.

To protract the war is the key to victory. Why must the war be protracted? Because if we compare our forces with those of the enemy, it is obvious that the enemy is still strong, and we are still weak. The enemy's country is an industrial one—ours is an agricultural country. The enemy has planes, tanks, warships; as for us, we have only rudimentary weapons. The enemy troops are well-trained, ours are not inured to war. If we throw the whole of our forces into a few battles to try and decide the outcome, we shall certainly be defeated and the enemy will win. On the other hand, if while fighting we maintain our forces, expand them, train our army and people, learn military tactics, strive to secure in sufficient quantities the things of which we are short, strengthen our weak points and at the same time wear down the enemy forces, we shall weary and discourage them in such a way that, strong as they are, they will become weak and will meet defeat instead of victory. In short, if we prolong the war, thanks to our efforts, our forces will grow stronger, the enemy forces will be weakened, their already low morale will become still lower, their already poor finances will become still poorer. The more we fight, the more united our people at home will be, and the more the world democratic movement will support us from outside. On the other hand, the more the enemy fights, the more the anti-war and democratic movement in France will check his hands; the revolutionary movement in the French colonies will oblige the enemy to divide his forces; and he will find himself in a position of isolation in the international arena. To achieve all these results, the war must be prolonged, and we must have time. Time works for us—time will be our best strategist, if we are determined to pursue the resistance war to the end.

Under the Tran dynasty, our people waged resistance three times in 31 years to defeat the Mongol invaders. Under the [l]ater Le dynasty, it took us ten years of resistance to wipe out the cruel Ming [Chinese] troops. The Chinese people carried out resistance for eight years to free themselves from Japanese occupation. The lesson of those long resistance wars is very clear. Those who want "lightning war and rapid victory", who want to bring the whole of our forces to the battle-front to win speedy victory and rapidly to decide the outcome of the war, do not profit from the invaluable experiences of history; indeed, they understand nothing of the strategy necessary to our people in this resistance war. They do not believe in the power of the masses for resistance. All that they would achieve would be the premature sacrifice of the bulk of our forces in a few adventurous battles; they would commit heroic but useless suicide. They pretend to underestimate the enemy. Yet they are the very ones who are afraid of the enemy and of a long resistance war.

What is our line in the fighting? It is to attack actively, and rapidly to decide every battle.

We are attacked. The enemy is stronger than we are. If we only remain on the defensive, only defend ourselves where we are attacked, the more we fight the weaker we shall become—the more we fight the more we shall be defeated. Therefore, in every campaign and battle, the weak points of the enemy must be discovered and attacked, and we must attack actively to annihilate his forces. If we attack, we must do it quickly and decide the battle rapidly. (From the strategic viewpoint, we must prolong the war; but in every individual campaign and from a tactical viewpoint, we must achieve rapid settlements.) It is only by applying the tactics of quick attack that we can destroy the enemy sector by sector. The upshot of many battles in which the enemy is destroyed sector by sector, will be to weaken his forces as a whole, to demoralize them. Our forces, on the other hand, will increase and our fighters' morale will be enhanced. We shall go on in this way until we reach the point at which we are sufficiently strong to launch a general counter-offensive to defeat the enemy on all battle-fronts and to recover the whole of our territory. . . .

Guerilla warfare is the method of fighting in partisan units or with relatively small groups of the regular army disguised as civilians and mingling with the people. Though these forces are armed only with rudimentary weapons, they are extremely active. They attack the enemy from behind, outflank him or launch sudden attacks on his weak points. They pretend to attack the enemy's right flank while actually attacking his left, they concentrate for attack and disperse to dodge the enemy's reply. They cut communication lines, harass the enemy while he is eating or sleeping, wear out his strength, cause him weariness and distress, render his forces lame, lost, hungry, thirsty . . . The three most generally employed tactics of guerilla warfare are: surprise attack, ambush and harassment . . .

Mobile warfare is fighting by the regular army, or by guerilla forces mustered into relatively big units and cooperating with the regular army, using more or less advanced weapons, concentrating themselves rapidly and launching lighting attacks: encircling the enemy in order to destroy him, working round positions to attack him, attacking from behind [rather] than launching frontal attacks, advancing rapidly and withdrawing quickly . . .

To achieve good results in guerilla and mobile warfare, we must mobilize the people to support our armed forces enthusiastically and to fight the enemy together with them. The people are the eyes and ears of the army, they feed and keep our soldiers. It is they who help the army in sabotage and in battle. *The people are the water and our army the fish.* The people constitute an inexhaustible source of strength to the army. To increase their numbers, the troops must recruit new fighters from among the people. That is why the entire people must be armed, guerilla movements must be initiated, the actions of the regular army and guerilla forces coordinated. We must act in such a way that wherever the enemy goes, he meets the resistance forces of the entire Vietnamese people who, arms in hand, fight against him, ready to die rather than return to slavery . . .

To wage a long resistance war, the entire people must be united and single-minded. It is the same with our people as with a bundle of chopsticks. If the chopsticks are bound together it is difficult to break them. But if they are separated, nothing is easier than to snap them one by one until the last.

But uniting the whole people doesn't mean that we blithely shut our eyes and allow a handful of Vietnamese traitors to betray their country freely, that we permit them freely to sabotage the resistance, become the henchmen of the enemy, and deceive and massacre our compatriots. To fight the enemy and to crush the national traitors are two tasks which must be undertaken simultaneously.

DOCUMENT 2.2

France Seeks International Support

Telegram from Léon Pignon, French High Commissioner in Indochina, to the Ministry of Overseas France, "Mao Tse-tung's Recognition of Ho Chi Minh," January 24, 1950

The end of 1949 and the first weeks of 1950 dramatically changed the political and military situation in Southeast Asia. On October 1, 1949, Chinese communists led by Mao Zedong declared the establishment of the People's Republic of China, bringing communist rule to the northern border of Vietnam. The United States and France refused to recognize the new regime in Beijing, but Great Britain, much to the annoyance of Washington and Paris, took that step in January 1950. The new Chinese government solidified its relationship with the DRV by recognizing Ho Chi Minh's government on January 18 and promising to send military aid. All of these developments caused alarm among French leaders, who feared that Chinese aid would greatly embolden the Viet Minh war effort. In this telegram to the colonial ministry in Paris, the top French official in Indochina, High Commissioner Léon Pignon, takes stock of the new situation.

It seems to me obvious that the communists are now determined to push to the limit their advantage in South East Asia and above all in Indochina. When the British officially recognized the Chinese government and set off an avalanche of official recognitions, they probably had no idea of the extent to which they were making life easier for the agents of the Third International.

The speed with which Mao Tse-tung, who is now in Moscow along with [Chinese Premier] Chou Enlai, has made use of the international legitimization conferred on the Chinese Communist state is very worrying, especially the way in which it has encouraged the Chinese government to accelerate and reinforce actions directed against non-communist countries in South East Asia.

. . . If one considers events in the Far East alongside the extraordinary effort that the French Communist Party is now making to sabotage the "dirty war," one must conclude that the Cominform has shifted its political and military aggression to the Far East, where it has found exceptionally favorable conditions for success. These conditions, which I have pointed out on several occasions and which the government knows well, now take on new urgency because everything suggests that a large combined action is close at hand.

On the eve of a possibly decisive challenge, we must bear in mind our principal weaknesses so that we can take them into account in studying ways to shore up the security of South East Asia.

▓ the inability of newly independent states to resist politically and militarily the communist assault.

▓ the total lack of organization of the democratic front in this part of the world and the slowness with which the Anglo-Saxons have moved toward a new policy.

▓ the relative weakness of democratic bloc forces stationed in [South East Asia, and] the dangerous illusion, too often fostered, that one can save Asia from communism simply through economic aid and economic development.

▓ the considerable advantage that the communists hold in exploiting local nationalism, which inspires fierce fighting under their leadership to win an independence that is described as real but in fact brings a danger of [communist] subjugation later on.

In the face of the challenge posed by Communist Chinese recognition of Ho Chi Minh, the democratic powers can adopt only two positions:

[First, they can] accept a fait accompli, recognize that their enemy, undeterred by either world opinion or respect for constitutional procedures, has defeated them in the Far East, and retreat to defensive positions.

If this approach were chosen, I must insist that it will be impossible for France alone to sustain the fight against a resolute and tireless adversary, which now is showing its true face. In this case, we would have to study with our allies the role that our forces—the most important white forces in Asia—could play in a withdrawal plan.

If, on the other hand, the U.S., Great Britain and the Dominions, and some Asian countries that now recognize the results of their short-sighted policies decide to put up a common front and continue to consider the integrity of Vietnam crucial to the defense of their positions, especially if they recognize the Bao Dai government, it is no longer possible for them to delay taking positions aimed at stopping the growing threat of communist expansion.

Now that we have full knowledge of the scope and aims of our adversaries' plan, we can no longer ignore the facts: Far Eastern problems must be considered in their entirety, on the international level and with reference to global military strategy. It is therefore urgent to take stock of the resources available to us from everywhere and to decide together on possible means of defense in the Far East.

It is in the framework of such a study that the defense of Indochina should be considered. This approach is even more appropriate since we failed to keep the "Indochina affair" an entirely Franco-Vietnamese matter, and events long ago pushed it to the level of a major international problem.

Thus, even if we leave aside the military dimension, we cannot avoid interference from multiple global powers in this problem. Any effort to maintain a solitary position—a desirable thing, if it were possible—will doubtlessly end up depriving us of effective material and moral support from the Anglo-Saxons while preventing our allies from making use of the significant assistance that the Associated States of Indochina, Vietnam in particular, can offer.

It is in this larger and more international framework that we must find our support and guarantees. The delaying effect that we have produced to the benefit of the democratic world has become fully evident today, when Mao Tse-tung has revealed Ho Chi Minh as an agent of communist imperialism. Our role in the second phase of action—the phase of international war—will still be considerable. We must stress this contribution since it is only in return for recognition of our sacrifices that we can accept the burden.

But it is obvious that French troops in Indochina, weak in numbers and burdened with mounting problems, will not be able to take on new tasks at the frontiers of Tonkin if they are not quickly supplied with materiel that will enable them to maintain overwhelming technological superiority, the only kind of superiority that we can envisage.

It is also obvious that our financial resources must be significantly increased in order to help our cause at the political and economic level. I know perfectly well that the government does not now have the means which I believe are necessary, but in my opinion we can reasonably ask our allies to supply these funds as the minimum cost of keeping this country out of the communist empire. It would also be important that this help be distributed to the Associated States through us.

Finally, it will be essential that the Anglo-Saxons, after they officially recognize Bao Dai, declare without ambiguity that they consider themselves the guarantors of the frontiers of the new state and that they begin increasing their military presence in Indochina through regular and well-publicized visits of warships and planes.

To sum up, the collapse of Nationalist China had completely changed the nature of the Indochina problem. The policies originally established to solve the problem could not take into account the international situation that has slowly evolved in South East Asia. It will probably not be difficult to demonstrate that our effort in Indochina has reached the breaking point and that it is time for other countries to help us effectively if they do not want to see us abandon our efforts.

DOCUMENT 2.3

Korea and Vietnam

Political Cartoon, *Rochester Times-Union*, September 25, 1950

As French leaders hoped, Washington decided in May 1950 to send military and economic aid to support the war in Indochina. American assistance, just

a trickle at first, increased dramatically following the start of the Korean War on June 25. With communist North Korean troops advancing into pro-Western South Korea in the early days of the fighting, U.S. policymakers feared that the two wars were prongs of a coordinated offensive directed by Moscow to extend communist rule throughout the Far East. Artist Elmer Messner captured U.S. fears in a cartoon published in the *Rochester (New York) Times-Union* three months after the outbreak of war in Korea. The cartoon appeared under the caption "That Firebug Again."

DOCUMENT 2.4

The Risks of Communist Takeover

CIA Study, "Consequences to the US of Communist Domination of Mainland Southeast Asia," October 13, 1950

The United States had few interests in Southeast Asia before the Second World War. For a time after 1945, moreover, American leaders hoped that the European powers would be able to manage the region by facilitating the transition of colonial territories into moderate, Western-oriented nations. By mid-1950, however, Washington regarded the region with utmost urgency and had begun pumping resources into the area to bolster friendly forces, including Bao Dai's regime in Vietnam. Underlying such behavior was a strong sense, illustrated in the following analysis by the Central Intelligence Agency, that losing Southeast Asia to the communist bloc would have an array of devastating strategic, economic, military, and psychological repercussions.

Communist domination of mainland Southeast Asia would not be critical to US security interests but would have serious immediate and direct consequences. The gravest of such consequences would be a spreading of doubt and fear among other threatened non-Communist countries as to the ability of the US to back up its proclaimed intention to halt Communist expansion everywhere. Unless offset by positive additions to the security of non-Communist countries in other sensitive areas of the world, the psychological effect of the loss of mainland Southeast Asia would not only strengthen Communist propaganda that the advance of Communism is inexorable but would encourage countries vulnerable to Soviet pressure to adopt "neutral" attitudes in the cold war, or possibly even lead them to an accommodation with Communism.

Domination of the Southeast Asian mainland would increase the threat to such Western outposts in the Pacific as the island chain extending from Japan to Australia and New Zealand. The extension of Communist control, via Burma, to the borders of India and Pakistan would augment the slowly developing Communist threat to the Indian subcontinent. The fall of the Southeast Asian mainland would increase the feeling of insecurity already present in Japan as a result of Communist successes in China and would further underline the apparent economic advantages to the Japanese of association with a Communist-dominated Asian sphere.

The countries of mainland Southeast Asia produce such materials on the US strategic list as rubber, tin, shellac, kapok, and teak in substantial volume. Although access to these countries is not considered to be "absolutely essential in an emergency" by the National Security Resources Board, US access to this area is considered "desirable." Unlimited Soviet access to the strategic materials of Southeast Asia would probably be "desirable" for the USSR but would not be "absolutely essential in an emergency" and therefore denial of the resources of the area to the Soviet Union would not be essential to the US strategic position. Communist control over the rice surpluses of the Southeast Asian mainland would, however, provide the USSR with considerable bargaining power in its relations with other countries of the Far East.

Loss of the area would indirectly affect US security interests through its important economic consequences for countries aligned with the US. Loss of Malaya would deprive the UK of its greatest net dollar earner. An immediate consequence of the loss of Indochina might be a strengthening of the defense of Western Europe since French expenditures for men and materiel in Indochina would be available to fulfill other commitments. Exclusion of Japan from trade with Southeast Asia would seriously frustrate Japanese prospects for economic recovery.

Communist domination of mainland Southeast Asia would place unfriendly forces astride the most direct and best-developed sea and air routes between the Western Pacific and India and the Near East. The denial to the US of intermediate routes in mainland Southeast Asia would be significant because communications between the US and India and the Near East would be essential in a global war.

In the event of such a war, the development of Soviet submarine and air bases in mainland Southeast Asia probably would compel the detour of US and allied shipping and air transportation in the Southeast Asia region via considerably longer alternate routes to the south. This extension of friendly lines of communication would hamper US strategic movements in this region and tend to isolate the major non-Communist bases in the Far East—the offshore island chain and Australia— from existing bases in East Africa and the Near and Middle East, as well as from potential bases on the Indian sub-continent.

Besides disrupting established lines of communication in the area, the denial of actual military facilities in mainland Southeast Asia—in particular, the loss of the major naval operating bases at Singapore—would compel the utilization of less desirable peripheral bases. Soviet exploitation of the naval and air bases in mainland Southeast Asia probably would be limited by the difficulties of logistic support but would, nevertheless, increase the threat to existing lines of communication.

The loss of any portion of mainland Southeast Asia would increase possibilities for the extension of Communist control over the remainder. The fall of Indochina would provide the Communists with a staging area in addition to China for military operations against the rest of mainland Southeast Asia, and this threat might well inspire accommodation in both Thailand and Burma. Assuming Thailand's loss, the already considerable difficulty faced by the British in maintaining security in Malaya would be greatly aggravated. Assuming Burma's internal collapse, unfavorable trends in India would be accelerated. If Burma were overcome by external aggression, however, a stiffening of the attitude of the Government of India toward International Communism could be anticipated.

DOCUMENT 2.5

Appraising the Revolution
Ho Chi Minh's Report to the Second Congress of the Vietnam Workers' Party, February 1951

By early 1951, the DRV had achieved major military and diplomatic successes. The DRV army, a ragtag force just a few years earlier, scored a sweeping victory over the French the previous fall, destroying French fortifications along the border between Vietnam and China. Meanwhile, Ho Chi Minh's regime won diplomatic recognition from China and the Soviet Union in early 1950, and Beijing began sending military support by the end of that year. When the executive committee (politburo) of the North Vietnamese communist party met in February 1951, however, Ho Chi Minh offered a mixed assessment of the war to date.

It can be said that since the founding of the Party, its policies on the whole have been correct. If they were not, how could we have recorded such tremendous achievements? But we have also shown major shortcomings and weaknesses:

Doctrinal studies are still inadequate, many Party cadres and members are not yet mature ideologically and their theoretical level is still low. As a result, in the carrying out of the politics of the Party and the Government there have occurred erroneous tendencies, either "leftist" or "rightist" . . . Our organization work is also still weak, and often cannot ensure correct implementation of the policies of the Party and the Government.

Therefore, to study our doctrine, sharpen our ideology, raise our theoretical level and perfect our organization are urgent tasks for the Party . . .

Efforts must be made to develop the strength of the troops and the people in order to win success after success and advance towards the general counter-offensive. This task aims at these main points:

- *In the building and development of the army*, all-out efforts must be made towards the organization and consolidation of political and military work among our troops. Their political consciousness, tactics, and techniques, and self-imposed discipline must be heightened. Our army must become a genuine people's army.

Simultaneously, the militia and guerilla units must be developed and consolidated in organization, training, leadership and combat strength. They must make up a vast and solid steel net spread all over the country so that wherever the enemy goes he will get enmeshed.

- *To enhance patriotism*. Our people are inspired by ardent patriotism. This is an invaluable tradition of ours. At all times, whenever the Fatherland is invaded, this patriotism forms an immensely powerful wave sweeping away all dangers and difficulties and drowning all traitors and aggressors.

Many great wars of resistance in our history are proofs of our people's patriotism. We can be proud of the glorious pages of history written by our people in the days of the Trung Sisters, Lady Trieu, Tran Hung Dao, Le Loi, Quang Trung, etc. We must engrave in our minds the achievements of our national heroes because they are the symbols of the heroic nation.

Our fellow countrymen today are worthy of their forefathers. White-haired folk, children, people residing abroad, people living in the area still under enemy control, in the plains, in the highlands—all are imbued with ardent love for the country and hatred for the aggressor. Fighters at the front go hungry for days on end in order to remain in contact with the enemy and annihilate him. Government employees in the rear go hungry for the sake of the troops. Women urge their husbands to enlist in the army while they themselves help to transport supplies. Combatants' mothers take care of the troops as they would their own children. Workers and peasants of both sexes emulate one another to increase production, shrinking from no hardships in order to contribute their part to the Resistance. Landowners offer their lands to the Government. These lofty gestures are all different; yet they are similar for they stem from the same ardent patriotism. Patriotism is like valuable objects. Sometimes these are exhibited in a glass or a crystal vase and are thus clearly visible. But at other times they may be discreetly hidden in a trunk or a suitcase. Our duty is to bring all these hidden valuables into full view. That is, every effort must be made in explanation, propaganda, organization and leadership so that the patriotism of all may find expression in work benefiting the country and the Resistance.

Genuine patriotism is altogether different from the chauvinism of the reactionary imperialist. It is part and parcel of internationalism. It was thanks to their patriotism that the army and the people of the Soviet Union crushed the German and Japanese fascists and safeguarded their socialist Fatherland, thereby helping the working class and the oppressed peoples of the world. It was thanks to their patriotism that the Chinese Liberation Army and the Chinese people destroyed the traitorous Chiang Kai-shek clique and drove out the American imperialists. It is thanks to their patriotism that the Korean troops and people, together with the Chinese Volunteers, are routing the American imperialists and their henchmen. It is also thanks to their patriotism that our troops and people have for long years endured untold sufferings and hardships, determined to smash the colonialist aggressors and the Vietnamese traitors, and to build an independent, re-unified, democratic, free, and prosperous Viet Nam, a new democratic Viet Nam.

- *To step up patriotic emulation.* First, let the troops emulate one another to exterminate the enemy and score feats of arms; second, let the people emulate one another to increase production. We must devote ourselves heart and soul to these two tasks . . .

- *Concerning the land policy*, in the free zones, we must strictly implement the reduction of land rent and interest rates, confiscate lands belonging to the French and the Vietnamese traitors and temporarily distribute them to the poor peasants and the families of army-men, with a view to improving the livelihood of the peasants, heightening their spirit, an fostering their forces for the Resistance.

- *Concerning the economy and finance*, we must safeguard and develop our economic bases and fight the enemy in the economic field. There must be an equitable and rational tax system. A balance must be achieved in receipts and expenditures in order to ensure supplies for the army and the people.

- *Cultural work* must be speeded up to form the new man and train new cadres for the Resistance and for national construction. All vestiges of colonialism and the enslaving influence of imperialist culture must be systematically rooted out. Simultaneously, we must develop the fine traditions of our national culture and assimilate the new in the world progressive culture in order to build a Vietnamese culture with a national, scientific and popular character.

Following our victories, the areas still under temporary enemy control will be liberated one after another. Therefore, preparations must be made to consolidate the newly liberated areas in all respects . . .

We are waging our war of resistance, the brotherly Cambodia and Lao nations are also waging theirs. The French colonialists and the American interventionists are the common enemy of our three nations. Consequently, we must strive to help our Cambodian and Lao brothers and their wars of resistance, and proceed to set up a Vietnam-Cambodia-Laos Front.

DOCUMENT 2.6
A Problematic Partnership
Telegram from Philip W. Bonsal, Counselor at the U.S. Embassy in Paris, to
William Lacy, Director of the State Department's Office of Philippine and
Southeast Asian Affairs, March 31, 1952

In the opinion of nearly all observers, the partnership among the Americans,
French, and the pro-Western Vietnamese regime under Bao Dai did not go
well. The Americans pressed the French to wage the war more aggressively
and to grant greater autonomy to Bao Dai's regime; the French dragged their
feet on greater autonomy and resisted U.S. military advice; Bao Dai's government remained dependent on France and had little direct contact with the
Americans. With public opinion in France turning against the war in early
1952, two U.S. officials in Paris wrote the following note to William Lacy, the
director of the State Department bureau that handled Indochinese affairs.
The telegram was signed by Philip Bonsal, a counselor at the U.S. embassy
who would soon move to Washington to replace Lacy, but it was co-authored
by Philip D. Sprouse, the first secretary of the embassy.

I am writing you . . . to stress my conviction that, while from the financial and
supply point of view there is no immediate anticipation of any change in the
continued bearing by the French of their Indochinese burden, the situation
nevertheless is changing for the worse from the psychological aspect. And
that, in a sense, leads us to the very crux of the whole problem. If the [Indo-
china] effort is to be anything more than a holding operation, a climate of confidence must be created—and that means among the Vietnamese, French and
Americans. Such confidence does not seem to exist here and, from the reports
reaching us from Saigon and on the basis of the accomplishments of the [Bao
Dai] Government to date, there seems to be *at least* a partial lack of confidence
in Indochina. You are better able than I to estimate the degree of confidence in
Washington.

But, how to create this confidence? It seems to me that, if we continue to look at
the problem as merely one of continued appropriations for and deliveries of military and economic aid, we can expect it to be simply a holding operation. As long
as the Chinese Communists sit on the other side of the border and feed in the ingredients necessary to a continuation of the Vietminh rebellion, there seems to be
no hope of a purely military decision. This, in my opinion, serves to emphasize the
inextricably woven pattern of the politico-military aspects of the situation. Certainly there can be no confidence without the military security which would reduce
the Vietminh threat. But that alone is not enough and never will be, unless we are
willing to throw in overwhelming forces to aid the French and stay until the job is
done. I take it that such a course of action is not even worthy of consideration,
given present world conditions. We must, therefore, behind the screen of military
protection find some means of building up confidence which would increase the

effectiveness both of the Vietnamese Government and of its national army. There certainly seems to be some kind of mystique behind the Vietminh which makes its troops, who are also "Vietnamese," continue the fight and create the uneasiness among the native people which results in less than full support of the [Bao Dai] Government and creates attentism.

In searching for the means by which we can build up this confidence, the first thing that comes to my mind—and this is not a new idea by any means—is the long-range outcome to all this effort. Given the present state of mind of Asiatics and the state of world affairs in terms of the strength of the Occident, is there any reason to believe that a Vietnamese Government strong enough to make a decisive contribution to the effort against the Communist-led rebellion will ever be willing to settle at the end of the battle for anything less than complete independence or, at best, a status comparable to that of India or Pakistan? Have we, and more importantly, have the French thought this through to the end? They, and we, speak of the creation and building up of a Vietnamese national army as a means of obtaining the repatriation of French forces in Indochina to the Metropole, where they can make the essential contribution to the rearmament effort in Europe. If the French are to bring back a sizable portion of their forces now in Indochina, it will flow either from the success of the Vietnamese forces or from a military disaster ending in their eviction. In either case the French are faced in the long run with a dynamic Vietnamese Government or a Communist Vietminh regime. If these assumptions have any validity—and I am laying aside the assumption that the whole thing is only a holding operation, since that is defeatist—then the French Government should face up to the long-range end result.

I know that in doing this they face the ever-present problem of how to justify the French effort in Indochina if it is only in order to hand over the country to the Vietnamese when it is all over. There is the vital question whether the National Assembly would have any heart for a contribution of French funds and blood if that was the only end in sight. There is also the important question of the effect of such action on the rest of the French Union, particularly North Africa. These two aspects of the problem—that is, the difficulty of obtaining from the National Assembly the continued necessary appropriations and the possible effect on North Africa—may represent insurmountable obstacles.

It seems to me that we have the following alternatives (there may be others): (1) The French withdraw, cut their losses and have Ho Chi-minh take over immediately. (2) The French hang on with our aid in a holding operation, frankly recognized as such, thus continuing the heavy drain financially and militarily, accompanied by the risk that at some point the burden becomes unbearable and they are forced to withdraw. If it is a holding operation, it becomes worthwhile only as an operation against the day when World War III breaks, at which time they might withdraw in an effort to save what forces they could for use elsewhere. In either case the French are finished in Indochina. (3) The French face up to the probability that the only way they can ease their burden is by the creation of native forces which will allow a partial French withdrawal and will bring about a greater and more effective Vietnamese effort. If this policy (which is that now being tried by the French Government if their own words are to be believed) is followed to its ultimate end and *is successful*, we will have a native government which will be in a position to face up to the French and perhaps tell them in effect "so sorry, this our garden now" (to paraphrase Ogden Nash). If the French are reluctant, they might get pushed out and thereby end the possibility of any kind of understanding with the Vietnamese. Here again, the end result is the end of France in Indochina.

Against the background of the foregoing, it seems to me that the French might well be asked what their view of the end result is and what they are prepared to do about it . . . The French Government could do much worse than realize the probable end results and then tell the Vietnamese, both privately and publicly, that when the bloodshed is over and the Vietminh rebellion is ended, the Vietnamese will be allowed to make their own choice—to remain in the French Union or to become completely independent. There is inevitably the risk that they might choose the latter, but if they, in the face of a hostile Communist China, decided that membership within the French Union had its advantages (don't forget that one of France's commitments in the constitution is to defend the French Union), then France and the free world would have gained. In the interim, the attentists would no longer have an excuse for attentism on the grounds that the French had no aim other than to maintain their control. It would provide an answer to the Nehrus of this world. And, the French might then save something from the ruins in the investment field, which would not otherwise be the case . . . The French have not convinced enough Indochinese that the real enemies are Ho Chi-minh and the Chinese Communists.

DOCUMENT 2.7
U.S. Leaders Weigh Intervention
Notes on a Meeting of the National Security Council, March 25, 1954

As the French lost ground at Dien Bien Phu, U.S. leaders confronted the question of whether to intervene in the fighting in order to prevent a communist victory. That possibility seemed to grow more likely in mid-March 1954, when the president's special committee on Indochina recommended that the United States work with its allies to prolong the war, including through the commitment of U.S. air, naval, and ground forces, if the French accepted a deal that "fell short of achieving real security and independence" for Vietnam, Cambodia, and Laos. The Joint Chiefs of Staff also pressed for decisions about the possibility of intervention. On March 25, President Eisenhower met with his National Security Council to consider these matters. Participants in the meeting included Secretary of State John Foster Dulles, Secretary of Defense Charles E. Wilson, Army Chief of Staff Matthew Ridgeway, Foreign Operations Administration Director Harold Stassen, and National Security Adviser Robert Cutler.

Secretary Dulles referred to a memorandum which set forth the views of the Joint Chiefs of Staff with respect to what the United States might do in the event of a French withdrawal or defeat in Indochina. He read paragraph 11 of the JCS memo, which read: "The National Security Council [should] consider now the extent to which the United States would be willing to commit its resources in support of the Associated States in the effort to prevent the loss of Indochina to the Communists either: *a.* In concert with the French; or *b.* In the event the French elect to withdraw, in concert with other allies or, if necessary, unilaterally." Secretary Dulles recommended that the Council instruct the [interagency] Planning Board to prepare the desired report, and explained that Secretary Wilson also favored this proposal.

Mr. Cutler replied that the Planning Board would undertake the study at once, but inquired whether it should envisage U.S. intervention with military forces . . .

The President replied to Mr. Cutler by stating that what he was asking was the extent to which we should go in employing ground forces to save Indochina from the Communists. The President pointed out, however, that there were certain omissions in the JCS memorandum. There was, for example, no reference to the UN taking cognizance of the aggression in Indochina. While he knew that the French were much opposed to any appeal to the UN, he himself did not see how the United States or other free world nations could go full-out in support of the Associated States without UN approval and assistance.

Secretary Dulles expressed the belief that while it might not be impossible to get a two-thirds UN vote in favor of intervention in Indochina, it would be far from easy, since we could count on the opposition of the Asian-Arab bloc, among others.

The President said he believed that the UN would certainly not intervene merely on the strength of a French appeal, but might do so if Vietnam called for assistance and particularly cited Chinese Communist aid to the rebels. In any case, said the President, he was clear that the Congress would have to be in on any move by the United States to intervene in Indochina. It was simply academic to imagine otherwise.

Secretary Wilson raised the question of what our reaction should be in the event that the Chinese Communists sent in MIG aircraft for operations over Indochina. Mr. Cutler answered that the existing policy paper on Southeast Asia was quite clear on this point. If the Chinese Communists flew aircraft into Indochina they would be guilty of overt aggression, and our response to such aggression had been clearly set forth in NSC [paper] 5405 [calling for U.S. intervention].

Secretary Dulles agreed with Mr. Cutler's response to Secretary Wilson's question, but pointed out that even so, the Executive would still have to go to Congress before intervening in the Indochina war. He then reminded the Council that the Attorney General was presumably preparing an opinion with respect to the prerogatives of the President and of the Congress in the matter of using U.S. military forces to counter aggression, and he hoped that the Attorney General would hasten completion of his report. The President suggested that Mr. Cutler prod the Attorney General, and suggested that this might be the moment to begin to explore with the Congress what support could be anticipated in the event that it seemed desirable to intervene in Indochina.

Secretary Dulles expressed the opinion that a lot more work needed to be done by the NSC on this problem before we were ready to take it up with Congress. He pointed out that the fighting season in Indochina would end soon, and he believed would end without a clear military decision. Furthermore, he thought it quite unlikely that the Chinese Communists would engage their MIGs in battle over Indochina prior to the Geneva Conference. The Communists were seeking a political rather than a military victory at this stage, and we could therefore safely discount overt Chinese intervention in Indochina. Nevertheless, the United States would certainly have to reach a clear-cut decision vis-à-vis the French. We were witnessing, said Secretary Dulles, the collapse or evaporation of France as a great power in most areas of the world. The great question was, who should fill the void left by the collapse of French power, particularly in the colonial areas. Would it be the Communists, or must it be the U.S.? In its consideration of the problem of U.S. intervention in Indochina, the Planning Board should give consideration to the fact that the United States could not move into the position abandoned by France in Indochina without estimating the repercussions in other parts of the world. Secretary Dulles expressed the belief that the French had actually reached a point where they would rather abandon Indochina than save it through United States intervention and assumption of French responsibilities. All this constituted primarily a political rather than a military problem. Accordingly, it could be settled after the end of the fighting season in May. In any event, Secretary Dulles did not believe that there was any need for the Council to proceed on the assumption of an imminent French military withdrawal. There was, accordingly, time allowed us to work out some kind of suitable UN action . . .

The President raised the question of what specific nations might be induced to join us in a broadened effort to save Indochina. It might be done, he thought, on the basis of expanding the ANZUS defense treaty with Australia and New Zealand. There were in any case only two possible ways of carrying this thing through. One was to induce the United Nations to intervene. The other was to get Vietnam to invite certain specific nations to come to its assistance on the basis of a treaty between Vietnam and each of the assisting nations. This latter offered the United States a good chance, since we could in all probability get the necessary two-thirds majority vote in the Senate on such a treaty. There was the added advantage, continued the President, that this procedure avoided solely Occidental assistance to Vietnam . . .

Governor Stassen expressed the belief that the best way to proceed to give the Associated States the necessary outside assistance would be to call for an economic conference of the Asian nations and thereafter gradually introduce the military security factor. That, in essence, was how NATO got started.

After further discussion of the governments and nations who might be approached to assist the Associated States, the President said that he thought that such a grouping of nations would probably have to be confined to those nations in or near Southeast Asia itself. If an attempt were made to expand the number to include, for instance, Japan and Korea, we would run up against the hostility which exists between so many of the Asian nations. It would perhaps be better, therefore, to consider Australia, New Zealand, the Philippines, Formosa, the free nations of Southeast Asia, the British, and the French. That was enough, wasn't it?

Secretary Dulles commented that of course the real problem which one immediately encountered in trying to decide on procedure was France. Either it would be necessary for the United States to beat the French into line, or else to accept a split with France. Both courses of action involved the gravest difficulty, particularly in relation to [the European Defense Community] . . .

Secretary Wilson asked whether it would be sensible to forget about Indochina for a while and concentrate on the effort to get the remaining free nations of Southeast Asia in some sort of condition to resist Communist aggression against themselves. The President expressed great doubt as to the feasibility of such a proposal, since he believed that the collapse of Indochina would produce a chain reaction which would result in the fall of all of Southeast Asia to the Communists.

3

BETWEEN TWO STORMS

INTERNATIONAL AGREEMENTS signed in July 1954 brought peace to Indochina. Military forces disengaged, and Vietnamese leaders turned their attention to vast economic and administrative problems created by eight years of war. In the late 1950s, however, war returned to Vietnam, fighting that would ultimately draw in U.S. combat forces. The peace that settled over Vietnam in 1954 turned out to be a mere calm between two storms.

Tensions that led to new fighting flowed from the peculiarities of the peace accord. DRV negotiators insisted on the independence and unity of their nation, but the great powers had other ideas: American leaders opposed the unification of Vietnam under communist control, and the Soviet and Chinese governments wanted to ease Cold War tensions more than they wanted to back their Vietnamese ally. In the end, the powers divided Vietnam at the seventeenth parallel, with the DRV administering the north and a pro-Western regime in charge in the south. Elections were to be held in 1956 for a single government that would knit the country back together.

Ho Chi Minh's government, desperate to end the fighting and hopeful of peaceful reunification in 1956, accepted this solution. Before long, however, it became clear that elections would never take place. The Saigon regime, led by staunch anti-communist Ngo Dinh Diem, rejected the idea, and the U.S. government quietly backed Diem. Thereafter, the two Vietnams increasingly looked like separate nations—the DRV in the north and the Republic of Vietnam in the South—divided by a border at the seventeenth parallel.

Although each Vietnamese government claimed to rule the entire country, both focused on resolving enormous internal problems in the first years after the Geneva agreements. In the DRV, commonly known as North Vietnam, Ho Chi Minh's government struggled with economic woes. A radical program of land redistribution between 1953 and 1956 compounded the challenges by unleashing a wave of ideologically inspired violence that killed tens of thousands of farmers and stirred widespread hostility to the regime.

In the Republic of Vietnam, known as South Vietnam, Ngo Dinh Diem's government also confronted major problems. In contrast to the North, the South was deeply fractured into rival political and religious groupings and lacked robust governmental institutions. So serious were Diem's problems that many American observers feared he stood no chance of establishing a viable state. They were therefore impressed when he not only survived numerous challenges to his authority but also vanquished his rivals between 1954 and 1956. Diem's government became one of the biggest recipients in the world of U.S. aid and a cornerstone of Western influence in Southeast Asia.

The ruthlessness with which Diem consolidated his authority turned out, however, to be a liability. Most importantly, the government's efforts to stamp out communist influence in the countryside, while effective for a time, alienated many peasants and ultimately helped provoke a new insurgency. Assassinations of South Vietnamese officials and attacks on South Vietnamese installations increased dramatically in 1958 and 1959.

At first, the government in Hanoi took a cautious approach to surging revolutionary violence in the South. Communist leaders continued to prioritize the internal development of North Vietnam, while the Soviet Union and China opposed a new war. In 1959, however, Hanoi changed course, authorizing military activity in the South and laying plans to send supplies and troops across the seventeenth parallel. The next year, Southern revolutionaries, with Hanoi's blessing, established the National Liberation Front (NLF) with the goal of overthrowing the government in Saigon.

DOCUMENT 3.1

Gloomy U.S. Predictions for South Vietnam

National Intelligence Estimate, "Probable Developments in South Vietnam, Laos, and Cambodia Through July 1956," November 23, 1954

Following the Geneva conference, American officials had little confidence that a communist takeover of South Vietnam could be prevented. Ngo Dinh Diem's regime confronted a staggering array of problems, including the hostility of the Hoa Hao and Cao Dai religious sects, the Binh Xuyen crime syndicate, key officers in the national army, and the French political and military establishments, which remained powerful despite the end of the war. The Central Intelligence Agency and other U.S. intelligence organizations collaborated to study all of these problems in the following report dated November 23, 1954.

The political situation in Vietnam south of the 17th parallel is one of almost total paralysis, caused primarily by the struggle for political power between Prime Minister Ngo Dinh Diem and his supporters on the one hand and a motley array of opposing elements on the other.

In the existing situation problems of extreme urgency have been neglected, and the authority of the South Vietnam state has remained nominal. The government has been largely ineffective in meeting vital tasks such as maintaining domestic order, performing the normal functions of civil administration, dealing with the extraordinary problems created by the armistice, and overcoming long-standing problems such as inefficiency and corruption.

The Vietnamese National Army is demoralized and disorganized, and its capability even for dealing with internal disorder is low. It lacks trained leadership and an aggressive spirit.

On the other hand, the Viet Minh in North Vietnam appears to have adjusted to the post-Geneva phase with continuing and unimpaired confidence. The Viet Minh derived from the Geneva Conference international recognition and greatly enhanced power and prestige. It is methodically consolidating its control over North Vietnam and continuing to plan for the extension of this control over South Vietnam as well. The Communist psychological offensive against the free areas of Indochina continues unabated, and the Viet Minh is continuing to develop networks of agents and political cadres throughout South Vietnam, Laos, and Cambodia . . .

The conclusion of the armistice greatly weakened non-Communist Vietnam morally and materially. Partition at the 17th parallel is abhorred by all Vietnamese, who regard unity of the three regions of Vietnam as a prerequisite of nationhood. The non-Communist state has been shorn of large territories, important resources, and above all of a considerable segment of its more homogenous and energetic population, particularly the Catholics and anti-Viet Minh nationalists of Tonkin.

Moreover, efforts to develop a strong state in South Vietnam are hindered by geographic and ethnic differences and wide social, cultural, and political heterogeneity. Cochinchina, rich and populous, is a mixture of diverse and divergent political, social, and religious forces: the apathetic rice-growing masses of the Mekong Delta; the large urbanized populations in cities like Saigon; the 1,500,000 adherents of the Caodai and the 500,000 adherents of the Hoa Hao, autonomous politico-religious sects which control large areas; the strong and homogeneous groups of Catholics; large overseas Chinese and Cambodian minorities; and approximately 300,000 destitute refugees from North Vietnam. Moreover, coastal south Annam has been in Communist hands without interruption since 1945, and has consequently been subjected to prolonged Communist indoctrination. Finally, the mass of the south Vietnamese have seen such a succession of crises in the last decade that they have become in effect inured to political developments and unresponsive to appeals.

Leadership elements in South Vietnam are drawn broadly from the following groups: (a) monarchists and court followers close to Bao Dai; (b) rich merchants and landlords whose interests are linked with those of French economic groups in Indochina; (c) former administrative officials; (d) professional men and intellectuals, nationalistic but not given to action; (e) a small number of professional politicians and intriguers; (f) leaders of the politico-religious sects, warlords who exploit every opportunity for wealth and power; and *(g)* army leadership—personified by General Hinh—a new-comer group whose influence is not completely known. These elements have for years accommodated themselves to French control and to a world of half-peace, half-war. In this climate, expediency has in most instances substituted for integrity and personal aggrandizement for devotion to public service . . .

Should the Diem government fall, it would probably be succeeded by an uneasy coalition drawn from the self-interested individuals and groups now contesting Diem's position. Almost certainly, however, any successor to the Diem government would be hampered by the incessant political intrigues which have plagued Diem. Moreover, no successor government is likely to be effective. A government tied closely to and politically supported by the French can have little popular following. But a government which does not have the benefit of the maintenance of public order by the French coupled with French non-interference in the local political scene, is not likely to be able to maintain itself for any length of time.

The internal security situation will remain precarious. The French will continue reluctant to commit their forces in internal security operations, believing that such action would antagonize the population and in the end might create greater problems than it would solve. Moreover, during the period of this estimate, Vietnamese forces will lack the capacity to maintain order unless the present political deterioration is reversed . . .

We believe that the Viet Minh will continue to gain in political strength and prestige and, with Chinese aid, to increase its military striking power in North Vietnam. The Viet Minh probably now feels that it can achieve control over all Vietnam without initiating large-scale warfare. Accordingly, we believe that the Communists will exert every effort to accomplish their objectives through means short of war. Viet Minh agents will continue to subvert all susceptible elements of the population, to intrigue to prevent the coalescence of the various factions and the building of any strength in the south, and Viet Minh "shadow-governments" and politico-military networks will be established wherever the failure of the national government or the French to impose controls leaves the Communists a vacuum in which to operate. As a result of their activities and probable degree of penetration in South Vietnam, it is possible that the Communists will succeed in convincing most Vietnamese in the south of the inevitability of Communist control.

If, on the other hand, South Vietnam should appear to be gaining in strength or if elections were postponed over Communist objections, the Communists probably would step up their subversive and guerrilla activities in the South and if necessary would infiltrate additional armed forces in an effort to gain control over the area. However, we believe that they would be unlikely openly to invade South Vietnam at least prior to July 1956, the date set for national elections, because: *(a)* they would consider that their prospects of gaining control over the area without resort to invasion continued to be highly favorable; *(b)* they would be concerned over the possibility of US military counteraction; and *(c)* they would probably fear that invasion would induce the neutral nations in Asia to move toward open alignments with the West.

We believe, on the basis of present trends, it is highly unlikely that South Vietnam will develop the strength necessary to counter growing Communist subversion within its borders; it almost certainly would not be able to defeat the Communists in country-wide elections. Even before the elections scheduled for 1956, the probable growth of Communist influence in the South may result in strong pressures within South Vietnam for coalition with the North.

DOCUMENT 3.2
An American Appraisal of the Vietnamese Countryside
Report by Agriculture Specialist Wolf Ladejinsky, July 16, 1955

To the astonishment of many South Vietnamese and Americans, Ngo Dinh Diem skillfully consolidated his authority during 1955, subduing the Binh Xuyen crime syndicate as well as the Hoa Hao and Cao Dai religious sects, which had wielded substantial influence in southern Vietnam. With Diem's rule seeming to hang in the balance, few Americans worried much about the attitudes of ordinary farmers in the South Vietnamese countryside. An important exception was Wolf Ladejinsky, a Ukrainian-born agricultural economist sent to South Vietnam by the U.S. Agency for International Development in 1955. Drawing on his travels through rural South Vietnam, Ladejinsky warned Washington in several lengthy reports that Diem's regime was failing to address the needs of the peasantry. The following excerpt is drawn from a lengthy report that Ladejinsky wrote after a trip through four of South Vietnam's southernmost provinces in early 1955.

F act gathering in Vietnam is difficult. Nothing is arranged in neat columns from which one may deduce reasonably accurate information. The attitude of the farmer is often even more difficult to fathom; it is not easy to determine whether he speaks his innermost thoughts or the piece implanted in his mind by years of Viet Minh indoctrination. One is therefore never absolutely certain that the picture itself and the conclusions drawn from it are what they appear to be. The only corrective to this unsatisfactory situation is further probing, in the hope that it does not merely compound original errors. It is with these uneasy thoughts that I set out for South Vietnam twice again after my first two reports to observe conditions in the provinces of Tay Ninh, Soc Trang, Bac Lieu, and Can Tho.

The time of the visits, late May and middle and late June, is worth noting because the month of May is likely to be remembered as a crucial one in the history of modern Vietnam. It was the month of the defeat of the Binh Xuyen gangsters; the neutralization of the Cao Dai sect; the emergence of the national army as a fighting instrument; and, by the same token, the emergence of President Ngo Dinh Diem as the undisputed leader of [South] Vietnam. These are all elements pointing in the direction of unification and stabilization of the country.

On the face of it, one might have expected to find that the national government had extended its authority and that the land reform program was being more readily accepted. In reality, recent observations in South Vietnam do not support all of these seemingly logical assumptions. The salutary political effects of the victory over the Binh Xuyen was apparent in Tay Ninh, the stronghold of the Cao Dai; but it has failed as yet to have a similar effect upon the attitude of the farmers toward the reform and the national government. Nor has local administration been visibly affected by the significant events of the past two months . . .

With few exceptions, chiefs of provinces and district officers are disturbingly unconcerned; even the exceptional official tends to engage in merely verbalizing the need for the enforcement of the law rather than concentrating on what little he could do to gain the confidence of the farmers and persuade them to accept the national government as *their* government. The emphasis is on the word "little," for, in justice to this better type of local administrator, he cannot do much until and unless the national government does its part in helping create the climate of "acceptance." The much vaster job of the national government lies beyond the successful trial of arms—it is to demonstrate its appreciation and understanding of the fundamental aspirations of the farmers. Of that there is only the merest beginnings; the people close to the grass roots must shift for themselves as best they know how, and the best is none too good. Unless the situation is radically improved, it will continue to benefit the antigovernment forces . . .

When we talk of farmers in South Vietnam, we refer to tenants. In all of South Vietnam the majority of the farmers do not own the land they cultivate. The French claim that "No country in the world could have done so much for the native population as France has done in Indochina." This statement alludes above all to the development of rice culture in Cochin China. Viewed in this light, a good measure of the claim is not without validity, although in the process of opening the land the French did not fail to stake out for themselves hundreds of thousands of choice acres in Cochin China and a total of about 1,300,000 acres in all of Indochina. Rich Vietnamese followed suit, [and] many of the cultivators who followed the [big land-developers] found themselves with no land of their own, and became tenants on other men's land. The depression of the 1930s helped to swell the tenant ranks. They often continued working the same land, but on somebody else's terms . . .

Throughout the civil war [1946–1954] Ca Mau was one of the principal centers of Viet Minh activity in South Vietnam. It was also the staging center of Viet Minh armed forces preparatory to their removal to North Vietnam in compliance with the Geneva agreement. According to local officials, they left behind very potent ideas and agents among the farmers. How deep this influence runs or how numerous the agents are, no official would venture to guess; but the district chiefs of Gia

Rai and Ca Mau agree that in a free election held today the majority of the farmers would vote for the Viet Minh. Wherein lie the causes for this support and how can they be eliminated? . . . [T]he problem can be fruitfully touched upon . . . , particularly as the district chief of Ca Mau, a former laborer in the Communist vineyard, was willing to air his views on the subject . . .

Tenants, owner cultivators, and landlords all were subject to taxation under the Viet Minh, the scale ranging stiff-stiffer-stiffest. Exemptions were almost nonexistent, since the Communists levied a 6 percent tax even on those so-called producers whose output was only from 61 to 75 kilograms per capita, far below their own consumption requirements. To be sure, hardly any farmer in Vietnam produces that little, but the Viet Minh position that even the smallest of the small producers is subject to tax is significant . . .

We addressed [the question of why peasants supported the Viet Minh despite the heavy tax burden] to the ex-Viet Minh official. The principal answer he gave us is roughly the same we heard in central Vietnam and in other provinces of South Vietnam: the farmers did not look upon the rice tax as economic exploitation. If our informants' statements were correct, the famers themselves practically administered the rice tax because of their supposed conviction that theirs was but a voluntary contribution to the People's War for Liberation. To promote that particular goal, the Communist leadership succeeded in convincing large sections of the people that they, the people, truly matter and that the economic imposts and other hardships were self-imposed by the multitude rather than by a small group with interests all of their own. This altogether new approach of not merely telling the people what to do but of taking them into the Viet Minh confidence and consulting with them impressed and flattered the farmers. It gave them a sense of participation and belonging never experienced before, and the support of the Viet Minh was a natural development . . .

Terror as a method of enforcing the "will of the people" was among the noneconomic factors he cited. But in his opinion leadership and organization as a means of identifying the Viet Minh with the people were by far the more potent weapons.

DOCUMENT 3.3

Caught Between Peace and War
Le Duan, "The Path of Revolution in the South," 1956

Following the Geneva Accords, Vietnamese communists who believed they must press quickly for national reunification, even at the risk of renewed war, were overruled. The dominant faction within the party believed that the time had come to focus on consolidating the new North Vietnamese state and insisted that communists in the South restrict their activities to political agitation. Internationally, neither the Soviet Union, which backed "peaceful coexistence" with the West, nor China wished to see new violence in Vietnam. This situation left Vietnamese advocates of quick reunification in a difficult position. On the one hand, they were bound to respect the will of their party and of the communist powers. On the other, they chafed against the peaceful policy and sought to keep alive the possibility of forceful action. The awkwardness of this position is captured in the following declaration written in 1956 by Le Duan, a high-ranking Southern communist official who would rise to the pinnacle of power in Hanoi a few years later.

The [overall balance of power in the Cold War] forces bellicose states such as the U.S. and Britain to recognize that if they adventurously start a world war, they themselves will be the first to be destroyed, and thus the movement to demand peace in those imperialist countries is also developing strongly.

Recently, in the U.S. Presidential election, the present Republican administration, in order to buy the people's esteem, put forward the slogan "Peace and Prosperity," which showed that even the people of an imperialist warlike country like the U.S. want peace.

The general situation shows us that the forces of peace and democracy in the world have tipped the balance toward the camp of peace and democracy. Therefore we can conclude that the world at present can maintain long-term peace.

On the other hand, however, we can also conclude that as long as the capitalist economy survives, it will always scheme to provoke war, and there will still remain the danger of war.

Based on the above the world situation, the Twentieth Congress of the Communist Party of the Soviet Union produced two important judgments:

1. All conflicts in the world at present can be resolved by means of peaceful negotiations.
2. The revolutionary movement in many countries at present can develop peacefully.

Naturally in the countries in which the ruling class has a powerful military-police apparatus and is using fascist policies to repress the movement, the revolutionary parties in those countries must look clearly at their concrete situation to have the appropriate methods of struggle.

Based on the general situation and that judgment, we conclude that, if all conflicts can be resolved by means of peaceful negotiations, peace can be achieved.

Because the interest and aspiration of peaceful reunification of our country are the common interest and aspiration of all the people of the Northern and Southern zones, the people of the two zones [do] not have any reason to provoke war, nor to prolong the division of the country. On the contrary the people of the two zones are more and more determined to oppose the U.S.–Diem scheme of division and war provocation in order to create favorable conditions for negotiations between the two zones for peaceful unification of the country.

The present situation of division is created solely by the arbitrary U.S.–Diem regime, so the fundamental problem is how to smash the U.S.–Diem scheme of division and war-provocation.

As observed above, if they want to oppose the U.S.–Diem regime, there is no other path for the people of the South but the path of revolution. What, then, is the line and struggle method of the revolutionary movement in the South? If the world situation can maintain peace due to a change in the relationship of forces in the world in favor of the camp of peace and democracy, the revolutionary movement can develop following a peaceful line, and the revolutionary movement in the South can also develop following a peaceful line.

First of all, we must determine what it means for a revolutionary movement to struggle according to a peaceful line. A revolutionary movement struggling according to a peaceful line takes the political forces of the people as the base rather than using people's armed forces to struggle with the existing government to achieve their revolutionary objective. A revolutionary movement struggling according to a peaceful line is also different from a reformist movement in that a reformist movement relies fundamentally on the law and constitution to struggle, while a revolutionary movement relies on the revolutionary political forces of the masses as the base. And another difference is that a revolutionary movement struggles for revolutionary objectives, while a reformist movement struggles for reformist goals.

With an imperialist, feudalist, dictatorial, fascist government like the U.S.–Diem [regime], is it possible for a peaceful political struggle line to achieve its objectives?

We must recognize that all accomplishments in every country are due to the people. That is a definite law: it cannot be otherwise. Therefore the line of the revolutionary movement must be in accord with the inclinations and aspirations of the people. Only in that way can a revolutionary movement be mobilized and succeed.

The ardent aspiration of the Southern people is to maintain peace and achieve national unification. We must clearly recognize this longing for peace: the revolutionary movement in the South can mobilize and advance to success on the basis of grasping the flag of peace, in harmony with popular feelings. On the contrary, U.S.–Diem is using fascist violence to provoke war, contrary to the will of the people and therefore must certainly be defeated.

Can the U.S.–Diem regime, by using a clumsy policy of fascist violence, create a strong force to oppose and destroy the revolutionary movement? Definitely not, because the U.S.–Diem regime has no political strength in the country worth mentioning to rely on.

On the contrary, nearly all strata of the people oppose them. Therefore the U.S.–Diem government is not a strong government[;] it is only a vile and brutal government. Its vile and brutal character means that it not only has no mass base in the country but is on the way to being isolated internationally. Its cruelty definitely cannot shake the revolutionary movement, and it cannot survive for long.

The proof is that in the past two years, everywhere in the countryside, the sound of the gunfire of U.S.–Diem repression never ceased; not a day went by when they did not kill patriots, but the revolutionary spirit is still firm, and the revolutionary base of the people still has not been shaken.

Once the entire people have become determined to protect the revolution, there is no cruel force that can shake it. But why has the revolutionary movement not yet developed strongly? This is also due to certain objective and subjective factors. Objectively, we see that, after nine years of waging strong armed struggle, the people's movement generally speaking now has a temporarily peaceful character that is a factor in the change of the movement for violent forms of struggle to peaceful forms. It has the correct character of rebuilding to advance later.

With the cruel repression and exploitation of the U.S.–Diem [regime], the people's revolutionary movement definitely will rise up. The people of the South have known the blood and fire of nine years of resistance war, but the cruelty of the U.S.–Diem [regime] cannot extinguish the struggle spirit of the people.

On the other hand, subjectively, we must admit that a large number of cadres, those that have responsibility for guiding the revolutionary movement, because of the change in the method of struggle and the work situation from public to secret, have not yet firmly grasped the political line of the party, have not yet firmly grasped the method of political struggle, and have not yet followed correctly the mass line, and therefore have greatly reduced the movement's possibilities for development.

At present, therefore, the political struggle movement has not yet developed equally among the people, and a primary reason is that a number of cadres and masses are not yet aware that the strength of political forces of the people can defeat the cruelty, oppression and exploitation of the U.S.–Diem [regime], and therefore they have a half-way attitude and don't believe in the strength of their political forces.

We must admit that any revolutionary movement has times when it falls and times when it rises; any revolutionary movement has times that are favorable for development and times that are unfavorable. The basic thing is that the cadres must see clearly the character of the movement's development to lead the mass struggle to the correct degree, and find a way for the vast determined masses to participate in the movement. If they are determined to struggle from the bottom to the top, no force can resist the determination of the great masses . . .

There are those who think that the U.S.–Diem [regime's] use of violence is now aimed fundamentally at killing the leaders of the revolutionary movement to destroy the Communist Party, and that if the Communist Party is worn away to the point that it doesn't have the capacity to lead the revolution, the political struggle movement of the masses cannot develop.

This judgment is incorrect. Those who lead the revolutionary movement are determined to mingle with the masses, to protect and serve the interest of the masses and to pursue correctly the mass line. Between the masses and communists there is no distinction any more. So how can the U.S.–Diem [regime] destroy the leaders of the revolutionary movement, since they cannot destroy the masses? Therefore they cannot annihilate the cadres leading the mass movement.

DOCUMENT 3.4

South Vietnam's Challenges

Speech by South Vietnamese President Ngo Dinh Diem, National Press Club, Washington, D.C., May 10, 1957

Within two years of the Geneva agreements, South Vietnamese President Ngo Dinh Diem had defied expectations by consolidating his authority. Diem garnered praise for his accomplishments during a triumphant visit to the United States in May 1957. Basking in adulation, Diem delivered a series of speeches in which he boasted of his achievements but warned of remaining dangers to his rule. In the following address, delivered at the National Press Club in Washington, Diem thanked Americans for their help in the anticommunist struggle. But he also emphasized that U.S. prescriptions for transforming South Vietnam into a Western-style nation were inappropriate for a society like Vietnam.

D estiny has placed our country at the converging point of one of the great human migrations. It lies across one of the main roads of access to the reserves of raw materials of South East Asia. In addition to this critical situation, the Vietnamese masses, like the Asian masses, are now aware that their political and economic development were retarded by colonial domination. Their nationalist feeling and social resentment have thereby been exacerbated. They have become embittered and impatient. They want to catch up rapidly with the advanced western nations, and some are even prepared to accept totalitarian measures in order to achieve this end.

The Communists have taken advantage of this situation to extend their domination over continental China and over neighboring countries.

Thus Viet-Nam, by virtue of its geography and history, is subject both internally and externally to heavy pressure. Its future political and economic regime will be to a very large extent determined by this fact. The Vietnamese people will be able to defend their independence and freedom against the covetousness of expansionist nations and the seduction of totalitarianism, only to the extent that they possess the necessary intelligence and sense of discipline. You should not lose sight of these geographical, sociological and historical facts if you wish to appraise correctly and justly our present efforts, because the Viet-Nam problem is a complex one.

Viet-Nam is located at a strategic spot in Asia. Its people are sensitive to all the currents which are agitating the Asian world. The problems of Viet-Nam cannot be separated from those of Asia. None of us must forget that Asia is living in a state of high revolutionary tension. Nationalist feeling may be in a large measure satisfied by the recovery of political independence, but only on the condition that political independence be made meaningful by tangible economic independence. And this is precisely the key to the understanding of Asia's revolt. Revolutionary tension there is at a high pitch because for too long the peoples of Asia have been the victims of hunger, disease and illiteracy. They are impatient. They want to see a quick end to their miseries. But how?

Viet-Nam cannot shut itself off from this revolutionary atmosphere, because Asia's problems are Viet-Nam's problems. Furthermore, by virtue of its geopolitical situation, Viet-Nam lies in the midst of this tension itself.

We see from time to time some Asian statesmen or leaders adopt positions which do not agree with our viewpoint. They probably hope thereby to shelter their peoples and themselves against this climate of tension in order to examine their problems in greater tranquility, deal with them and solve them one by one, leisurely, surely. This attitude is very human. But I am afraid that I do not see the problem in the same fashion, because I think this revolutionary tension is not entirely external to us. It is in large measure of internal origin. It is an organic part of the general situation of Asia. Well, I myself stated in June, 1954, when I assumed office, that I wanted to carry out our national revolution peacefully in every respect.

You know that events have not complied with my wish . . . I was successful in stabilizing a situation seemingly past mending, thanks to the strong measures taken and thanks to the moral and material support of the American people. But more important and urgent tasks are arising all the time and require solution. The most important and urgent of these is the economic and social recovery of Viet-Nam . . .

Whether we like it or not, the revolution continues to be with us in Viet-Nam. And as in all revolutions, a period of centralization is necessary before we can pave the way for decentralization. This must be done if we want to avoid paralysis, anarchy, and with them, violent revolution or foreign intervention.

You know as well as I do that the possession of Viet-Nam is a great temptation for the Communists. Viet-Nam is the gateway to the invasion of South East Asia and to its immense resources in manpower and raw materials.

As long as Communism has not renounced world revolution and domination, we cannot let ourselves be lulled by the songs of peaceful coexistence. This is especially true since competitive coexistence has replaced peaceful coexistence as the war cry of the Communists after the last Congress of the Russian Communist party. Moreover, the Chinese Communist party proclaimed, in December 1956, the necessity of imposing the dictatorship of the proletariat by violent action. Because Communist pressure threatens to weigh heavily on all our land frontiers, Viet-Nam must be more watchful than in the past against this menace.

We are convinced that our neighbors are also concerned about the problems of internal subversion and that their efforts combined with ours can stem international Communism of which Red China is the active leader in all South East Asia.

I am certain that it is clear now that Viet-Nam is living in a volcanic situation. It is a focal point in this vast area of the world which is bound to experience, for many years to come, rapid, profound and violent transformations.

What to do then?

It is obvious that we must not allow fatalism and defeatism to overwhelm us. Neither must we be deluded into adopting seemingly easy solutions which consist in imitating Western methods blindly. America has had more than a century at her disposal to accomplish and digest its political, economic and social revolutions.

We must then find our own solution in the light of our own experience of the last two and a half years, in drawing from the experience of other democratic nations, and from our own Vietnamese traditions. We have endeavored to build a political and economic structure in conformity with our national character and the geopolitical realities of Viet-Nam, while retaining all the essential freedoms of men. Our task has been now to organize our political and economic life in such a way that our government will be strong enough to meet the enormous difficulties which beset us, flexible enough to deal rapidly with an ever-changing situation, and open enough to allow more freedom as the dangers which threaten us subside.

Our experience is hard. But it is also exalting, because we are not alone: the United States is with us. We can never repeat often enough how effective the moral and material aid of the American people to Viet-Nam has been. This aid has met complete success. Nobody can deny it. We want the American people to know it.

We also want the American people to know that their unselfish and effective aid to Viet-Nam is a good example for other peoples of South East Asia. In this connection I am pleased to tell you that, now that the economy has begun to recover, principally thanks to American aid, the people of Viet-Nam are increasing their own contribution to the general welfare. New and higher taxes were recently imposed, national conscription has been decreed, and a new policy for foreign private investment has been announced.

DOCUMENT 3.5

Revolutionary Stirrings in the Countryside
Reminiscences by Nguyen Thi Dinh of Events in 1959–1960, Published in 1966

As the insurgency against Ngo Dinh Diem's government expanded in the late 1950s, the regime responded with new initiatives to crack down on revolutionaries. In February 1959, Saigon authorities began building agrovilles, fortified villages to which it aimed to relocate the rural population in order to insulate peasants from revolutionary influence and improve surveillance. Later in 1959, the government enacted Decree 10/59, which gave security forces authority to arrest, try, imprison, and execute suspected insurgents. Both measures generated strong resistance in the countryside. In the following passage, Nguyen Thi Dinh, a Southern communist leader who became one of the highest-ranking women in the revolutionary movement, recalls the reaction of peasants in her native Ben Tre province when the regime began constructing an agroville designed to quash antigovernment activism. The abuses and broad resistance that Nguyen Thi Dinh reports were apparently widespread. The government ended the program in 1961, though it quickly initiated a new population-relocation policy known as Strategic Hamlets.

At the end of 1959, I was busily engaged in my work when I was urgently called to help provide guidance for dealing with the enemy's plot of setting up an agroville in Thanh Thoi village, Mo Cay district. The villagers were angry and up-in-arms because they had been ordered by Diem and the Americans to tear down their houses and move within a month. An entire area of fertile rice fields, luxuriant fruit trees, and densely populated settlements . . . had to be completely evacuated for the establishment of an agroville. The enemy's plot was to assemble all families with relatives who had regrouped to the North and those of the cadres who had left to work for the revolution, and patriotic people, in this hell on earth.

Diem and the Americans had chosen Thanh Thoi village as a testing ground to develop the experience which they would then apply all over the South. When they met us, the villagers said:

— If we're going to die, we're going to die right here, we're not going anywhere.

We were very happy to hear the people say this because only by relying on the unity and determination of the people could we foil the cruel scheme of the enemy. As anticipated, a month passed without any villagers obeying the order to dismantle their houses, although the enemy exerted intense pressure and blatantly resorted to force . . . Every day, they set fire to houses, cut down trees, and crushed lush rice fields with tractors. The brutes poured toward the house of sister Tu. Her husband had been killed in action fighting for the Resistance. After the Dien Bien Phu victory the revolution gave her three *cong* of land to farm and support her five young children. After peace returned, she painstakingly built an embankment to grow tangerines, clod of earth by clod of earth. The tangerines were beginning to ripen when the soldiers came to cut them down. Watching them destroy what she had constructed with sweat and tears, she shouted in anger:

— Heavens above, what kind of government is this that can be so cruel?

Her children rushed in and tried to prevent the soldiers from cutting down the trees, but the soldiers were unmoved for they could not care less whether the people starved and died.

All the young people were conscripted to do forced labor, and anyone who resisted was arrested and jailed. Under the burning sun, about five thousand villagers— young and old, men and women—were gathered and forced to destroy hundreds of acres of lush rice plants already bearing young grains bursting with milky sap. The soldiers took measurements and as soon as they finished measuring the people would have to start digging. The villagers huddled together in one spot and refused to dig . . .

Mrs. Bay stepped forward and said:

— Look, my husband and myself along with our nine children depend entirely on the income from our five *cong* of fruit grove[s] to live, now you've forced us to cut all the trees down. Then you forced my husband to do corvee work. You don't give him any rice to eat and beat him violently besides. Let me ask you, how is our family going to survive? . . .

As Tet drew near the Americans and Diem intensified their pressure to have the agroville completed. They even brought in conscripted laborers from all six provinces of Central Nam Bo to work on the agroville. Every day, more than ten thousand people lived at the site in extremely crowded conditions. The flames of hatred smoldered in the hearts of the people, ready to erupt at the right opportunity. One day, [government official] Ba Huong ordered the buildings spruced up to welcome Diem who was coming to inspect the agroville. The villagers went looking for the [revolutionary] cadres to relay the news and to solicit their opinion. On the appointed day, the soldiers beat the drums, making a dreadful din, searched each house, and forced the people to hang out flags and don new clothes to welcome "President Diem." That day, I stayed close by to keep track of the situation. Following the cadres' instructions faithfully, the village notables—formally dressed, petitions hidden in the sleeves of their robes—stood in the front row. The villagers called out to each other to go and welcome the president, and with everyone bustling about, the atmosphere was very different from the one prevailing normally. The security police and the militia were overjoyed, convinced they would be rewarded for their work this time around.

That morning, wherever Diem went, telephones rang to announce his movement. He went to Mo Cay, Thom, and then arrived in Thanh Thoi. The moment his car came to a stop the villagers—defying the thick ring of security and regular police—took off the outer layer of clothing and appeared in ragged and filthy clothes. They wrapped their heads in mourning bands and rushed onto the road, moaning and weeping as though they were at a funeral. It was complete chaos. The policemen blew their whistles, tried to hold the people back with their rifle butts, and fired madly into the air, but could not prevent the ring of people from closing around Ngo Dinh Diem's car. The notables handed their petitions directly to Diem, while the people handed theirs to the soldiers and reporters. Seizing this opportunity, many women and children clung to Diem and the officers by hanging on their jackets, weeping pitifully, and demanding the release of their husbands and parents. Ngo Dinh Diem, greatly embarrassed, stood up to make a few promises and then fled from the scene. After this defeat, at the orders of the Americans and Diem, their lackeys took revenge on the people and launched a fierce wave of repression in Mo Cay district and all over Ben Tre province.

Also in this period Diem concocted the 10/59 decree, an extremely fascist law under which anyone who entertained thoughts of opposition—even if he did not take any concrete action to oppose the regime—would be labeled Viet Cong and guillotined. The mobile guillotine was taken everywhere and prisons mushroomed.

Newspapers [controlled by Diem] clamored for on-the-spot executions of Communists without hesitation . . .

The sympathetic villagers in Mo Cay district wept and told me:

— Sister, we must arm ourselves in order to survive, otherwise we'll die. If you permit us to kill the security police agents to obtain weapons, we'll do it right away. The Americans and Diem have torn up the Geneva Accords long ago. We can't be kind to the devil! Whenever the call for armed resistance is issued, just let us know and we'll leave at once. If we go on like this, they'll burn down our houses and kill us one of these days. We won't have anything with which to fight back and it will be unbearable.

Whenever they ran into me the comrades from every district in the province impatiently asked:

— We heard that Hong Ngu [District, Kien Tuong province] and Dong Thap [The Plain of Reeds] have taken up arms. How about our province? Have we been allowed to strike back?

I told them my true feeling:

— I share your wishes.

DOCUMENT 3.6

Applying Pressure on Ngo Dinh Diem

Memorandum Handed to President Ngo Dinh Diem by the U.S. Ambassador in Saigon, Elbridge Durbrow, October 15, 1960

The growing insurgency and the rise of urban discontent in South Vietnam stirred intense anxiety among U.S. officials. Among the most vexing problems was Ngo Dinh Diem's apparent unwillingness to consider major reforms in order to shore up his position. The U.S. ambassador in Saigon, Elbridge Durbrow, wanted to apply strong pressure on Diem to change his ways, but many officials in Washington preferred a gentler approach. The two sides compromised in mid-1960. Durbrow received permission to lean on Diem but not to go as far as threatening to withhold U.S. military aid. At a meeting with Diem on October 15, 1960, Durbrow read a French-language version of the following memorandum. Durbrow reported to Washington later in the day that Diem had listened patiently to the American ideas. The proposals included bringing the Can Lao party—the secret political organization controlled by Diem's brother, Ngo Dinh Nhu—out into the open or dissolving it altogether. In a separate memo that he also read to Diem, Durbrow proposed that Nhu, a focus of American criticism, be relieved of his duties and sent abroad as an ambassador.

Mr. President, in your struggle for survival against the Viet Cong, you have taken many wise steps with respect to the security forces of the Government, and I understand that you are in the process of setting up a national Internal

Security Council and a centralized intelligence agency as important and necessary additional steps toward giving effective guidance to and making maximum use of the security forces. We have recognized the increased security threat to your Government and the additional needs of your security forces. We have shown this recognition by the comprehensive program for training, equipping, and arming the Civil Guard which I have just explained, by our furnishing special forces personnel needs of ARVN for the war against the guerrillas.

Our serious concern about the present situation is based, however, not only on the security threat posed by the Viet Cong, but also on what to us seems to be a decline in the popular political support of your Government brought on in part, of course, by Viet Cong intimidation. As your friend and supporter, Mr. President, I would like to have a frank and friendly talk with you on what seems to be the serious political situation confronting your Government. While I am aware that the matters I am raising deal primarily with internal affairs and, therefore, in ordinary circumstances would be no concern of mine, I would like with your permission and indulgence to talk to you frankly as a friend and try to be as helpful as I can by giving you the considered judgment of myself and some of my friends and your friends in Washington on what we hope would be appropriate measures to assist you in the present crucial situation.

I believe that your speech to the National Assembly on October 3, in which you stated that your Government has decided to reorganize certain of its institutions and to rationalize and simplify its working methods, indicates that we may be thinking to some extent at least along the same lines.

I would like particularly to stress the desirability of actions to broaden and increase your popular support prior to the 1961 Presidential elections. It would seem to me that some sort of psychological shock effect would be helpful in order to take the initiative from the Communist propagandists as well as the non-Communist oppositionists, and to convince the population that your Government is taking effective political as well as security measures to deal with the present situation. It would appear that, unless fully effective steps are taken to reverse the present adverse political trend, your Government will face an increasingly difficult internal security situation. It is our carefully considered view that small or gradual moves are not adequate. To attain the desired effect, moves, major in scope and with extensive popular appeal, should be taken at once. Specific actions which we would suggest are as follows:

1. We suggest that you consider Cabinet changes as a necessary part of the effective moves needed to build up popular interest and support. One Cabinet change that we believe would be helpful would be the appointment of a full-time Minister of National Defense in order to permit you to devote your attention to developing over-all policies. To achieve maximum benefit it is suggested that you issue firm directives to assure that there is adherence to channels of command both up and down and that firm action be taken to eliminate any feeling that favoritism and political considerations enter into the promotion and assignment of personnel in

the armed forces. Removal of this latter feeling is of great importance if the morale of the armed forces is not to be adversely affected during their mortal struggle against the Viet Cong . . .

2. In rationalizing and simplifying the Government's methods of work, we suggest you seek to find new methods to encourage your Cabinet Members to assume more responsibility rather than frequently submitting relatively minor matters to the Presidency for decision, thus allowing you more time to deal with basic policy matters . . .

3. We would suggest that you consider altering the nature of the Can Lao Party from its present secret character to that of a normal political party which operates publicly, or even consider disbanding it. If the first alternative is adopted, various methods of convincing the population that the action has been taken might be used, such as party publication of a list of its members. The purpose of this action would be to eliminate the atmosphere of secrecy and fear and reduce the public suspicion of favoritism and corruption, which the Can Lao Party's secret status has fostered according to many reports we have heard in and out of the Government.

4. We suggest that the National Assembly be authorized to investigate any department or agency of the Government. The Assembly should be authorized to conduct its investigations through public hearings and to publish the findings. This investigative authority for the Assembly would have a three-fold purpose: (a) to find some mechanism for dispelling through public investigation the persistent rumors about the Government and its personalities; (b) to provide the people with an avenue of recourse against arbitrary actions by certain Government officials; and (c) to assuage some of the non-Communist opposition to the Government.

We further suggest that the National Assembly be asked to establish requirements for the behavior of public servants . . .

5. We suggest that you issue a warning that you may require every public official to make a declaration, for possible publication, listing his property and sources of income.

6. We suggest that you announce that, if the press will take a responsible role in policing itself, the controls exercised over it by the Government would be reduced. In this connection you might wish to consider the appointment of a committee, including representatives of the press and some members of the opposition, to draft a press code which the press would police . . .

Providing timely and more ample information would . . . help to reduce anti-Government rumors. Means to accomplish this include freer access for the press to responsible members of the Government, and frequent public statements from the Presidency and fireside chats, transmitted to the people by radio, sound film, tape recordings, and through the press. The more these media are encouraged to reach the provinces, the more effective will they be in bringing the people closer to your Government by providing a means of transmitting ideas from one to the other.

7. We would like to suggest that you liberalize arrangements for Vietnamese wishing to study [abroad], and for this purpose make more foreign exchange available . . .

8. We suggest that you consider some appropriate means by which villagers could elect at least some of their own officials. Such elections at the village level would be a means of associating the population with the Government and of eliminating arbitrary actions by local government officials by demonstrating to them that they will periodically be judged at the polls.

9. We suggest prompt adoption of the following measure for the enhancement of the Government's support in rural areas:

  a. Take action which will result in an increase in the price which peasants actually will receive for [rice] paddy before the new harvest.

  b. Liberalize the terms of credit extended to the small rice farmers.

  c. Continue to expand expenditures for agricultural development and diversification, particularly in the Mekong Delta area.

  d. Institute a system of modest Government payment for all community development labor whether on agrovilles or on other Government projects.

  e. Institute a system of limited subsidies to the inhabitants of agrovilles during the period of their readjustment . . . This should help to develop a favorable popular attitude toward the agrovilles by covering some of the expenses incurred in moving to and getting settled in the agrovilles . . .

4

THE DEEPENING CRISIS

BY 1961, SOUTH VIETNAM was a nation at war. NLF forces, dubbed the Vietcong ("Vietnamese communists") by South Vietnamese President Ngo Dinh Diem, held the upper hand in the fighting. The situation caused mounting anxiety in Washington, where the new Kennedy administration drastically increased the U.S. commitment to the defense of South Vietnam in 1962 and 1963. Likewise, Hanoi steadily stepped up its support for the insurgency. For the moment, however, both the United States and North Vietnam held back from all-out intervention in the fighting.

The advent of the Kennedy administration brought to power a group of men with remarkable confidence in American power and eagerness to wage the Cold War more aggressively, especially in the decolonizing world. After visiting South Vietnam in mid-1961, two of Kennedy's aides, General Maxwell Taylor and Deputy National Security Adviser Walt Rostow, recommended bold U.S. action. They urged that the administration not only send more aid and military advisers but also dispatch several thousand combat troops. Kennedy, eager to prevent the collapse of South Vietnam but wary of a full-fledged role in the war, accepted the first recommendation but not the second. His decision to follow a middle path established a pattern that would hold through the end of 1964.

For a time, it appeared as though Kennedy's approach might work. Expanded American aid helped the South Vietnamese fight more effectively in 1962. The trend did not last, however. On the battlefield, the Vietcong devised new methods to cope with helicopters and other sophisticated weaponry sent by the United States. Just as worrying to U.S. leaders, the South Vietnamese government confronted powerful new political opposition in 1963, especially from Buddhists. U.S. officials pleaded with Diem to enact reforms to quell unrest and broaden his base of support or at least to drop his brother, Ngo Dinh Nhu, from the government. But the South Vietnamese president gave little ground. Alarmed that Diem's authoritarianism was undermining the anticommunist war effort, U.S. officials backed a coup on November 1, 1963.

U.S. leaders hoped that new South Vietnamese leaders would stabilize the political situation and reenergize the war effort, but in fact the coup created fresh problems for Washington. Eliminating Diem opened the way not to stability but to a series of ineffective military juntas that did little to rally support for the South Vietnamese government. The coup also emboldened North Vietnam. Concerned that mounting problems in Saigon would lead to all-out intervention by the United States, leaders in Hanoi decided in late 1963 to escalate the fighting in hopes of achieving victory before the United States could bring its power fully to bear.

Thus did Lyndon Johnson, who became president following Kennedy's assassination on November 22, 1963, inherit a rapidly deteriorating situation in Vietnam. Although numerous policymakers, members of Congress, journalists, and foreign leaders urged Johnson to seek a negotiated settlement of the war, the administration remained committed to longstanding American goals in South Vietnam. U.S. officials began to consider bombing North Vietnam and sending American combat troops to stave off defeat. In the short term, Johnson made no bold move to put these plans into operation. The president believed that his chances in the November 1964 presidential race would be enhanced by a cautious tone on Vietnam. Only after his landslide electoral victory did Johnson break with Kennedy's approach and dispatch American combat forces.

DOCUMENT 4.1

The Challenge of Modernization
Speech by Deputy National Security Adviser Walt W. Rostow, June 29, 1961

To many Americans, instability in Vietnam seemed just one expression of a worrying global trend. As European empires crumbled in the years after the Second World War, dozens of new states emerged in Africa, the Middle East, and Asia. These former colonies often suffered political turmoil and even bloodshed as rival factions struggled to establish independent nations. A growing number of American policymakers, scholars, and political commentators believed that communists were well positioned to exploit such instability and insisted that the United States take an active role in helping young nations toward pro-Western "modernity." One of the most striking expressions of this view came in a speech delivered in the early days of the Kennedy administration by Walt W. Rostow, an eminent economist who joined Kennedy's "New Frontier" as deputy national security adviser. Rostow delivered the address at a graduation ceremony at the U.S. Army Special Warfare School at Fort Bragg, North Carolina, where his audience included foreign military officers who had received training in counterinsurgency warfare.

What is happening throughout Latin America, Africa, the Middle East, and Asia is this: Old societies are changing their ways in order to create and maintain a national personality on the world scene and to bring to their peoples the benefits modern technology can offer. This process is truly revolutionary. It touches every aspect of the traditional life—economic, social, and political. The introduction of modern technology brings about not merely new methods of production but a new style of family life, new links between the villages and the cities, the beginnings of national politics, and a new relationship to the world outside.

Like all revolutions, the revolution of modernization is disturbing. Individual men are torn between the commitment to the old familiar way of life and the attractions of a modern way of life. The power of old social groups—notably the landlord, who usually dominates the traditional society—is reduced. Power moves toward those who can command the tools of modern technology, including modern weapons. Men and women in the villages and the cities, feeling that the old ways of life are shaken and that new possibilities are open to them, express old resentments and new hopes.

This is the grand arena of revolutionary change which the Communists are exploiting with great energy. They believe that their techniques of organization—based on small disciplined cadres of conspirators—are ideally suited to grasp and to hold power in these turbulent settings. They believe that the weak transitional governments that one is likely to find during this modernization process are highly vulnerable to subversion and to guerrilla warfare . . .

It is on the weakest nations, facing their most difficult transitional moments, that the Communists concentrate their attention. They are the scavengers of the modernization process. They believe that the techniques of political centralization under dictatorial control—and the projected image of Soviet and Chinese Communist economic progress—will persuade hesitant men, faced by great transitional problems, that the Communist model should be adopted for modernization, even at the cost of surrendering human liberty. They believe that they can exploit effectively the resentments built up in many of these areas against colonial rule and that they can associate themselves effectively with the desire of the emerging nations for independence, for status on the world scene, and for material progress.

This is a formidable program; for the history of this century teaches us that communism is not the long-run wave of the future toward which societies are naturally drawn. On the contrary. But it is one particular form of modern society to which a nation may fall prey during the transitional process. Communism is best understood as a disease of the transition to modernization . . .

What is our reply to this historical conception and strategy? What is the American purpose and the American strategy? We, too, recognize that a revolutionary process is under way. We are dedicated to the proposition that this revolutionary process of modernization shall be permitted to go forward in independence, with increasing degrees of human freedom. We seek two results: first, that truly independent nations shall emerge on the world scene; and, second, that each nation will be permitted to fashion, out of its own culture and its own ambitions, the kind of modern society it wants. The same religious and philosophical beliefs which decree that we respect the uniqueness of each individual make it natural that we respect the uniqueness of each national society. Moreover, we Americans are confident that, if the independence of this process can be maintained over the coming years and decades, these societies will choose their own version of what we would recognize as a democratic, open society . . .

Thus our central task in the underdeveloped areas, as we see it, is to protect the independence of the revolutionary process now going forward. This is our mission, and it is our ultimate strength. For this is not—and cannot be—the mission of communism. And in time, through the fog of propaganda and the honest confusions of men caught up in the business of making new nations, this fundamental difference will become increasingly clear in the southern half of the world. The American interest will be served if our children live in an environment of strong, assertive, independent nations, capable, because they are strong, of assuming collective responsibility for the peace . . .

The United States has the primary responsibility for assisting the economies of those hard-pressed states on the periphery of the Communist bloc, which are under acute military or quasi-military pressure which they cannot bear from their own resources; for example, South Korea, Viet-Nam, Taiwan, Pakistan, Iran. The United States has a special responsibility of leadership in bringing not merely its own resources but the resources of all the free world to bear in aiding the long-run development of those nations which are serious about modernizing their economy and their social life . . .

Finally, the United States has a role to play—symbolized by your presence here and by mine—in learning to deter guerrilla warfare, if possible, and to deal with it, if necessary . . .

I do not need to tell you that the primary responsibility for dealing with guerrilla warfare in the underdeveloped areas cannot be American. There are many ways in which we can help—and we are searching our minds and our imaginations to learn better how to help; but a guerrilla war must be fought primarily by those on the spot. This is so for a quite particular reason. A guerrilla war is an intimate affair, fought not merely with weapons but fought in the minds of the men who live in the villages and in the hills, fought by the spirit and policy of those who run the local government. An outsider cannot, by himself, win a guerrilla war. He can help create conditions in which it can be won, and he can directly assist those prepared to fight for their independence. We are determined to help destroy this international disease; that is, guerrilla war designed, initiated, supplied, and led from outside an independent nation.

Although as leader of the free world the United States has special responsibilities which it accepts in this common venture of deterrence, it is important that the whole international community begin to accept its responsibility for dealing with this form of aggression. It is important that the world become clear in mind, for example, that the operation run from Hanoi against Viet-Nam is as clear a form of aggression as the violation of the 38th parallel by the North Korean armies in June 1950 . . .

I am confident that we can deal with the kind of operation now under way in Viet-Nam. It is an extremely dangerous operation, and it could overwhelm Viet-Nam if the Vietnamese—aided by the free world—do not deal with it. But it is an unsubtle operation, by the book, based more on murder than on political or psychological appeal.

When Communists speak of wars of national liberation and of their support for "progressive forces," I think of the systematic program of assassination now going forward in which the principal victims are the health, agriculture, and education officers in the Viet-Nam villages. The Viet Cong are not trying to persuade the peasants of Viet-Nam that communism is good; they are trying to persuade them that their lives are insecure unless they cooperate with them. With resolution and confidence on all sides and with the assumption of international responsibility for [defending against cross-border subversion], I believe we are going to bring this threat to the independence of Viet-Nam under control.

DOCUMENT 4.2

Kennedy's Doubts

Notes of a National Security Council Meeting, November 15, 1961

John F. Kennedy delighted in bold rhetoric about America's purpose in the world. Most famously, he proclaimed in his inaugural speech that the United States would "pay any price, bear any burden, meet any hardship, support any friend, oppose any foe" in the defense of liberty. Whether the new administration would act on such ambitious pronouncements was a different matter. One test of Kennedy's approach came in fall 1961, when key aides, alarmed by the worsening situation in South Vietnam, urged him to send vast new military aid, larger numbers of military advisers, and even combat troops. In a meeting with his National Security Council to consider these proposals (outlined in a draft memorandum dated two days earlier), the president voiced numerous doubts about prospects for achieving American goals in Vietnam and balancing problems in Asia with the ongoing crisis over Berlin. Participants in the meeting included Secretary of State Dean Rusk, Secretary of Defense Robert S. McNamara, and Lyman Lemnitzer, the chairman of the Joint Chiefs of Staff. Ultimately, Kennedy gratified his aides by endorsing more military assistance and advisers, but he refused to send combat soldiers.

Mr. Rusk explained the Draft of Memorandum on South Viet Nam. He added the hope that, in spite of the magnitude of the proposal, any U.S. actions would not be hampered by lack of funds nor failure to pursue the program vigorously. The President expressed the fear of becoming involved simultaneously on two fronts on opposite sides of the world. He questioned the wisdom of involvement in

Viet Nam since the basis thereof is not completely clear. By comparison he noted that Korea was a case of clear aggression which was opposed by the United States and other members of the U.N. The conflict in Viet Nam is more obscure and less flagrant. The President then expressed his strong feeling that in such a situation the United States needs even more the support of allies in such an endeavor as Viet Nam in order to avoid sharp domestic partisan criticism as well as strong objections from other nations of the world. The President said that he could even make a rather strong case against intervening in an area 10,000 miles away against 16,000 guerrillas with a native army of 200,000, where millions have been spent for years with no success. The President repeated his apprehension concerning support, adding that none could be expected from the French, and Mr. Rusk interrupted to say that the British were tending more and more to take the French point of view. The President compared the obscurity of the issues in Viet Nam to the clarity of the positions in Berlin, the contrast of which could even make leading Democrats wary of proposed activities in the Far East.

Mr. Rusk suggested that firmness in Viet Nam in the manner and form of that in Berlin might achieve desired results in Viet Nam without resort to combat. The President disagreed with the suggestion on the basis that the issue was clearly defined in Berlin and opposing forces identified whereas in Viet Nam the issue is vague and action is by guerrillas, sometimes in a phantom-like fashion. Mr. McNamara expressed an opinion that action would become clear if U.S. forces were involved since this power would be applied against sources of Viet Cong power including those in North Viet Nam. The President observed that it was not clear to him just where these U.S. forces would base their operations other than from aircraft carriers which seemed to him to be quite vulnerable. General Lemnitzer confirmed that carriers would be involved to a considerable degree and stated that Taiwan and the Philippines would also become principal bases of action.

With regard to sources of power in North Viet Nam, Mr. Rusk cited Hanoi as the most important center in North Viet Nam and it would be hit. However, he considered it more a political target than a military one and under these circumstances such an attack would "raise serious questions." He expressed the hope that any plan of action in North Viet Nam would strike first of all any Viet Cong airlift into South Viet Nam in order to avoid the establishment of a procedure of supply similar to that which the Soviets have conducted for so long with impunity in Laos . . .

The President returned the discussion to the point of what will be done next in Viet Nam rather than whether or not the U.S. would become involved. He cautioned that the technique of U.S. actions should not have the effect of unilaterally violating Geneva accords. He felt that a technique and timing must be devised which will place the onus of breaking the accords on the other side and require them to defend their actions. Even so, he realized that it would take some time to achieve this condition and even more to build up world opinion against Viet Cong . . .

The President asked what nations would possibly support the U.S. intervention in Viet Nam, listing Pakistan, Thailand, the Philippines, Australia, New Zealand . . .

Mr. Rusk replied that they all would but the President implied doubts because of the pitfalls of the particular type of war in Viet Nam. He described it as being more a political issue, of different magnitude and (again) less defined than the Korean War . . .

The President asked the Secretary of Defense if he would take action if SEATO did not exist and McNamara replied in the affirmative. The President asked for justification and Lemnitzer replied that the world would be divided in the area of Southeast Asia on the sea, in the air and in communications. He said that Communist conquest would deal a severe blow to freedom and extend Communism to a great portion of the world. The President asked how he could justify the proposed courses of action in Viet Nam while at the same time ignoring Cuba. General Lemnitzer hastened to add that the JCS feel that even at this point the United States should go into Cuba.

The President stated the time had come for neutral nations as well as others to be in support of U.S. policy publicly. He felt that we should aggressively determine which nations are in support of U.S. policy and that these nations should identify themselves. The President again expressed apprehension on support of the proposed action by the Congress as well as by the American people. He felt that the next two or three weeks should be utilized in making the determination as to whether or not the proposed program for Viet Nam could be supported. His impression was that even the Democratic side of Congress was not fully convinced. The President stated that he would like to have the Vice President's views in this regard and at that point asked if there was information on the Vice President's arrival. The President then stated that no action would be taken during the meeting on the proposed memorandum and that he would discuss these subjects with the Vice President.

DOCUMENT 4.3

Motives for the Coup Against Ngo Dinh Diem
Reminiscence by General Tran Van Don Concerning Events in 1962 and 1963, Published in 1978

Opponents of Ngo Dinh Diem and his government included numerous senior officers in the South Vietnamese army. Disaffected generals resented not only Diem's unwillingness to wage the anticommunist war more assertively but also the regime's practice of giving promotions or desirable jobs to reward loyalty to the government rather than professional achievement. Such grievances led to unsuccessful coup attempts in 1960 and 1962 and then to the overthrow of Diem in November 1963. In the following passage from his memoir published in 1978, General Tran Van Don, one of the leaders of the 1963 coup, recalls his mounting disillusionment with the Diem government in 1962 and 1963. Don was born in France and served in the Vietnamese army that fought under French command in the First Indochina War.

He then held various high-level positions in the South Vietnamese army, including army chief of staff. In this excerpt, Don refers to General Duong Van Minh ("Big Minh"), who led the junta that replaced Diem's government, and General Le Van Kim.

My responsibility was to maintain peace and order in the five northern provinces: Quang Tri, Thua Thien, Quang Nam, Quang Tin, and Quang Ngai. To carry out this extensive mission, I had only two divisions, about thirty thousand men, under my command dispersed throughout these provinces over thousands of square miles. We had to provide security, attack the enemy in secret hideouts, and prepare for an anticipated North Vietnamese invasion across the 17th parallel. One would think that I would have been given full control of all forces in my region and been allowed to carry out operations as I deemed necessary. This was decidedly not the case. No officials, military or civilian, were allowed to carry out any plan without the personal approval of Ngo Dinh Can, President Diem's brother and advisor in charge of Central Vietnam . . .

Government operations against the NLF forces were being conducted against dedicated guerrillas who lived and worked with the villagers. I can remember on one such strike in Quang Nam province that a farmer came to me and openly disapproved of our actions. He said, "You came here with artillery, trucks, and well-equipped soldiers to fight against our own people. You have plenty of supplies while we are poor and have nothing. You blame us for giving the NLF soldiers rice, but you must remember that they are living here with us, sharing our poor lot and protecting us. They are our own children and brothers and belong to our village."

All I could do was to shake my head sadly because I had no logical answer for him. Everything he said was true. The NLF never told the villagers that they were Communists, only that they were trying to help them against governmental interference in their lives.

I found in my corps area many patriotic nationalist leaders who were definitely anti-Communist but had as much trouble accepting the government programs as I did. They were civil servants, professors, and prominent businessmen who had been meeting secretly and discussing the problems of the country. Our ambitions were mutual: to build a true democratic society, improve living conditions of the people, and continue the struggle against the Communists—eventually bringing a genuine peace to the country. We met every two or three months to exchange ideas and information and, over a period of time, my plans for leading a coup d'état against the Diem government took more concrete shape.

In mid-December 1962, I was transferred back to Saigon to become the commander of the army. This position, with its headquarters and a strength of eighty men, was newly established by presidential decree. Although bearing the title, in reality I was not allowed to command any army unit and did not have the proper authority to operate as a commander. Simultaneously, General Big Minh's field command headquarters was dissolved and he was assigned to a new job as military advisor to the president. Giving him this function was like putting him on an extended vacation because he was the advisor of nobody and had no authority or responsibility.

In my own case, I could not stand to stay inactive in Saigon. Therefore, I asked the president to let me go out and inspect field units and observe the establishment of the strategic hamlets throughout the country. He agreed, and through these visits I was able to ascertain the true state of morale in the army and what was going on in the minds of the citizenry. I tried to go to as many places as I could, from the Ben Hai River in the north to the point of Ca Mau. The more I saw, the more I realized that the situation throughout the country was even worse than I had previously thought. I was certainly able to see that if the situation was not improved, the country would fall rapidly into the hands of the Communists.

After each inspection tour, I made extensive reports to the president on the local situation, with suggested measures for improvement. I told him about declining morale in the officer corps because of promotion for religious preference or party loyalty instead of ability. I made specific suggestions that various incompetent military leaders be dismissed and others advanced, but my pleas fell on deaf ears. I told him of the terrible conditions of the soldiers' families and recommended possible solutions that might help. I told him of the mistreatment of poor villagers by his corrupt officials, and suggested they be charged for their crimes and punished. Again, I was met with silence by the implacable mandarin. In addition, of course, I was also able to bring back much accurate information for our coup plot for discussions with Generals Minh and Kim.

In June 1963, Big Minh and I were sent to observe a demonstration of SEATO forces in Thailand. Here we had an opportunity to meet various foreigners and to read foreign newspapers and magazines. We discovered that world opinion was violently against the Ngo Dinh Diem government, particularly after the fiery suicide of the Buddhist bonze, Thich Quang Duc.

When we returned home at the end of June, we were surprised to see how far downhill the political situation had gone. The suicides of several Buddhists, combined with demonstrations and riots, caused what I can only characterize as a boiling atmosphere with people furious all over. The turmoil existed directly in the nation's capital and in other principal cities throughout the country, but still the government did not come up with any kind of effective solution. We three, Minh, Kim, and Don, saw that every day the National Liberation Front was making further gains because of the disgust of the common people with the government. Our suggestions to President Diem and Ngo Dinh Nhu were met with vague promises or by simple silence.

We began our detailed planning for the coup at this time.

DOCUMENT 4.4

Lodge Favors a Coup

Telegram from Henry Cabot Lodge Jr., U.S. Ambassador in Saigon, to the State Department, August 29, 1963

American alarm about South Vietnam reached new levels of intensity during 1963. On the battlefield, the insurgency gained strength, but the bigger concern for U.S. leaders was a growing political crisis in South Vietnam's cities. The problem began in May when Buddhists began demonstrating against the regime, complaining of religious persecution by the Catholic-led government. By midsummer, the protests had grown into a major nationwide movement against the Diem regime. Violence escalated on August 21, when Diem's troops raided Buddhist pagodas throughout South Vietnam, killing hundreds of protesters. Revolted by Diem's crackdown, some U.S. officials called for a coup to install a new South Vietnamese government that would end the political crisis and wage the anticommunist war more assertively. Disgruntled South Vietnamese generals had already indicated their interest in taking that step and solicited U.S. support. One American who championed a coup was the new U.S. ambassador in Saigon, Henry Cabot Lodge Jr. He sent the following cable to Washington on August 29 after a three-hour meeting with Diem in which the South Vietnamese president defended his government's policies and blamed the American press for exaggerating the crisis. At two points in the document, Lodge refers to General Paul D. Harkins, the U.S. commander in South Vietnam.

We are launched on a course from which there is no respectable turning back: The overthrow of the Diem government. There is no turning back in part because U.S. prestige is already publicly committed to this end in large measure and will become more so as facts leak out. In a more fundamental sense, there is no turning back because there is no possibility, in my view, that the war can be won under a Diem administration, still less that Diem or any member of the family can govern the country in a way to gain the support of the people who count, i.e., the educated class in and out of government service, civil and military—not to mention the American people. In the last few months (and especially days), they have in fact positively alienated these people to an incalculable degree . . .

The chance of bringing off a Generals' coup depends on them to some extent; but it depends at least as much on us.

We should proceed to make all-out effort to get Generals to move promptly. To do so we should have authority to do following:

(a) That General Harkins repeat to Generals personally messages previously transmitted by CAS officers. This should establish their authenticity. (General Harkins should have order from President on this.)

(b) If nevertheless Generals insist on public statement that all U.S. aid to Vietnam through Diem regime has been stopped, we would agree, on express understanding that Generals will have started at same time. (We would seek persuade Generals that it would be better to hold this card for use in event of stalemate. We hope it will not be necessary to do this at all.)

Vietnamese Generals doubt that we have the will power, courage, and determination to see this thing through. They are haunted by the idea that we will run out on them even though we have told them pursuant to instructions, that the game had started.

We must press on for many reasons. Some of these are:

(a) Explosiveness of the present situation which may well lead to riots and violence if issue of discontent with regime is not met. Out of this could come a pro-Communist or at best a neutralist set of politicians.

(b) The fact that war cannot be won with the present regime.

(c) Our own reputation for steadfastness and our unwillingness to stultify ourselves.

(d) If proposed action is suspended, I believe a body blow will be dealt to respect for us by Vietnamese Generals. Also, all those who expect U.S. to straighten out this situation will feel let down. Our help to the regime in past years inescapably gives us a large responsibility which we cannot avoid.

I realize that this course involves a very substantial risk of losing Vietnam. It also involves some additional risk to American lives. I would never propose it if I felt there was a reasonable chance of holding Vietnam with Diem.

... I would not hesitate to use financial inducements if I saw a useful opportunity ...

General Harkins thinks that I should ask Diem to get rid of [Ngo Dinh Nhu and his wife, Tran Le Xuan ("Madame Nhu")] before starting the Generals' action. But I believe that such a step has no chance of getting the desired result and would have the very serious effect of being regarded by the Generals as a sign of American indecision and delay. I believe this is a risk which we should not run. The Generals distrust us too much already. Another point is that Diem would certainly ask for time to consider such a far-reaching request. This would give the ball to Nhu.

With the exception of [the previous] paragraph above General Harkins concurs in this telegram.

DOCUMENT 4.5

Hanoi Calls for Escalation

Resolution of the Ninth Plenum of the Central Committee of the Vietnam Workers' Party, December 1963

North Vietnamese leaders faced critical decisions in late 1963, when the overthrow of Ngo Dinh Diem seemed to suggest that the United Sates would greatly expand its role in the war. Some policymakers in Hanoi advocated a negotiated settlement, thereby avoiding a major war with the Americans and enabling their country to concentrate on internal priorities. But the dominant faction, including General Secretary Le Duan, wished to intensify the war in the hope of achieving victory before the United States could act. The hawks' supremacy became clear in December 1963, when communist leaders met in Hanoi for the Ninth Plenum of the Vietnam Workers' Party. Although the final resolution, excerpted here, paid lip service to old ideas about the necessity of a protracted war, it also insisted that North Vietnam was ready to intensify the fight. The document expressed hope that the United States would continue to wage a "special war" (keeping the main burden of combat on South Vietnamese troops) but expressed confidence that communist forces could prevail even if U.S. leaders opted for "limited war" (sending large numbers of American combat soldiers to take charge of the fighting).

Based on the resolutions and directives of the Party on the Revolution in SVN and the previous experiences gained by our people during the past years, this Resolution gives further clarification on the prospect of the revolutionary movement in SVN and on the struggle guidelines for the Southern compatriots; at the same time, it sets forth the guidelines and missions in order to attain new, bigger victories in the coming period . . .

We . . . have the capability to check and defeat the enemy in his "special war." This capability will increase if we are determined to fight the U.S. imperialists and their henchmen, if we have a clever stratagem, and know how to exploit the contradictions in the enemy's internal organizations, contradictions between the U.S. imperialists and the other imperialists, . . . contradictions between the U.S. and their henchmen in South Viet-Nam and the bourgeois ruling clique in Southeast Asia . . .

However, we must always be vigilant and prepared to cope with the U.S. if she takes the risk of turning the war in South Viet-Nam into a limited war. The possibility that a limited war in South Viet-Nam would turn into a world war is almost nonexistent because the purpose and significance of this war cannot generate conditions leading to a world war.

In the framework of the "special war," there are two possibilities:

- First, the Americans would carry on the war at the present or slightly higher level.

- Second, the Americans would intensify the war by bringing in troops many times larger [than the present number] or both American troops and troops from the Southeast Asian aggressive bloc will intervene in the war . . .

Through our subjective efforts, let us strive to deal with the first eventuality[;] at the same time, let us also positively prepare to defeat the enemy should the second eventuality materialize.

We have sufficient conditions to quickly change the balance of forces in our favor. And whether the U.S. maintains its combat strength at the present level or increases it, she must still use her henchmen's army as a main force. However, this army becomes weaker day by day due to the serious decline of its quality, the demoralization of its troops and the disgust of the latter for the Americans and their lackeys. These are the factors that cause the collapse of Americans' and their lackeys' troops. No U.S. financial assistance or weapons can prevent this collapse . . .

If the U.S. imperialists send more troops to Viet-Nam to save the situation after suffering a series of failures, the Revolution in Viet-Nam will meet more difficulties, the struggle will be stronger and harder but it will certainly succeed in attaining the final victory. With 800,000 well-trained troops, the French imperialists could not defeat the 12 million courageous Algerians and finally had to give independence and freedom to them. For the same reason, the U.S. imperialists cannot win over 14 million Vietnamese people in the South who have taken arms to fight the imperialists for almost 20 years, and who, with all the compatriots throughout the country, have defeated the hundreds of thousands [of] troops of the French expeditionary force. Now the South Vietnamese people show themselves capable of beating the enemy in any situation. They certainly have the determination, talents, strength and patience to crush any U.S. imperialists' schemes and plans, and finally to force them to withdraw from Viet-Nam as the French imperialists did.

There is the possibility that the South Viet-Nam Revolution must go through a transitional period which entails complex forms and methods of struggling before it attains the final victory. The reunification of the country must be carried out step by step. In the present national democratic revolutionary phase in South Viet-Nam, we must strive to attain victory step by step and gradually push back the enemy before reaching the General Offensive and Uprising to win complete victory . . . In any case, we must encourage the entire Party, people, and army to attain the maximum victory, and we should not have a hesitating attitude or . . . pause at the transitional period. If we are highly determined to win and prepared to face any situation, the final victory will certainly be in the hands of our people . . .

[W]e must thoroughly understand the guidelines for protracted struggle but on the other hand we must also seize the opportunities to win victories in a not too long period of time. In a revolutionary war, which is at the same time a war against aggression and a domestic war, as in SVN, we should be ready to take advantage of sudden changes in the situation to turn our struggle into a large revolutionary movement to disintegrate the enemy's troops and government. There is no contradiction in the concept of a protracted war and the concept of taking advantage of opportunities to gain victories in a short time, because the method to gain victory in our people's revolution in SVN is to make efforts to build and develop forces in all aspects . . . [T]he key point at the present time is to make outstanding efforts to rapidly strengthen our military forces in order to create a basic change in the balance of forces between the enemy and us in South Viet-Nam.

We should pay due concern to coordinating political and military struggles.

The political struggle plays a decisive and fundamental role. First, because our basic strength is in the political field, and the basic weakness of the enemy is also in the political field. From the start we have the absolute superiority over the enemy in the political field. Second, the enemy cannot refrain from resorting to such political schemes as using the false labels of "nation, people, democracy" in order to woo the people; therefore we must, and can, take advantage of this to hit back at the enemy. Third, the SVN people have had long political struggle traditions and experiences . . .

Armed struggle also plays a very basic and decisive role: First, because only with the support of armed struggle can the masses' prestige and position be brought into full play . . . Second, because the enemy is using military power as a principal tool to maintain his domination and using the anti-revolutionary war to oppose the people, the latter must use revolutionary war to counter the enemy's anti-revolutionary war in order to protect their lives and property and liberate themselves.

If we do not defeat the enemy's military forces, we cannot overthrow his domination and bring the Revolution to victory . . .

[N]ot only the Party and people in the South must make outstanding efforts but the Party and people in the North must make outstanding efforts as well . . . [I]t is time for the North to increase aid to the South, the North must bring into fuller play its role as the revolutionary base for the whole nation.

There should be a strong evolution in leadership concerning the support and aid for the Revolution in South Viet-Nam; we should thoroughly understand that under the leadership of the Party, our people are peacefully building North Viet-Nam, and at the same time conducting the anti-American war in South Viet-Nam. It is our nation's responsibility to struggle against the U.S. and their henchmen . . .

We should indoctrinate cadre, Party members, and the people in North Viet-Nam about their responsibility toward the Revolution in South Viet-Nam in order to increase their revolutionary spirit, their fighting determination, their patriotism, and to encourage them to work harder, and to be ready to fulfill their obligation toward the southern Revolution under any form and in any circumstance.

We should plan to aid the South to meet the requirements of the Revolution, and because of this aid, we must revise properly our plan for building North Viet-Nam.

We must understand that the favorable development of the Revolution in the South depends on our unceasing efforts to strengthen North Viet-Nam. Therefore, we must increase our economic and defensive strength in North Viet-Nam. We should increase our vigilance at all times and be ready to face the enemy['s] new schemes. At the same time, we should be prepared to cope with the eventuality of the expansion of the war into North Viet-Nam.

British Pessimism and Reticence

Memorandums by Robert Thompson, Head of the British Advisory Mission in South Vietnam, and J. E. Cable, Chief of the South East Asia Department of the British Foreign Office, August 13 and 17, 1964

As the political and military situation worsened for the South Vietnamese regime in 1963 and 1964, many governments friendly to the United States concluded that the war could not be won at a reasonable cost. A few allied leaders, most notably French President Charles de Gaulle, spoke up, calling publicly for a negotiated settlement and warning U.S. counterparts that escalation would bring only frustration and ultimate defeat. Others were more cautious about offending Washington and more guarded about expressing their pessimism. In the following documents, senior British policymakers agree about the basic situation in Vietnam but disagree over how strongly to challenge U.S. policy. In the first, Robert Thompson, head of the British Advisory Mission in South Vietnam (and an occasional consultant to both the Kennedy and Johnson administrations), warns that the government of Nguyen Khanh had done nothing to improve South Vietnam's prospects and calls on leaders in London to insist on negotiations to end the fighting. But in the second document, J. E. Cable, the head of the Foreign Office's South East Asia Department, urges that Britain keep quiet. Cable's view carried the day.

I am now convinced that we are passing the point of no return within South Vietnam whatever the Americans may do anywhere short of war with North Vietnam and China. Recent events show that Khanh's Government is unable and even unwilling to take the measures necessary to retrieve the situation . . . The Government is also split and is becoming increasingly repressive and irresponsible. Even [U.S. Ambassador Maxwell] Taylor seems to have little control over it. Defeat by the Viet Cong, through subversion and increased guerrilla activity, is therefore inevitable in 1965 and this prospect will become gradually more apparent over the next few months. Whether it will remain sufficiently obscure until after the American Presidential elections in November I cannot say, but it will be plain for all to see early in 1965.

Excluding a miracle, such as the collapse of the Communist regime in North Vietnam, there might be a very faint ray of hope, at least of a longer delaying action, if Khanh was succeeded by a group of dedicated young officers . . . who were prepared to hand over effective control to the Americans and provided that the latter were prepared to accept this role, which I doubt, and support it with some combat forces if necessary.

You will realize just how faint this ray is and, if it is excluded, then I strongly advocate that the earliest possible opportunity should be taken to open negotiations while a measure of control remains in South Vietnam. This too is a bleak and unpalatable prospect but I am afraid that, otherwise, the Americans may eventually be faced with a situation where they could be forced to insert combat troops in some strength not to retrieve the position but merely to extricate themselves.

. . . [T]he Americans are battling on against all the odds and past experience of Vietnamese performance (there is no institutional memory). Naturally they must publicly maintain an air of confidence. In this I fully support them and will continue to do so but we must prepare to face reality.

Mr. Thompson thinks the situation in South Viet-Nam is so hopeless that we should advise the United States Government to open negotiations while a measure of control remains in South Viet-Nam. Otherwise, he fears, the U.S. Government might eventually have to send in combat troops in order to extricate their 17,000-odd military advisers when South Viet-Namese resistance collapses.

Mr. Thompson may be right and [British embassies in] both Saigon and Washington have recently reported acute pessimism in the junior ranks of U.S. officials concerned with Viet-Nam. Nevertheless my own inclination is . . . that we should keep quiet. With the electoral campaign as well as American prestige at stake, the U.S. Government would not welcome advice from us and it might only result in our being made the scapegoat for their own failures. Moreover, though I share Mr. Thompson's pessimism about the eventual outcome of the struggle in South Viet-Nam, I doubt whether the debacle will necessarily come as soon as he thinks. If the position can be held until after the U.S. elections, it will be less difficult to discuss these problems if President Johnson is re-elected.

DOCUMENT 4.7

Estimating U.S. Intentions
Conversation between Chinese Leader Mao Zedong and North Vietnamese Prime Minister Pham Van Dong in Beijing, October 5, 1964

U.S. leaders sent conflicting messages about their intentions in Vietnam throughout 1964. On the one hand, the Johnson administration ordered bombing raids against North Vietnam in August after U.S. warships reported coming under attack in the Gulf of Tonkin, and the president obtained a resolution from Congress authorizing further military action. On the other hand, Johnson, posturing as a foreign-policy moderate during his campaign for the presidency, declared that he would never send "American boys" to do a job that South Vietnamese soldiers should do for themselves. Unsurprisingly, leaders in the communist world had difficulty interpreting these moves. In the following record of a meeting on October 5, Chinese leader Mao Zedong and North Vietnamese Prime Minister Pham Van Dong speculate on what the Americans had in mind and how North Vietnam might respond. Among other sources of uncertainty was whether U.S. leaders would send American soldiers to take charge of the fighting—whether, in North Vietnamese terminology, Washington would shift from "special war" (support for the South Vietnamese military) to "limited war" (large-scale U.S. intervention). Also unclear was whether Americans might go so far as to invade North Vietnam or attack the Chinese air force.

MAO ZEDONG: According to Comrade Le Duan, you had the plan to dispatch a [North Vietnamese] division [to the South]. Probably you have not dispatched that division yet. When . . . you dispatch it, the timing is important. Whether or not the United States will attack the North, it has not yet made the decision. Now, [the United States] is not even in a position to resolve the problem in South Vietnam. If it attacks the North, [it may need to] fight for one hundred years, and its legs will be trapped there. Therefore, it needs to consider carefully. The Americans have made all kinds of scary statements. They claim that they will run after [you], and will chase into your country, and that they will attack our air force. In my opinion, the meaning of these words is that they do not want us to fight a big war, and that [they do not want] our air force to attack their warships. If [we] do not attack their warships, they will not run after you. Isn't this what they mean? The Americans have something to hide.

PHAM VAN DONG: This is also our thinking. The United States is facing many difficulties, and it is not easy for it to expand the war. Therefore, our consideration is that we should try to restrict the war in South Vietnam to the sphere of special war, and should try to defeat the enemy within the sphere of special war. We should try our best not to let the U.S. imperialists turn the war in South Vietnam into a limited war, and try our best not to let the war be expanded to North Vietnam. We must adopt a very skillful strategy, and should not provoke [the United States] . . .

MAO ZEDONG: Yes.

PHAM VAN DONG: If the United States dares to start a limited war, we will fight it, and will win it.

MAO ZEDONG: Yes, you can win it. The South Vietnamese [regime] has several hundred thousand troops. You can fight against them, you can eliminate half of them, and you can eliminate all of them. To fulfill these tasks is more than possible. It is impossible for the United States to send many troops to South Vietnam. The Americans altogether have 18 army divisions. They have to keep half of these divisions, i.e., nine of them, at home, and can send abroad the other nine divisions. Among these divisions, half are in Europe, and half are in the Asian-Pacific region . . .

PHAM VAN DONG: Comrade Le Duan has reported Chairman Mao's opinions to our Central Committee. We have conducted an overall review of the situations in the South and the North, and our opinion is the same as that of Chairman Mao's. In South Vietnam, we should actively fight [the enemy]; and in North Vietnam, we should be prepared [for the enemy to escalate the war]. But we should also be cautious.

MAO ZEDONG: Our opinions are identical. Some other people say that we are belligerent. As a matter of fact, we are cautious . . .

The more thoroughly you defeat them, the more comfortable they feel. For example, you beat the French, and they became willing to negotiate with you. The Algerians defeated the French badly, and France became willing to come to peace with Algeria . . .

It is not completely a bad thing to negotiate. You have already earned the qualification to negotiate. It is another matter whether or not the negotiation will succeed.

5

AMERICANIZATION

BETWEEN NOVEMBER 1964 AND JULY 1965, U.S. leaders committed the nation fully to war in Vietnam. Numerous influential Americans and foreign leaders opposed the move, but President Johnson and his top advisers saw no good alternative to escalation in order to prevent a communist takeover of South Vietnam. By the end of 1965, approximately 185,000 American soldiers were stationed in the country. Meanwhile, increasing numbers of North Vietnamese soldiers came down the Ho Chi Minh Trail to fight in the South. Thus began a major war involving not just Southern insurgents and South Vietnamese soldiers but also major U.S. and North Vietnamese forces.

The Vietnamese Communist Party's decision in 1963 to send Northern troops across the seventeenth parallel began to take effect at the end of 1964, when Hanoi dispatched units of its regular army, not just Southern-born fighters who had moved north after 1954, to fight alongside the Vietcong. Around the same time, the Johnson administration began to expand American military activity to shore up the deteriorating situation in the South. To be sure, administration officials had been considering escalation for months, but the process began in earnest only after Johnson had won a landslide victory in the November 1964 election.

Following a Vietcong assault on the U.S. base at Pleiku on February 7, 1965, Johnson ordered bombing of North Vietnam to bolster morale in the South, disrupt the flow of supplies across the seventeenth parallel, and punish Hanoi for its support of the insurgency. A few weeks later, Johnson sent the first American combat troops. Their function was merely to guard the American airbase at Da Nang, but within weeks, the administration expanded their mission to include offensive operations.

In the United States and around the world, innumerable political leaders, media commentators, and activists decried the burgeoning war and urged both sides to seek a negotiated settlement. But those appeals accomplished nothing. In Hanoi as in Washington, top decision-makers remained wedded to their longstanding objectives and saw little to be gained through talks in the near term. To be sure, leaders on both sides expected that a war would be long and difficult, but both sides were confident that fighting would bring ultimate victory.

In July, the Johnson administration made its boldest decision to "Americanize" the war, approving a U.S. force of 175,000 soldiers for Vietnam. Americans increasingly assumed the burden of the anticommunist fight, mounting "search and destroy" operations all over South Vietnam. Meanwhile, Washington steadily intensified the bombing of North Vietnam and expanded the areas where American aircraft were allowed to mount attacks.

DOCUMENT 5.1

The Logic of Bombing

Telegram from National Security Adviser McGeorge Bundy to President Lyndon Johnson, February 7, 1965

President Johnson sent his national security adviser, McGeorge Bundy, and a team of aides to South Vietnam in early February to study the deteriorating situation and make recommendations. On February 7, while Bundy was in Saigon, Vietcong guerrillas attacked the U.S. air base at Pleiku, killing eight Americans and wounding more than a hundred. Bundy wrote the following memorandum for the president a few hours after that attack while flying home to Washington. Johnson accepted Bundy's advice to begin "sustained reprisal" bombing of North Vietnam. That relatively limited campaign of "tit-for-tat" strikes gave way to the program of continuous bombing, code-named Operation Rolling Thunder, on March 2.

The situation in Vietnam is deteriorating, and without new U.S. action defeat appears inevitable—probably not in a matter of weeks or perhaps even months, but within the next year or so. There is still time to turn it around, but not much.

The stakes in Vietnam are extremely high. The American investment is very large, and American responsibility is a fact of life which is palpable in the atmosphere of Asia, and even elsewhere. The international prestige of the United States, and a substantial part of our influence, are directly at risk in Vietnam. There is no way of unloading the burden on the Vietnamese themselves, and there is no way of negotiating ourselves out of Vietnam which offers any serious promise at present. It is possible that at some future time a neutral non-Communist force may emerge, perhaps under Buddhist leadership, but no such force currently exists, and any negotiated U.S. withdrawal today would mean surrender on the installment plan.

The policy of graduated and continuing reprisal outlined [below] is the most promising course available, in my judgment. That judgment is shared by all who accompanied me from Washington, and I think by all members of the country team.

The events of the last twenty-four hours have produced a practicable point of departure for this policy of reprisal, and for the removal of U.S. dependents. They may also have catalyzed the formation of a new Vietnamese government. If so, the situation may be at a turning point . . .

For the last year—and perhaps for longer—the overall situation in Vietnam has been deteriorating. The Communists have been gaining and the anti-Communist forces have been losing. As a result there is now great uncertainty among Vietnamese as well as Americans as to whether Communist victory can be prevented. There is nervousness about the determination of the U.S. Government. There is recrimination and fear among Vietnamese political leaders. There is an appearance of wariness among some military leaders. There is a worrisome lassitude among the Vietnamese generally. There is a distressing absence of positive commitment to any serious social or political purpose. Outside observers are ready to write the patient off. All of this tends to bring latent anti-Americanism dangerously near to the surface.

To be an American in Saigon today is to have a gnawing feeling that time is against us. Junior officers in all services are able, zealous and effective within the limits of their means. Their morale is sustained by the fact that they know that they are doing their jobs well and that they will not have to accept the responsibility for defeat. But near the top, where responsibility is heavy and accountability real, one can sense the inner doubts of men whose outward behavior remains determined.

The situation is not all black. The overall military effectiveness of the Vietnamese armed forces in open combat continues to grow. The month of January was one of outstanding and genuine success in offensive military action, showing the highest gross count of Viet Cong dead of any month of the war, and a very high ratio also of enemy to friendly losses. We believe that General Westmoreland is right . . . when he says that the Viet Cong do not now plan to expose themselves to large-scale military engagements in which their losses on the average would be high and their gains low . . .

Moreover, the Vietnamese people, although war weary, are also remarkably tough and resilient, and they do not find the prospect of Communist domination attractive. Their readiness to quit is much lower than the discouraging events of recent months might lead one to expect. It is probable that most Vietnamese think American withdrawal is more likely than an early switch to neutralism or surrender by major elements within Vietnam.

Nevertheless the social and political fabric is stretched thin, and extremely unpleasant surprises are increasingly possible—both political and military.

And it remains a stubborn fact that the percentage of the countryside which is dominated or threatened by the Viet Cong continues to grow. Even in areas which are "cleared," the follow-on pacification is stalled because of widespread belief that the Viet Cong are going to win in the long run. The areas which can be regarded as truly cleared and pacified and safe are few and shrinking . . .

Next only to the overall state of the struggle against the Viet Cong, the shape and structure of the government is the most important element of the Saigon situation . . .

For immediate purposes—and especially for the initiation of reprisal policy, we believe that the government need be no stronger than it is today with General Khanh as the focus of raw power while a weak caretaker government goes through the motions. Such a government can execute military decisions and it can give formal political support to joint US/GVN policy. That is about all it can do.

In the longer run, it is necessary that a government be established which will in one way or another be able to maintain its political authority against all challenges over a longer time than the governments of the last year and a half . . .

The prospect in Vietnam is grim. The energy and persistence of the Viet Cong are astonishing. They can appear anywhere—and at almost any time. They have accepted extraordinary losses and they come back for more. They show skill in their sneak attacks and ferocity when cornered. Yet the weary country does not want them to win.

There are a host of things the Vietnamese need to do better and areas in which we need to help them. The place where we can help most is in the clarity and firmness of our own commitment to what is in fact as well as in rhetoric a common cause. There is one grave weakness in our posture in Vietnam which is within our own power to fix—and that is a widespread belief that we do not have the will and force and patience and determination to take the necessary action and stay the course.

This is the overriding reason for our present recommendation of a policy of sustained reprisal. Once such a policy is put in force, we shall be able to speak in Vietnam on many topics and in many ways, with growing force and effectiveness . . .

At its very best the struggle in Vietnam will be long. It seems to us important that this fundamental fact be made clear and our understanding of it be made clear to our own people and to the people of Vietnam. Too often in the past we have conveyed the impression that we expect an early solution when those who live with this war know that no early solution is possible. It is our own belief that the people of the United States have the necessary will to accept and to execute a policy that rests upon the reality that there is no short cut to success in South Vietnam . . .

A Policy of Sustained Reprisal

We believe that the best available way of increasing our chance of success in Vietnam is the development and execution of a policy of sustained reprisal against North Vietnam—a policy in which air and naval action against the North is justified by and related to the whole Viet Cong campaign of violence and terror in the South.

While we believe that the risks of such a policy are acceptable, we emphasize that its costs are real. It implies significant U.S. air losses even if no full air war is joined, and it seems likely that it would eventually require an extensive and costly effort against the whole air defense system of North Vietnam. U.S. casualties would be higher—and more visible to American feelings—than those sustained in the struggle in South Vietnam. Yet measured against the costs of defeat in Vietnam, this program seems cheap. And even if it fails to turn the tide—as it may—the value of the effort seems to us to exceed its cost . . .

This reprisal policy should begin at a low level. Its level of force and pressure should be increased only gradually—and as indicated above it should be decreased if VC terror visibly decreases. The object would not be to "win" an air war against Hanoi, but rather to influence the course of the struggle in the South . . .

Predictions of the effect of any given course of action upon the states of mind of people are difficult. It seems very clear that if the United States and the Government of Vietnam join in a policy of reprisal, there will be a sharp immediate increase in optimism in the South, among nearly all articulate groups . . .

While emphasizing the importance of reprisals in the South, we do not exclude the impact on Hanoi. We believe, indeed, that it is of great importance that the level of reprisal be adjusted rapidly and visibly to both upward and downward shifts in the level of Viet Cong offenses. We want to keep before Hanoi the carrot of our desisting as well as the stick of continued pressure. We also need to conduct the application of the force so that there is always a prospect of worse to come.

We cannot assert that a policy of sustained reprisal will succeed in changing the course of the contest in Vietnam. It may fail, and we cannot estimate the odds of success with any accuracy—they may be somewhere between 25% and 75%. What we can say is that even if it fails, the policy will be worth it. At a minimum it will damp down the charge that we did not do all that we could have done, and this charge will be important in many countries, including our own. Beyond that, a reprisal policy—to the extent that it demonstrates U.S. willingness to employ this new norm in counter-insurgency—will set a higher price for the future upon all adventures of guerrilla warfare, and it should therefore somewhat increase our ability to deter such adventures. We must recognize, however, that that ability will be gravely weakened if there is failure for any reason in Vietnam.

DOCUMENT 5.2

An Appeal for Negotiations

Memorandum from Vice President Hubert H. Humphrey to President Lyndon B. Johnson, February 17, 1965

In the months following his resounding electoral triumph in November 1964, President Johnson made momentous decisions to escalate U.S. military involvement in Vietnam. Fearing that these steps would commit the United States to a difficult and unnecessary war, critics demanded a change of course. One such appeal came from Vice President Hubert H. Humphrey, who called attention to the domestic-political risks of escalation and criticized the president for adopting policies associated with his defeated Republican rival, Arizona Senator Barry Goldwater. In a memorandum to the president ten days after the beginning of "sustained reprisal" bombing, Humphrey warned that the American public had little enthusiasm for a major war and that escalation might damage both the administration and the Democratic Party more generally. Although there is no definitive evidence that Johnson read the memo, one of Johnson's aides, Bill Moyers, later stated that he had given it to the president.

I would like to share with you my views on the political consequences of certain courses of action that have been proposed in regard to U.S. policy in Southeast Asia. I refer both to the domestic political consequences here in the United States and to the international political consequences.

A. Domestic Political Consequences

1. 1964 Campaign.

Although the question of U.S. involvement in Vietnam is and should be a nonpartisan question, there have always been significant differences in approach to the Asian question between the Republican Party and the Democratic Party. These came out in the 1964 campaign. The Republicans represented both by Goldwater, and the top Republican leaders in Congress, favored a quick, total military solution in Vietnam, to be achieved through military escalation of the war.

The Democratic position emphasized the complexity of a Vietnam situation involving both political, social and military factors; the necessity of staying in Vietnam as long as necessary; recognition that the war will be won or lost chiefly in South Vietnam. In Vietnam, as in Korea, the Republicans have attacked the Democrats either for failure to use our military power to "win" a total victory, or alternatively for losing the country to the Communists. The Democratic position has always been one of firmness in the face of Communist pressure but restraint in the use of military force; it has sought to obtain the best possible settlement without provoking a nuclear World War III; it has sought to leave open face-saving options to an opponent when necessary to avoid a nuclear show-down. When grave risks have been necessary, as in the case of Cuba, they have been taken. But here again a face-saving option was permitted the opponent. In all instances the Democratic position has included a balancing of both political and military factors.

Today the Administration is being charged by some of its critics with adopting the Goldwater position on Vietnam. While this is not true of the Administration's position as defined by the President, it is true that many key advisors in the Government are advocating a policy markedly similar to the Republican policy as defined by Goldwater.

2. Consequences for other policies advocated by a Democratic Administration.

The Johnson Administration is associated both at home and abroad with a policy of progress toward detente with the Soviet bloc, a policy of limited arms control, and a policy of new initiatives for peace. A full-scale military attack on North Vietnam—with the attendant risk of an open military clash with Communist China—would risk gravely undermining other U.S. policies. It would eliminate for the time being any possible exchange between the President and Soviet leaders; it would postpone any progress on arms control; it would encourage the Soviet Union and China to end their rift; it would seriously hamper our efforts to strengthen relations with our European allies; it would weaken our position in the United Nations; it might require a call-up of reservists if we were to get involved in a large-scale land war—and a consequent increase in defense expenditures; it would tend to shift the Administration's emphasis from its Great Society oriented programs to further military outlays; finally and most important it would damage the image of the President of the United States—and that of the United States itself.

3. Involvement in a full scale war with North Vietnam would not make sense to the majority of the American people.

American wars have to be politically understandable by the American public. There has to be a cogent, convincing case if we are to have sustained public support. In World Wars I and II we had this. In Korea we were moving under UN auspices to defend South Korea against dramatic, across-the-border conventional aggression. Yet even with those advantages, we could not sustain American political support for fighting the Chinese in Korea in 1952.

Today in Vietnam we lack the very advantages we had in Korea. The public is worried and confused. Our rationale for action has shifted away now even from the notion that we are there as advisors on request of a free government—to the simple argument of our "national interest." We have not succeeded in making this "national interest" interesting enough at home or abroad to generate support.

4. From a political viewpoint, the American people find it hard to understand why we risk World War III by enlarging a war under terms we found unacceptable 12 years ago in Korea, particularly since the chances of success are slimmer . . .

5. Absence of confidence in the Government of South Vietnam.

Politically, people can't understand why we would run grave risks to support a country which is totally unable to put its own house in order. The chronic instability in Saigon directly undermines American political support for our policy.

6. Politically, it is hard to justify over a long period of time sustained, large-scale U.S. air bombardments across a border as a response to camouflaged, often non-sensational, elusive, small-scale terror which has been going on for 10 years in what looks like a civil war in the South.

7. Politically, in Washington and across the country, the opposition is more Democratic than Republican.

8. Politically, it is always hard to cut losses. But the Johnson Administration is in a stronger position to do so than any Administration in this century. 1965 is the year of minimum political risk for the Johnson Administration. Indeed it is the first year when we can face the Vietnam problem without being preoccupied with

the political repercussions from the Republican right. As indicated earlier, the political problems are likely to come from new and different sources if we pursue an enlarged military policy very long (Democratic liberals, Independents, Labor, Church groups).

9. Politically, we now risk creating the impression that we are the prisoner of events in Vietnam. This blurs the Administration's leadership role and has spill-over effects across the board. It also helps erode confidence and credibility in our policies.

10. The President is personally identified with, and admired for, political ingenuity. He will be expected to put all his great political sense to work now for international political solutions. People will be counting upon him to use on the world scene his unrivalled talents as a political leader.

They will be watching to see how he makes this transition. The best possible outcome a year from now would be a Vietnam settlement which turns out to be better than was in the cards because the President's political talents for the first time came to grips with a fateful world crisis and so successfully. It goes without saying that the subsequent domestic political benefits of such an outcome, and such a new dimension for the President, would be enormous.

11. If on the other hand, we find ourselves leading from frustration to escalation, and end up short of a war with China but embroiled deeper in fighting with Vietnam over the next few months, political opposition will steadily mount. It will underwrite all the negativism and disillusionment which we already have about foreign involvement generally—with direct spill-over effects politically for all the Democratic internationalist programs to which we are committed—AID, UN, disarmament, and activist world policies generally.

B. International Political Implications of Vietnam

If ultimately a negotiated settlement is our aim, when do we start developing a political track, in addition to the military one, that might lead us to the conference table? I believe we should develop the political track earlier rather than later. We should take the initiative on the political side and not end up being dragged to a conference as an unwilling participant. This does not mean we should cease all programs of military pressure. But we should distinguish carefully between those military actions necessary to reach our political goal of a negotiated settlement, and those likely to provoke open Chinese military intervention.

We should not underestimate the likelihood of Chinese intervention and repeat the mistake of the Korean War. If we begin to bomb further north in Vietnam, the likelihood is great of an encounter with the Chinese Air Force operating from sanctuary bases across the border . . .

Confrontation with the Chinese Air Force can easily lead to massive retaliation by the Chinese in South Vietnam. What is our response to this? Do we bomb Chinese air bases and nuclear installations? If so, will not the Soviet Union honor its treaty of friendship and come to China's assistance? I believe there is a good chance that it would—thereby involving us in a war with both China and the Soviet Union. Here again, we must remember the consequences for the Soviet Union of not intervening if China's military power is destroyed by the U.S.

The NLF Vows to Persevere
Statement by the National Liberation Front about U.S. Escalation, March 22, 1965

Communist General Secretary Le Duan and other party leaders failed in their attempt to achieve victory in South Vietnam before the United States could bring its power fully to bear on the side of the Saigon government. The start of U.S. bombing against North Vietnam and the introduction of American ground troops clearly spelled hardship for North Vietnam and the Southern insurgents. Yet communist leaders left no doubt in their public statements of their determination to carry on with the war, no matter the cost. The National Liberation Front, ostensibly an independent Southern revolutionary organization but in fact tightly controlled by Hanoi, issued the following statement two weeks after the arrival of the first U.S. combat troops.

Though deeply attached to peace, the South Vietnamese people are determined not to sit back with folded arms and let the U.S. aggressors and their henchmen trample upon their homeland. Rather to die than live in slavery, the fourteen million valiant South Vietnamese have stood up like one man in an undaunted struggle to defeat the U.S. aggressors and the native traitors so as to liberate their territory and achieve independence, democracy, peace and neutrality in South Viet Nam, in contribution to the maintenance of peace in Indochina and Southeast Asia. Their war of liberation fully conforms to the most elementary and basic principles of international law concerning the people's rights to self-determination and their right to wage a patriotic war against foreign aggression. In this sacred war of liberation they have used all kinds of weapons to fight against their enemy. The chief and biggest arms purveyor of their forces is none other than the U.S. imperialists themselves, who have sustained heavy and repeated setbacks over the years.

With bare hands at the beginning, the South Vietnamese people have achieved a great work and recorded glorious feats of arms. They are firmly convinced that with their own strength and the wholehearted support of the people throughout the world, they will certainly win complete victory. The U.S. imperialists and their lackeys find themselves in a desperate blind alley. They are being knocked down in the powerful storm of the South Vietnamese people's revolution and are madly writhing before reconciling themselves to their defeat. To retrieve this situation, the U.S. imperialists are plunging headlong into extremely dangerous military adventures. . . .

Viet Nam is one country, the Vietnamese people are one nation. North and South Viet Nam are of the same family. This sentiment is loftier than mountains and deeper than the sea. This truth is shining like the rising sun; nothing can tarnish it. In this boiling situation and in this life-and-death struggle against the U.S. imperialists and their lackeys, our heart cannot but suffer when our hands are cut. That the people in North Viet Nam are resolved to accomplish their duty toward their kith and kin in the South fully conforms to sentiment and reason . . .

The South Viet Nam [NLF] and people are not only strong with the justice of their cause; their material and organizational strength are rapidly increasing. They have been and are the glorious victors. The more they fight, the more ardent they become and the more victories they win; and the more they win, the stronger they grow and the greater their victories. Worthy heirs to the traditions of the Dien Bien Phu fighters and of the Vietnamese people who possess a 4,000-year history of heroic struggle against foreign invasion, we have developed these traditions to a high degree. Moreover, the [NLF] and the people of South Viet Nam are conducting their valiant fight in an extremely favourable condition afforded by the present time when the oppressed nations in Asia, Africa and Latin America have risen up like tidal waves. The socialist countries and the forces of democracy and peace around the world are an important factor stimulating the advance of mankind, overwhelming and smashing imperialism and colonialism under whatever disguise. If the U.S. imperialists and their henchmen are rash enough to fan the flames of war all over Indochina, the people of this area and Southeast Asia as a whole will resolutely stand up like one man and drive them out into the ocean . . .

Even if we are to carry out the struggle for ten, twenty years or longer, and to suffer great difficulties and hardships, we are prepared to fight up until not a single American aggressor is seen on our soil.

DOCUMENT 5.4

The Rationale for Escalation

Speech by President Lyndon B. Johnson at Johns Hopkins University, "Peace Without Conquest," April 7, 1965

President Johnson hoped to attract as little attention as possible to his decisions to escalate the U.S. role in Vietnam. He worried above all that vigorous national discussion of the war would distract attention and resources from his domestic agenda, the array of reform measures known as the Great Society. Inescapably, however, U.S. decisions drew intense scrutiny. Antiwar activists staged the first "teach-ins" and large demonstrations in March and April. Conservative hawks, meanwhile, insisted that the United States step up its role in Vietnam more boldly than Johnson intended. Anxious to dampen criticism from both sides, the president delivered a major speech on the war on April 7, 1965, at Johns Hopkins University in Baltimore. The next day, the North Vietnamese government responded by laying out four conditions for a peaceful resolution of the war: U.S. withdrawal from Vietnam, respect for the Geneva agreements, implementation of the NLF political program in the South, and peaceful reunification of Vietnam.

Tonight Americans and Asians are dying for a world where each people may choose its own path to change.

This is the principle for which our ancestors fought in the valleys of Pennsylvania. It is the principle for which our sons fight tonight in the jungles of Viet-Nam.

Viet-Nam is far away from this quiet campus. We have no territory there, nor do we seek any. The war is dirty and brutal and difficult. And some 400 young men, born into an America that is bursting with opportunity and promise, have ended their lives on Viet-Nam's steaming soil.

Why must we take this painful road?

Why must this Nation hazard its ease, and its interest, and its power for the sake of a people so far away?

We fight because we must fight if we are to live in a world where every country can shape its own destiny. And only in such a world will our own freedom be finally secure.

This kind of world will never be built by bombs or bullets. Yet the infirmities of man are such that force must often precede reason, and the waste of war, the works of peace.

We wish that this were not so. But we must deal with the world as it is, if it is ever to be as we wish.

The world as it is in Asia is not a serene or peaceful place.

The first reality is that North Viet-Nam has attacked the independent nation of South Viet-Nam. Its object is total conquest.

Of course, some of the people of South Viet-Nam are participating in attack on their own government. But trained men and supplies, orders and arms, flow in a constant stream from north to south.

This support is the heartbeat of the war.

And it is a war of unparalleled brutality. Simple farmers are the targets of assassination and kidnapping. Women and children are strangled in the night because their men are loyal to their government. And helpless villages are ravaged by sneak attacks. Large-scale raids are conducted on towns, and terror strikes in the heart of cities.

The confused nature of this conflict cannot mask the fact that it is the new face of an old enemy.

Over this war—and all Asia—is another reality: the deepening shadow of Communist China. The rulers in Hanoi are urged on by Peking. This is a regime which has destroyed freedom in Tibet, which has attacked India, and has been condemned by the United Nations for aggression in Korea. It is a nation which is helping the forces of violence in almost every continent. The contest in Viet-Nam is part of a wider pattern of aggressive purposes.

Why are these realities our concern? Why are we in South Viet-Nam?

We are there because we have a promise to keep. Since 1954 every American President has offered support to the people of South Viet-Nam. We have helped to build, and we have helped to defend. Thus, over many years, we have made a national pledge to help South Viet-Nam defend its independence.

And I intend to keep that promise.

To dishonor that pledge, to abandon this small and brave nation to its enemies, and to the terror that must follow, would be an unforgivable wrong.

We are also there to strengthen world order. Around the globe, from Berlin to Thailand, are people whose well-being rests, in part, on the belief that they can count on us if they are attacked. To leave Viet-Nam to its fate would shake the confidence of all these people in the value of an American commitment and in the value of America's word. The result would be increased unrest and instability, and even wider war.

We are also there because there are great stakes in the balance. Let no one think for a moment that retreat from Viet-Nam would bring an end to conflict. The battle would be renewed in one country and then another. The central lesson of our time is that the appetite of aggression is never satisfied. To withdraw from one battlefield means only to prepare for the next. We must say in southeast Asia—as we did in Europe—in the words of the Bible: "Hitherto shalt thou come, but no further." . . .

Our objective is the independence of South Viet-Nam, and its freedom from attack. We want nothing for ourselves—only that the people of South Viet-Nam be allowed to guide their own country in their own way.

We will do everything necessary to reach that objective. And we will do only what is absolutely necessary.

In recent months attacks on South Viet-Nam were stepped up. Thus, it became necessary for us to increase our response and to make attacks by air. This is not a change of purpose. It is a change in what we believe that purpose requires.

We do this in order to slow down aggression.

We do this to increase the confidence of the brave people of South Viet-Nam who have bravely borne this brutal battle for so many years with so many casualties.

And we do this to convince the leaders of North Viet-Nam—and all who seek to share their conquest—of a very simple fact: We will not be defeated. We will not grow tired.

We will not withdraw, either openly or under the cloak of a meaningless agreement.

We know that air attacks alone will not accomplish all of these purposes. But it is our best and prayerful judgment that they are a necessary part of the surest road to peace.

We hope that peace will come swiftly. But that is in the hands of others besides ourselves. And we must be prepared for a long continued conflict. It will require patience as well as bravery, the will to endure as well as the will to resist . . .

Once this is clear, then it should also be clear that the only path for reasonable men is the path of peaceful settlement.

Such peace demands an independent South Viet-Nam—securely guaranteed and able to shape its own relationships to all others, free from outside interference—tied to no alliance—a military base for no other country.

These are the essentials of any final settlement.

We will never be second in the search for such a peaceful settlement in Viet-Nam.

There may be many ways to this kind of peace: in discussion or negotiation with the governments concerned; in large groups or in small ones; in the reaffirmation of old agreements or their strengthening with new ones.

We have stated this position over and over again, fifty times and more, to friend and foe alike. And we remain ready, with this purpose, for unconditional discussions.

DOCUMENT 5.5
Political Cartoon from the Washington Post, June 15, 1965

The overthrow of Ngo Dinh Diem in November 1963 yielded not greater political stability in South Vietnam, as U.S. leaders hoped, but heightened turbulence. Six changes of government took place in 1964 and three more in early 1965, sometimes with the same leaders reshuffled in different roles. The *Washington Post*'s Herbert Block captured American frustrations in this cartoon, published on June 15, 1965. The seemingly endless cycle of coups ended that same month, when Nguyen Van Thieu and Nguyen Cao Ky, two generals who would lead South Vietnam for nearly a decade, came to power.

DOCUMENT 5.6

Deliberating a Major War

Minutes of a Meeting at the White House, July 21, 1965

The first U.S. combat troops arrived in South Vietnam on March 8, 1965, a major escalation of American involvement in the war. Yet the U.S. commitment of ground forces remained relatively limited for several weeks. Between March and July, the Johnson administration increased troop strength in small increments, expanded their mission cautiously, and did little to inform the American public of any significant shift. The decision to fight a major war, with large numbers of U.S. troops bearing the main burden of the fighting, came in late July, following a trip by Secretary of Defense Robert S. McNamara to assess the situation in Vietnam. Upon his return, McNamara recommended that the United States increase its force to 175,000 troops and prepare for further deployments thereafter. Between July 21 and 28, President Johnson held a series of meetings with senior advisors to discuss these proposals, the closest the administration came to a thorough, high-level discussion of the issues involved. Presidential aide Jack Valenti took the following notes during a session held at the White House on July 21. Participants included McNamara, Secretary of State Dean Rusk, Joint Chiefs of Staff Chairman Earle G. Wheeler, Undersecretary of State George Ball, CIA Director William F. Raborn, U.S. Information Agency Director Carl Rowan, and the U.S. ambassador to South Vietnam, Henry Cabot Lodge Jr.

President: What has happened in recent past that requires this decision on my part? What are the alternatives? Also, I want more discussions on what we expect to flow from this decision. Discuss in detail.

Have we wrung every single soldier out of every country we can? Who else can help? Are we the sole defenders of freedom in the world? Have we done all we can in this direction? The reasons for the call up? The results we can expect? What are the alternatives? We must make no snap judgments. We must consider carefully all our options.

We know we can tell SVN "we're coming home." Is that the option we should take? What flows from that.

The negotiations, the pause, all the other approaches—have all been explored. It makes us look weak—with cup in hand. We have tried.

Let's look at all our options so that every man at this table understands fully the total picture.

McNamara: This is our position a year ago (shows President a map of the country with legends). Estimated by country team that VC controls 25%—SVN 50%—rest in white area, VC in red areas.

VC tactics are terror, and sniping.

President: Looks dangerous to put US forces in those red areas.

McNamara: You're right. We're placing our people with their backs to the sea—for protection. Our mission would be to seek out the VC in large scale units.

Wheeler: Big problem in Vietnam is good combat intelligence. The VC is a creature of habit. By continuing to probe we think we can make headway.

Ball: Isn't it possible that the VC will do what they did against the French—stay away from confrontation and not accommodate us?

Wheeler: Yes, but by constantly harassing them, they will have to fight somewhere.

McNamara: If VC doesn't fight in large units, it will give ARVN a chance to re-secure hostile areas.

We don't know what VC tactics will be when VC is confronted by 175,000 Americans.

Raborn: We agree—by 1965, we expect [North Vietnam] will increase their forces. They will attempt to gain a substantial victory before our build-up is complete.

President: Is anyone of the opinion we should not do what the memo says—If so, I'd like to hear from them.

Ball: I can foresee a perilous voyage—very dangerous—great apprehensions that we can win under these conditions. But, let me be clear, if the decision is to go ahead, I'm committed.

President: But is there another course in the national interest that is better than the McNamara course? We know it's dangerous and perilous. But can it be avoided?

Ball: There is no course that will allow us to cut our losses. If we get bogged down, our cost might be substantially greater. The pressures to create a larger war would be irresistible. Qualifications I have are not due to the fact that I think we are in a bad moral position.

President: What other road can I go?

Ball: Take what precautions we can—take losses—let their government fall apart—negotiate—probable take over by Communists. This is disagreeable, I know.

President: Can we make a case for this—discuss it fully?

Ball: We have discussed it. I have had my day in court.

President: I don't think we have made a full commitment. You have pointed out the danger, but you haven't proposed an alternative course. We haven't always been right. We have no mortgage on victory.

I feel we have very little alternative to what we are doing.

I want another meeting before we take this action. We should look at all other courses carefully. Right now I feel it would be more dangerous for us to lose this now, than endanger a greater number of troops.

Rusk: What we have done since 1954-61 has not been good enough. We should have probably committed ourselves heavier in 1961.

Rowan: What bothers me most is the weakness of the Ky government. Unless we put the screws on the Ky government, 175,000 men will do us no good.

Lodge: There is no tradition of a national government in Saigon. There are no roots in the country. Not until there is tranquility can you have any stability. I don't think we ought to take this government seriously. There is no one who can do anything. We have to do what we think we ought to do regardless of what the Saigon government does.

As we move ahead on a new phase—it gives us the right and duty to do certain things with or without the government's approval.

President: George, do you think we have another course?

Ball: I would not recommend that you follow McNamara's course.

President: Are you able to outline your doubts—and offer another course of action? I think it is desirable to hear you out—and determine if your suggestions are sound and ready to be followed.

Ball: Yes. I think I can present to you the least bad of two courses. What I would present is a course that is costly, but can be limited to short term costs.

President: Then, let's meet at 2:30 this afternoon to discuss Ball's proposals. Now let Bob tell us why we need to risk those 600,000 lives.

(McNamara and Wheeler outlined the reasons for more troops.) 75,000 now just enough to protect bases—it will let us lose slowly instead of rapidly. The extra men will stabilize the situation and improve it. It will give ARVN breathing room. We limit it to another 100,000 because [Vietnam] can't absorb any more. There is no major risk of catastrophe.

President: But you will lose greater number of men.

Wheeler: The more men we have the greater the likelihood of smaller losses.

President: What makes you think if we put in 100,000 men Ho Chi Minh won't put in another 100,000?

Wheeler: This means greater bodies of men—which will allow us to cream them.

President: What are the chances of more NVN men coming?

Wheeler: 50-50 chance. He would be foolhardy to put 1/4 of his forces in SVN. It would expose him too greatly in NVN.

President: (to Raborn) Do you have people in NVN?

Raborn: Not enough. We think it is reliable.

President: Can't we improve intelligence in NVN?

Raborn: We have a task force working on this.

[Meeting adjourns at 1 p.m. and resumes at 2:30 p.m.]

Ball: We can't win. Long protracted. The most we can hope for is messy conclusion. There remains a great danger of intrusion by Chicoms.

Problem of long war in US:

1. Korean experience was galling one. Correlation between Korean casualties and public opinion . . . showed support stabilized at 50%. As casualties increase, pressure to strike at jugular of the NVN will become very great.
2. World opinion. If we could win in a year's time—win decisively—world opinion would be alright. However, if long and protracted we will suffer because a great power cannot beat guerrillas.
3. National politics. Every great captain in history is not afraid to make a tactical withdrawal if conditions are unfavorable to him. The enemy cannot even be seen; he is indigenous to the country.

Have serious doubt if an army of westerners can fight orientals in Asian jungle and succeed.

President: This is important—can westerners, in absence of intelligence, successfully fight orientals in jungle rice-paddies? I want McNamara and Wheeler to seriously ponder this question.

Ball: I think we have all underestimated the seriousness of this situation. Like giving cobalt treatment to a terminal cancer case. I think a long protracted war will disclose our weakness, not our strength.

The least harmful way to cut losses in SVN is to let the government decide it doesn't want us to stay there. Therefore, put such proposals to SVN government that they can't accept, then it would move into a neutralist position—and I have no illusions that after we were asked to leave, SVN would be under Hanoi control.

What about Thailand? It would be our main problem. Thailand has proven a good ally so far—though history shows it has never been a staunch ally. If we wanted to make a stand in Thailand, we might be able to make it.

Another problem would be South Korea. We have two divisions there now. There would be a problem with Taiwan, but as long as Generalissimo is there, they have no place to go. Indonesia is a problem—insofar as Malaysia. There we might have to help the British in military way. Japan thinks we are propping up a lifeless government and are on a sticky wicket. Between long war and cutting our losses, the Japanese would go for the latter . . .

President: Wouldn't all those countries say Uncle Sam is a paper tiger—wouldn't we lose credibility breaking the word of three presidents—if we set it up as you proposed. It would seem to be an irreparable blow. But, I gather you don't think so.

Ball: The worse blow would be that the mightiest power in the world is unable to defeat guerrillas.

President: Then you are not basically troubled by what the world would say about pulling out?

Ball: If we were actively helping a country with a stable, viable government, it would be a vastly different story. Western Europeans look at us as if we got ourselves into an imprudent fashion [situation].

President: But I believe that these people are trying to fight. They're like Republicans who try to stay in power, but don't stay there long . . .

McNamara: Ky will fall soon. He is weak. We can't have elections until there is physical security, and even then there will be no elections because as Cabot said, there is no democratic tradition. (Wheeler agreed about Ky—but said Thieu impressed him.)

President: Two basic troublings:

1. That Westerners can ever win in Asia.
2. Don't see how you can fight a war under direction of other people whose government changes every month.

Now go ahead, George, and make your other points.

Ball: The cost, as well as our Western European allies, is not relevant to their situation.

What they are concerned about is their own security—troops in Berlin have real meaning, none in VN.

President: Are you saying pulling out of Korea would be akin to pulling out of Vietnam?

Bundy: It is not analogous. We had a status quo in Korea. It would not be that way in Vietnam.

Ball: We will pay a higher cost in Vietnam.

This is a decision one makes against an alternative.

On one hand—long protracted war, costly, NVN is digging in for long term. This is their life and driving force. Chinese are taking long term view—ordering blood plasma from Japan.

On the other hand—short-term losses. On balance, come out ahead of McNamara plan. Distasteful on either hand.

Bundy: Two important questions to be raised—I agree with the main thrust of McNamara. It is the function of my staff to argue both sides.

To Ball's argument: The difficulty in adopting it now would be a radical switch without evidence that it should be done. It goes in the face of all we have said and done.

His whole analytical argument gives no weight to loss suffered by other side. A great many elements in his argument are correct.

We need to make clear this is a somber matter—that it will not be quick—no single action will bring quick victory.

I think it is clear that we are not going to be thrown out.

Ball: My problem is not that we don't get thrown out, but that we get bogged down and don't win.

Bundy: I would sum up: The world, the country, and the VN would have alarming reactions if we got out.

Rusk: If the Communist world finds out we will not pursue our commitment to the end, I don't know where they will stay their hand.

I am more optimistic than some of my colleagues. I don't believe the VC have made large advances among the VN people.

We can't worry about massive casualties when we say we can't find the enemy. I don't see great casualties unless the Chinese come in.

Lodge: There is a greater threat to World War III if we don't go in. Similarity to our indolence at Munich.

6
THE WIDER WAR

IN AUGUST 1964, PRESIDENT JOHNSON declared that he sought "no wider war" in Vietnam. By the middle of 1965, however, American troops were flooding into South Vietnam. Over the next two-and-a-half years, both Washington and Hanoi continued to expand their commitments in hopes of gaining the upper hand. But greater exertions and higher levels of violence did not result in any breakthroughs. Rather, the war settled into a bloody stalemate.

U.S. bombing of North Vietnam destroyed much of the country's industrial infrastructure as the target list grew between 1965 and 1968. American planes also pummeled the routes along which North Vietnamese troops and supplies entered the South. But Hanoi showed no sign up buckling. North Vietnam maintained domestic order and, with Chinese and Soviet aid, managed to increase its role in the war.

Below the seventeenth parallel, U.S. ground troops, supported by massive artillery strikes and aerial bombing, inflicted heavy casualties on communist forces. By this measure, the U.S. strategy, dubbed "Search and Destroy," was a success. American forces aimed to locate large concentrations of enemy troops and then, exploiting vastly superior mobility and firepower, kill as many as possible. Operations throughout South Vietnam—from the swampy Mekong Delta to the "Iron Triangle" near Saigon to the mountainous jungles of the interior highlands—almost always resulted in battlefield victories for U.S. and South Vietnamese forces.

Yet, as with the bombing campaign, American successes did not bring victory. Despite heavy losses, the Viet Cong and the North Vietnamese army expanded their forces and avoided decisive defeats. Morale among American troops suffered as they fell victim to the communists' hit-and-run tactics, landmines, and booby traps and often had difficulty distinguishing friend from foe among the Vietnamese population.

Compounding American frustrations were a variety of political problems. For one thing, the regime in Saigon failed to gain support among the South Vietnamese population. Even South Vietnam's most robust institution, its army, suffered from high desertion rates and poor leadership. Meanwhile, the Johnson administration failed to coax major allies such as Britain, France, and Canada to join the fight alongside U.S. and South Vietnamese troops.

Perhaps most important of all, American leaders faced mounting opposition to the war within the United States, where many citizens came to view intervention as a terrible mistake or even as an expression of profound ills at the heart of American society. By the end of 1967 polls showed that majorities of Americans disapproved of President Johnson's management of the war and believed the United States was not winning.

The Pro-War Movement
Op-Ed by Admiral Arleigh Burke, *Human Events*, March 12, 1966

Antiwar activism received intensive media coverage as protests grew larger and polls showed Americans increasingly questioning the decision to intervene. But a substantial part of the American population strongly backed the decision to fight in Vietnam and demanded that the Johnson administration employ more force. Hawkish commentators differed over precisely how to wage the war, but most of them agreed that Johnson and his advisers were too anxious about provoking a confrontation with China and needed to commit the nation more fully to the conflict. The following op-ed by retired Admiral Arleigh Burke appeared in *Human Events*, a leading conservative newspaper. Burke had retired in 1961 after a 41-year career in the Navy, including six years as Chief of Naval Operations.

Half a world away, in Southeast Asia, the most powerful nation on earth is resisting a take-over by a small, backward country whose people are 80 percent illiterate.

The United States is blessed with a mighty economy, an advanced technology and superb fighting units. North Viet Nam is a nation of peasants, virtually without industry, food, or transportation.

And yet we are bogged down.

The reason is that our goals are too limited. Our fighting men are doing a magnificent job, but they are under restraints. Why? Because we, as a people, have delayed facing up to the ultimate problem and therefore are delaying the solution.

Our efforts to limit the action and our overtures toward negotiation seem, unfortunately, to have given the North Vietnamese and their fellow Communists in Peking and Moscow the impression that our will to win is uncertain.

It would be a much more difficult course, but a wiser one, to increase the intensity of the war now and convince our enemies that they are certain to lose.

By that I mean blockading North Viet Nam, mining Haiphong harbor, destroying all military installations in North Viet Nam regardless of location, and using whatever means necessary to prevent Communist supplies from entering South Viet Nam through Laos and Cambodia.

Such a course of action, some will say, risks direct conflict with Red China. It does, but so does our present course. If all our decisions are to be controlled by that remote possibility, we have no business being west of San Francisco.

It should be made clear to Red China and the world that we hope she will not come in, but that if she does it will be on her own initiative, and she will be courting disaster.

Actually, our present course of piecemeal escalation runs a greater risk of bringing in Red China by gradual involvement.

If we escalate the war slowly, as present policies recommend, we shall protract the war in terms of time and cost. If past cold-war crises have taught us anything, they should have taught us to act swiftly—before the Communists compound and complicate the crisis—and in such a manner that they are convinced we really mean it.

If we persist in bit-by-bit escalation, the total cost to the United States for eventually freeing South Viet Nam is likely to be far greater in men and substance.

Thus the choices confronting us are grave, but the alternative of withdrawal from South Viet Nam is unthinkable. Such a course means abdicating our position of world leadership . . .

A key to North Viet Nam's thinking—and therefore a key to what our strategy should be—may lie in recent history, specifically the battle of Dien Bien Phu in 1954.

The significance of that battle, in which the Indochinese defeated the French, is conspicuously important to our present situation. An oriental army equipped with obsolete or captured weapons vanquished a modern European force. An army with powerful air and naval support suffered an ignominious defeat by a force which had neither.

History teaches us also that the French campaign in Indochina failed not entirely because of combat conditions, but because of a lack of will on the part of the French government and people to pursue the war.

This was not accidental. It came about through continuous psychological warfare waged by Moscow through the French Communist party, bolstered by Communist organizations in other countries and supported by non-Communists who unwittingly accepted their propaganda.

The point, one which is vital to our strategy, is that the North Vietnamese convinced themselves they could drive out the French . . . It is logical for them to suppose, given their experience with the French and what may appear a lukewarm effort by the United States, that we, too, eventually will withdraw.

Certainly they have given no indication of willingness to negotiate, except on terms essentially requiring our withdrawal. Such conditions are, of course, unacceptable to the United States because they would endanger our national interests and security and those of the free people of Asia . . .

In any event, it should be made clear to the Red Chinese that our actions will be limited to North Viet Nam, but any move on their part to enter the conflict would be a signal for an all-out offensive against them.

In such a contingency the use of any weapons should not be precluded. To those who are shocked, it should be repeated that it is wiser to face this problem now than after the Red Chinese have launched human-wave attacks on our free-world friends—and us.

In war and world politics, the decision is never between two extremes. It is rather [to choose] the lesser of two evils, and postponing the choice will not, as some seem to hope, make it go away.

DOCUMENT 6.2

Johnson's Predicament
Political Cartoon from the *Sunday Telegraph*, London, June 3, 1966

OBSTACLE COURSE

The gradualness of American escalation in Vietnam partly reflected the Johnson administration's belief that it could use force in a limited, carefully calibrated way to achieve precise military and political results. But the administration's behavior also reflected the president's calculations about South Vietnamese and especially American public opinion—a tendency visible across the ocean to British political cartoonist John Jensen. As he made decisions about the war, Johnson was keenly aware that many Americans opposed deeper involvement, while others advocated bolder escalation.

The Impact of U.S. Intervention

Study by Leon Gouré, RAND Corporation, "Some Findings of the Viet Cong Motivation and Morale Study, January–June 1966: A Briefing to the Joint Chiefs of Staff," August 1, 1966

One of the persistent problems for U.S. officials in Vietnam was measuring how the war was going. Were South Vietnamese and U.S. forces making headway in suppressing the insurgency or beating back the North Vietnamese? Was the Saigon government gaining any ground with its population? It was extremely difficult to know with any certainty. One effort to ascertain answers was spearheaded by the RAND Corporation, a government-funded think tank. Throughout U.S. embroilment in Vietnam, RAND specialists interviewed communist prisoners and defectors, seeking insight into motives and morale among enemy forces. The following passage comes from a report written by RAND analyst Leon Gouré for the Joint Chiefs of Staff. It summarized the results of interviews with 150 prisoners and defectors between January and July 1966.

The shift of the initiative to GVN and U.S. forces and the intensification of ground and air operations has further increased the strain on VC and NVA soldiers and frequently disrupted their concentrations, plans, training, food collecting, and other activities. Many interviewees report growing fear of combat, discouragement, malingering, desertions, and defections among the troops. The high rate of sickness, especially among NVA troops in the highlands, which was said to incapacitate 20 to 30 percent of the men in some units at any given time, was reported to cause growing worries and even fear among the soldiers. Other interviewees, however, while admitting to some loss of "fighting spirit" in their units, said that the majority of the soldiers still fought well . . .

. . . [T]he available data indicate that VC and NVA discipline and controls, especially among Main Force units, are still largely effective and that their combat capability is still very considerable. By contrast, Local Force and guerrilla soldiers appear less able to bear the growing pressures and difficulties and also have better opportunities than Main Force soldiers to defect or desert home.

Although exposed to growing pressures, the enemy is very skillful at trying to reduce their effectiveness. The VC are very quick at identifying set patterns in GVN and American tactics, operations, movements, attacks or weapon employment and take advantage of them at avoid attacks or to reduce their effectiveness. The VC also make good use of their extensive intelligence network and intercepts of GVN and U.S. radio communications to give them warning of attacks or to facilitate their own operations . . .

The NVA forces in South Vietnam are increasingly bearing the main burden of fighting U.S. forces. They differ from the VC in that they are not a native force, do not depend to the same extent on the civilian population in the South nor participate in its control, and do not fight for personal gains or benefits but to support a revolution in the South. Furthermore, they are essentially a conventionally trained and organized force with none of the VC's experience in guerrilla warfare . . .

NVA interviewees increasingly mention that many soldiers did not like being sent South and that some deserted when they learned about their units' assignment. In many cases, 5 to 10 men were said to have deserted from each company in the North, including some cadres and Party members, while others sought to be exempted. The majority, however, felt that they had no choice but to obey their government.

All interviewed NVA soldiers . . . had made the entire trip on foot and had carried all of their weapons, including heavy ones, as well as some ammunition. Because of the disruption of rail and truck traffic in the North by U.S. air strikes, the troops spent from 20 to 30 days marching through North Vietnam, mainly at night, before crossing into Laos, thereby prolonging considerably the trip and adding to its hardships. Most reported having suffered on the trip from fatigue, inadequate rations, and a high rate of malaria, so that in many cases the units spent several months recuperating before being sent into combat.

Although many NVA interviewees complained of unexpected hardships, heavy losses, and fear of dying far from home, few seemed to think that they had any choice but to go on fighting. They could not desert home and feared that if they surrendered, they would never be able to return North or that they would be killed by the GVN or U.S. forces, as their cadres kept telling them.

Concerning U.S. forces, the interviewees agree that their presence has greatly changed the nature of the war and its intensity and deprived the VC of an early victory. Interviewees who have met U.S. troops in combat were impressed by their fire power, and some said the soldiers were afraid to fight U.S. troops. The great majority reported that contrary to VC propaganda they had been well treated by U.S. soldiers. Few had heard any information other than from VC or Hanoi sources on U.S. aims in Vietnam, and many appeared to have sincerely believed that the United States intends to colonize Vietnam and to keep its troops permanently there. A number of them reported instances where villagers who had received gifts of food, fertilizer, etc., from Americans had refused to heed VC propaganda about American aggression and that others had been glad to be pacified and secured by U.S. troops. Some complained, however, of the practice of U.S. troops during sweep operations of arresting many villagers as suspects while others blamed the prolongation of the war and the continuing misery of the population on the Americans.

DOCUMENT 6.4

Breaking with the President

Speech by Reverend Martin Luther King Jr., "A Time to Break Silence," Riverside Church, New York, April 4, 1967

Opposition to the war steadily mounted in 1966 and 1967. Perhaps most consequentially, antiwar opinions gradually spread from relatively small groups of committed activists to other parts of the American population. Among the most striking indications of this trend was a dramatic speech by the Reverend Martin Luther King Jr., the eminent civil rights leader. King had worked closely with President Johnson and other liberals to win passage of major civil rights legislation and had good reason to mute his criticism of the war. In 1967, however, he broke with the liberal establishment by speaking out against U.S. policy. King delivered the following speech before an audience of more than 3,000 at Riverside Church in New York. The address drew criticism from prominent liberal newspapers and from the National Association for the Advancement of Colored People (NAACP), which accused King of wrongly linking civil rights and the war. But King continued to condemn the war until his death a year later.

I come to this platform tonight to make a passionate plea to my beloved nation. This speech is not addressed to Hanoi or to the National Liberation Front. It is not addressed to China or to Russia. Nor is it an attempt to overlook the ambiguity of the total situation and the need for a collective solution to the tragedy of Vietnam. Neither is it an attempt to make North Vietnam or the National Liberation Front paragons of virtue, nor to overlook the role they must play in the successful resolution of the problem. While they both may have justifiable reasons to be suspicious of the good faith of the United States, life and history give eloquent testimony to the fact that conflicts are never resolved without trustful give and take on both sides. Tonight, however, I wish not to speak with Hanoi and the National Liberation Front, but rather to my fellow Americans.

Since I am a preacher by calling, I suppose it is not surprising that I have seven major reasons for bringing Vietnam into the field of my moral vision. There is at the outset a very obvious and almost facile connection between the war in Vietnam and the struggle I and others have been waging in America. A few years ago there was a shining moment in that struggle. It seemed as if there was a real promise of hope for the poor, both black and white, through the poverty program. There were experiments, hopes, new beginnings. Then came the buildup in Vietnam, and I watched this program broken and eviscerated as if it were some idle political plaything on a society gone mad on war. And I knew that America would never invest the necessary funds or energies in rehabilitation of its poor so long as adventures like Vietnam continued to draw men and skills and money like some demonic, destructive suction tube. So I was increasingly compelled to see the war as an enemy of the poor and to attack it as such.

Perhaps a more tragic recognition of reality took place when it became clear to me that the war was doing far more than devastating the hopes of the poor at home. It was sending their sons and their brothers and their husbands to fight and to die in extraordinarily high proportions relative to the rest of the population. We were taking the black young men who had been crippled by our society and sending them eight thousand miles away to guarantee liberties in Southeast Asia which they had not found in southwest Georgia and East Harlem. So we have been repeatedly faced with the cruel irony of watching Negro and white boys on TV screens as they kill and die together for a nation that has been unable to seat them together in the same schools. So we watch them in brutal solidarity burning the huts of a poor village, but we realize that they would hardly live on the same block in Chicago. I could not be silent in the face of such cruel manipulation of the poor.

My third reason moves to an even deeper level of awareness, for it grows out of my experience in the ghettos of the North over the last three years, especially the last three summers. As I have walked among the desperate, rejected, and angry young men, I have told them that Molotov cocktails and rifles would not solve their problems. I have tried to offer them my deepest compassion while maintaining my conviction that social change comes most meaningfully through nonviolent action. But they asked, and rightly so, "What about Vietnam?" They asked if our own nation wasn't using massive doses of violence to solve its problems, to bring about the changes it wanted. Their questions hit home, and I knew that I could never again raise my voice against the violence of the oppressed in the ghettos without having first spoken clearly to the greatest purveyor of violence in the world today: my own government. For the sake of those boys, for the sake of this government, for the sake of the hundreds of thousands trembling under our violence, I cannot be silent . . .

And as I ponder the madness of Vietnam and search within myself for ways to understand and respond in compassion, my mind goes constantly to the people of that peninsula. I speak now not of the soldiers of each side, not of the ideologies of the Liberation Front, not of the junta in Saigon, but simply of the people who have been living under the curse of war for almost three continuous decades now. I think of them, too, because it is clear to me that there will be no meaningful solution there until some attempt is made to know them and hear their broken cries.

They must see Americans as strange liberators. The Vietnamese people proclaimed their own independence in 1954—in 1945 rather—after a combined French and Japanese occupation and before the communist revolution in China. They were led by Ho Chi Minh. Even though they quoted the American Declaration of Independence in their own document of freedom, we refused to recognize them. Instead, we decided to support France in its reconquest of her former colony. Our government felt then that the Vietnamese people were not ready for independence, and we again fell victim to the deadly Western arrogance that has poisoned the international atmosphere for so long. With that tragic decision we rejected a revolutionary government seeking self-determination and a government that had been established not by China—for whom the Vietnamese have no great love—but by clearly indigenous forces that included some communists. For the peasants this new government meant real land reform, one of the most important needs in their lives . . .

After the French were defeated, it looked as if independence and land reform would come again through the Geneva Agreement. But instead there came the United States, determined that Ho should not unify the temporarily divided nation, and the peasants watched again as we supported one of the most vicious modern dictators, our chosen man, Premier Diem. The peasants watched and cringed as Diem ruthlessly rooted out all opposition, supported their extortionist landlords, and refused even to discuss reunification with the North. The peasants watched as all of this was presided over by United States influence and then by increasing numbers of United States troops who came to help quell the insurgency that Diem's methods had aroused. When Diem was overthrown they may have been happy, but the long line of military dictators seemed to offer no real change, especially in terms of their need for land and peace.

The only change came from America as we increased our troop commitments in support of governments which were singularly corrupt, inept, and without popular support. All the while the people read our leaflets and received the regular promises of peace and democracy and land reform. Now they languish under our bombs and consider us, not their fellow Vietnamese, the real enemy. They move sadly and apathetically as we herd them off the land of their fathers into concentration camps where minimal social needs are rarely met. They know they must move on or be destroyed by our bombs.

So they go, primarily women and children and the aged. They watch as we poison their water, as we kill a million acres of their crops. They must weep as the bulldozers roar through their areas preparing to destroy the precious trees. They wander into the hospitals with at least twenty casualties from American firepower for one Vietcong-inflicted injury. So far we may have killed a million of them, mostly children. They wander into the towns and see thousands of the children, homeless, without clothes, running in packs on the streets like animals. They see the children degraded by our soldiers as they beg for food. They see the children selling their sisters to our soldiers, soliciting for their mothers.

What do the peasants think as we ally ourselves with the landlords and as we refuse to put any action into our many words concerning land reform? What do they think as we test out our latest weapons on them, just as the Germans tested out new medicine and new tortures in the concentration camps of Europe? Where are the roots of the independent Vietnam we claim to be building? Is it among these voiceless ones? . . .

Perhaps a more difficult but no less necessary task is to speak for those who have been designated as our enemies. What of the National Liberation Front, that strangely anonymous group we call "VC" or "communists"? What must they think of the United States of America when they realize that we permitted the repression and cruelty of Diem, which helped to bring them into being as a resistance group in the South? What do they think of our condoning the violence which led to their own taking up of arms? How can they believe in our integrity when now we speak of "aggression from the North" as if there was nothing more essential to the war? . . .

At this point I should make it clear that while I have tried to give a voice to the voiceless in Vietnam and to understand the arguments of those who are called "enemy," I am as deeply concerned about our own troops there as anything else. For it occurs to me that what we are submitting them to in Vietnam is not simply the brutalizing process that goes on in any war where armies face each other and seek to destroy. We are adding cynicism to the process of death, for they must know after a short period there that none of the things we claim to be fighting for are really involved. Before long they must know that their government has sent them into a struggle among Vietnamese, and the more sophisticated surely realize that we are on the side of the wealthy, and the secure, while we create a hell for the poor . . .

I would like to suggest five concrete things that our government should do to begin the long and difficult process of extricating ourselves from this nightmarish conflict:

Number one: End all bombing in North and South Vietnam.

Number two: Declare a unilateral cease-fire in the hope that such action will create the atmosphere for negotiation.

Three: Take immediate steps to prevent other battlegrounds in Southeast Asia by curtailing our military buildup in Thailand and our interference in Laos.

Four: Realistically accept the fact that the National Liberation Front has substantial support in South Vietnam and must thereby play a role in any meaningful negotiations and any future Vietnam government.

Five: Set a date [when] we will remove all foreign troops from Vietnam in accordance with the 1954 Geneva Agreement . . .

These are revolutionary times. All over the globe men are revolting against old systems of exploitation and oppression, and out of the wounds of a frail world, new systems of justice and equality are being born. The shirtless and barefoot people of the land are rising up as never before. The people who sat in darkness have seen a great light. We in the West must support these revolutions.

It is a sad fact that because of comfort, complacency, a morbid fear of communism, and our proneness to adjust to injustice, the Western nations that initiated so much of the revolutionary spirit of the modern world have now become the arch antirevolutionaries. This has driven many to feel that only Marxism has a revolutionary spirit. Therefore, communism is a judgment against our failure to make democracy real and follow through on the revolutions that we initiated. Our only hope today lies in our ability to recapture the revolutionary spirit and go out into a sometimes hostile world declaring eternal hostility to poverty, racism, and militarism.

DOCUMENT 6.5

"Two, Three or Many Vietnams"
Speech by Ernesto "Che" Guevara, Havana, Cuba, April 16, 1967

The fighting in Vietnam generated different responses around the world. A few countries—South Korea, Australia, New Zealand, the Philippines, and Thailand—sent combat forces to fight alongside U.S. and South Vietnamese troops. But most nations friendly to the United States remained on the sidelines because of doubts about American policy and strong public pressure to avoid the conflict. Eastern Bloc nations sharply criticized American policy, though some of them participated in international peace initiatives. In the developing world, meanwhile, nations emerging from colonialism often identified strongly with the Vietnamese revolutionaries and viewed the U.S. war as an extension of old patterns of Western imperialism. Some maintained a relatively neutral position and joined efforts to make peace in Vietnam, but others condemned U.S. behavior in no uncertain terms. Among the latter was the Cuban government. Ernesto "Che" Guevara, who was born in Argentina but achieved fame for his role in revolutionary Cuba, delivered the following speech on April 16, 1967, to a gathering of leaders from Asian, African, and Latin American nations.

The solidarity of all progressive forces of the world towards the people of Vietnam today is similar to the bitter irony of the plebeians coaxing on the gladiators in the Roman arena. It is not a matter of wishing success to the victim of aggression, but of sharing his fate; one must accompany him to his death or to victory.

When we analyze the lonely situation of the Vietnamese people, we are overcome by anguish at this illogical moment of humanity.

U.S. imperialism is guilty of aggression—its crimes are enormous and cover the whole world. We already know all that, gentlemen! But this guilt also applies to those who, when the time came for a definition, hesitated to make Vietnam an inviolable part of the socialist world; running, of course, the risks of a war on a global scale—but also forcing a decision upon imperialism. And the guilt also applies to those who maintain a war of abuse and snares—started quite some time ago by the representatives of the two greatest powers of the socialist camp . . .

What role shall we, the exploited people of the world, play? The peoples of the three continents focus their attention on Vietnam and learn their lesson. Since imperialists blackmail humanity by threatening it with war, the wise reaction is not to fear war. The general tactics of the people should be to launch a constant and a firm attack in all fronts where the confrontation is taking place . . .

The fundamental field of imperialist exploitation comprises the three underdeveloped continents: America, Asia, and Africa. Every country has also its own characteristics, but each continent, as a whole, also presents a certain unity.

Our America is integrated by a group of more or less homogeneous countries and in most parts of its territory U.S. monopolist capitals maintain an absolute supremacy. Puppet governments or, in the best of cases, weak and fearful local rulers, are incapable of contradicting orders from their Yankee master. The United States has nearly reached the climax of its political and economic domination; it could hardly advance much more; any change in the situation could bring about a setback. Their policy is to maintain that which has already been conquered. The line of action, at the present time, is limited to the brutal use of force with the purpose of thwarting the liberation movements, no matter of what type they might happen to be . . .

America, a forgotten continent in the last liberation struggles, is now beginning to make itself heard . . . and, in the voice of the vanguard of its peoples, the Cuban Revolution, will today have a task of much greater relevance: creating a Second or a Third Vietnam, or the Second and Third Vietnam of the world . . .

While envisaging the destruction of imperialism, it is necessary to identify its head, which is no other than the United States of America.

We must carry out a general task with the tactical purpose of getting the enemy out of its natural environment, forcing him to fight in regions where his own life and habits will clash with the existing reality. We must not underrate our adversary; the U.S. soldier has technical capacity and is backed by weapons and resources of such magnitude that render him frightful. He lacks the essential ideological motivation which his bitterest enemies of today—the Vietnamese soldiers—have in the highest degree. We will only be able to overcome that army by undermining their morale—and this is accomplished by defeating it and causing it repeated sufferings . . .

We must carry the war into every corner the enemy happens to carry it: to his home, to his centers of entertainment; a total war. It is necessary to prevent him from having a moment of peace, a quiet moment outside his barracks or even inside; we must attack him wherever he may be; make him feel like a cornered beast wherever he may move. Then his moral fiber shall begin to decline. He will even become more beastly, but we shall notice how the signs of decadence begin to appear.

And let us develop a true proletarian internationalism; with international proletarian armies; the flag under which we fight would be the sacred cause of redeeming humanity. To die under the flag of Vietnam, of Venezuela, of Guatemala, of Laos, of Guinea, of Colombia, of Bolivia, of Brazil—to name only a few scenes of today's armed struggle—would be equally glorious and desirable for an American, an Asian, an African, even a European.

Each spilt drop of blood, in any country under whose flag one has not been born, is an experience passed on to those who survive, to be added later to the liberation struggle of his own country. And each nation liberated is a phase won in the battle for the liberation of one's own country.

The time has come to settle our discrepancies and place everything at the service of our struggle . . .

How close we could look into a bright future should two, three or many Vietnams flourish throughout the world with their share of deaths and their immense tragedies, their everyday heroism and their repeated blows against imperialism, impelled to disperse its forces under the sudden attack and the increasing hatred of all peoples of the world!

DOCUMENT 6.6

An Appraisal of Rolling Thunder
Study by the Central Intelligence Agency, "The Vietnam Situation: An Analysis and Estimate," May 23, 1967

U.S. intelligence agencies had no doubt that Rolling Thunder, the sustained bombing of North Vietnam begun in March 1965, inflicted enormous destruction in North Vietnam. As months passed and the bombing expanded in scope and intensity, however, they also repeatedly drew another conclusion: the bombing was having little effect on Hanoi's willingness or ability to carry on the war in the South. Each month, the Central Intelligence Agency compiled a progress report pointing to more or less the same conclusion. In spring 1967, CIA analysts sifted through all the data collected over the previous 27 months and prepared an overall assessment of Rolling Thunder. That document, excerpted here, analyzes both the operation's past results and future prospects.

The objectives of the bombing program are stated currently to be two-fold:

1. To limit or raise the cost of sending men and supplies to South Vietnam.
2. To make North Vietnam pay a price for its aggression against the South.

To the extent that any degradation of enemy capabilities or any penalties imposed on his aggressive conduct in South Vietnam are indicative of successful achievement of US objectives, the US bombing campaign must be judged to be meeting with some success. But the degree of success is limited. The bombing program has undoubtedly raised the cost and increased the burdens of maintaining the aggression in South Vietnam. These exactions appear to be within acceptable limits to the Hanoi regime. Given the continuing flow of economic and military aid from Communist China and the USSR, North Vietnam remains capable of maintaining and supplying its forces in South Vietnam at both present and higher levels of combat. The price of its aggression, with the exception of manpower losses, is being assumed by its Communist allies.

Despite the increased weight and broadening of the air attack, North Vietnam has increased its support of the insurgency in South Vietnam. There was a three-fold increase in the level of personnel infiltration in 1966 and additional thousands of troops have been positioned in an around the DMZ. The flow of material supplies to the VC/NVA forces in South Vietnam during the current dry season is at least equal to and may exceed the volume made available last year.

The North Vietnamese economy has suffered increasing damage, but this has had no decisive effect on the attitude of the regime toward the war, nor has it caused a deterioration of popular morale to the point where the regime has lost the support of its people. The performance of the domestic transportation system exceeds that achieved before the Rolling Thunder program; imports both by sea and by rail have moved to increasingly high levels. Deficiencies in domestic food supply are being met by the USSR and Communist China and food shortages have not attained serious proportions. The vital petroleum storage system, as currently dispersed, has survived the destruction of more than 85 percent of its major bulk storage capacities, and petroleum stocks have been maintained at essentially early 1966 levels. The neutralization of 70 percent of the country's electric power generating capacity has created severe shortages of power and disrupted much of North Vietnam's modern industrial economy. It is unlikely, however, that the loss of electric power can have a significant impact on military operations . . .

The outlook for marked success in achieving the current objectives of US bombing programs is not bright . . . The returns that can be realistically expected from the neutralization of the remaining economic, military, and land transport targets [listed by the Joint Chiefs of Staff] is small. The two most promising target systems—locks and mineable areas—have been unacceptable to date on humane grounds or because of the political problems their neutralization would create. The enemy's success in countering attacks on bridges and in sustaining traffic movement is too well catalogued to warrant further discussion. Attacks on military installations would have only limited effects. Many of these facilities are inactive, and contingency plans to counter their loss are undoubtedly well developed. Even if North Vietnam were denied complete access to its airfields, this alone would be unlikely to significantly alter the regime's attitude toward the war since it would have only a marginal effect, through increasing costs, on the flow of men and supplies to the South.

The neutralization of North Vietnam's remaining industry would extract a high price in terms of the elimination of the results of years of economic development, loss of foreign exchange earnings, and the displacement of the urban labor force, and would add to the burden of aid from other Communist countries. There is no apparent reason why such losses would force Hanoi to the negotiating table. The loss of its modern industrial sector is apparently a tolerable burden in a country that has an overwhelmingly agrarian economy. The contribution of North Vietnam's modern economy to the war effort is small and its loss can be countered as long as essential economic and military supplies can be obtained from the USSR and China . . .

The US would probably pay increasing costs—both political and military—in choosing any of the available options for escalation of the air war. The political costs in terms of both domestic US and international reactions would vary with the options chosen. US aircraft losses on the recent strikes in the Hanoi-Haiphong area have been at a rate of more than ten times those experienced during the 1966 campaign and in attacks on more isolated targets during 1967. The preponderance of the targets yet unstruck or warranting restrike are in the more heavily defended areas of North Vietnam . . .

The bombing has not weakened Hanoi's confidence that time is still on the side of the Communist forces in the South and that the US eventually will be compelled to scale down its objectives and modify its terms for negotiations. The airstrikes, moreover, have had no discernable effect on Hanoi's ability and intention to maintain at least a rough military stalemate in the South—which the North Vietnamese view above all as the essential prerequisite to forcing an eventual adjustment in American policy . . .

There is no evidence that the bombing has had any significant effect in impairing the morale of either the Hanoi regime or the population. Many non-Communist foreign visitors have testified to the North Vietnamese "unshakable will to resist" and to their "ability to deal with the situation" no matter how much the US increases its efforts. Hanoi officials have privately conceded that the bombing has caused great damage but they profess confidence that morale will remain high so long as population centers are not subjected to sustained and systematic attack.

DOCUMENT 6.7

An American Soldier Remembers

Reminiscence by Rifleman Antoine "Andy" Roy, 173rd Airborne Brigade, U.S. Army, of Fighting in November 1967

By the end of 1966, the United States had sent more than 385,000 soldiers to South Vietnam, and American forces were fighting all over the country. Individual soldiers' experiences varied enormously. Some served only in base camps, hospitals, or other rear-echelon facilities, while others endured grueling combat. Among combat soldiers, some served in the densely populated Mekong Delta and fought mostly against Vietcong guerrillas. Others were based in the remote Central Highlands and faced large concentrations of North Vietnamese regulars. Among the latter was Army rifleman Antoine "Andy" Roy, who served three tours of duty in Vietnam from 1967 to 1969. In the following reminiscence, recorded in 2003, Roy recounts his experience of intense combat on Hill 875, near Dak To, in November 1967. Roy first recalls his unit's arrival in the combat area and then describes a battle in which he participated.

It was starting to get dusk [when] we came into a . . . battalion-sized [North Vietnamese] base camp. There were dug-in kitchen areas and hammock areas and little bunkers. It had been occupied very recently and my guess to this day is that this was one of the positions where part of that regiment guarding Hill 875 had been set up . . . It was starting to get dark . . . I mean just literally pitch black. Inside triple canopy forest, I mean you literally can't see your hand two inches in front of your face. So we had to hold up—you put your rifle with the sling over your shoulder and the rifle slung perpendicular to your body with the butt to the rear, the muzzle in front. The man behind you would hold on to the butt of your rifle and then you'd hold on to the butt of the rifle of the man in front of you because if you didn't there was no way you could continue without getting separated . . .

As we went on the moon came up about, oh gee, 9:30 or so, maybe 10 o'clock. It was a full moon. It was bright and all of a sudden it went from darkness to this glow of heavy moonlight which you could hardly see through the trees. I remember we're going along and we're going along. Suddenly I looked around me and I could tell I was in an area where a lot of people had been because of the grass and the brush were trampled down. I expected it to be another abandoned enemy base camp. The column slowed down, real slow . . . We stopped for a second and I remember looking forward to my right front and right along the trail I could see what at first glance looked like a log laying there, but the log wasn't that long. At second glance I could tell suddenly it was a body. It was just a dark shape and then by the size of it I knew it was an American. It wasn't a Vietnamese. So we continued and we continued and it got—it thinned out more and more and more and suddenly off to the sides you could see other bodies laying there . . . I can remember there was still some little fires burning in the trees, especially in the bamboo, that would pop or snap a little bit. The scene was completely filled with moonlight. There were bodies everywhere, scattered. There were rucksacks on the ground. You could tell they had been rifled through. You could see little groups of Americans and it looked like they had formed a little circle to make a final defense because the attack had come in from three sides . . .

We were exhausted. We were just totally exhausted. The things we'd been through, the things we had seen had just mentally exhausted us. We set up [camp] and our impression was that we were inside the 2nd Battalion perimeter, but come to find out we weren't. We assumed we were being given a rest. Nobody had to pull guard duty. So nobody pulled guard. If the North Vietnamese had known it they could have walked right in on us, but again they had their serious problems. So we woke up in the morning, found out what was going on and started digging in right away.

Then we started receiving very, very heavy mortar fire . . . You hear a doong, doong, doonk-doong, doong doong, doong, and those are the tubes firing. So you have that split second to get down. Most of us got down, grabbed our rucksacks, pulled them over our backs and curled up underneath or, if you could, slide up next to a tree or something. They started impacting. About the third round I heard this guy screaming. He was screaming, "Oh my God, oh my God, oh my God, help me, oh my God," and it was a horrible, terrible scream. I'm envisioning, you know, he's looking at his entrails hanging out or his arm's been blown off or something like this. It just echoed. It was a scary, demoralizing sound for everybody. The mortar rounds walked up the line. They went right past my position. We started digging in even deeper. Luckily it was this nice orange clay that was easy to dig into. We'd have to stop periodically because then the mortars would come back in again and go back down the line, sometimes starting from the other direction . . .

Finally we got completely dug in. It took about an hour and a half because we kept having to stop when we were getting mortared or rocketed and get down. We got the land cleared in front us. Different companies were taking turns trying to assault the hill . . . So finally the word came down to get ready because it was our turn to assault. That's always a great anxiety provoker. So we formed up. Another company came in and took over our positions, and I don't remember who they were. Oh, just before that, some of the survivors of A Company, 2nd Battalion came by. I remember one guy asking them, "How many men did you lose?" They said, "We don't know. We have no idea, but it was just"—and the way he said it, it was just bunches and bunches . . .

So anyway we, we went over. We got on line. We were working our way up the hill along a trail and then we were going to take over the line from the company that was there and they were going to pull back . . .

I remember getting up to the area right where, just before the enemy positions, which you couldn't really figure out exactly. They were so well hidden and camouflaged, plus all the blown-down vegetation. This one area in between the lines had been hit so heavily it was virtually open, just stumps of trees and the like. We worked our way up, I remember, at a stoop. There [was] mortar fire coming in. Our artillery was still hitting. Even our own shrapnel was flying back on us. I stopped by a stump that was maybe three feet high of a big tree, maybe three, four feet in diameter . . . Next thing I know this tree stump that I'm behind is catching bullet after bullet after bullet . . . [A] few bullets actually came through, especially on the sides where it was thinner. They were hitting down low and I remember—I'm just crouching down lower and lower and lower and lower and just hoping that some North Vietnamese doesn't have a fifty-one caliber machine gun, which would go right through that. So, after about a minute of that—and there must have been at least two hundred rounds either hit that stump or go right past me—the firing stopped . . .

Just then, a sergeant called me over to the left. I didn't recognize the sergeant and I think he was from the unit that we were replacing on the firing line. He said,

"Get over here." I said, "I can't. I'm with my unit." He said, "God damn it, I said get over here. We have to get this man down the hill or he's going to die." It was a wounded man and he was laying on a poncho. He was unconscious . . . So, okay, I go over there and I grab a corner of the poncho. Suddenly I realize, wait a minute, we're going to have to stand up at a crouch at least to carry this guy, which means we're going to be exposed. I'm thinking, oh God. So the sergeant says, "Take him." So we all lift and we're at a crouch . . .

We got up and we went at this bent-over run, which isn't easy when you're carrying a lot of weight. We'd be able to advance twenty feet and then have to get down for a second. The first move we made, some bullets went by, not extremely close. The second move we made took us a little bit down the hill so it was kind of over the edge, but at the same time the whole hill on our side is constantly being mortared. The rounds are going off in the trees and there's shrapnel flying around. It took us several of those twenty-foot runs before we'd have to stop and let down. I can't truthfully tell you whether the guy was dead or alive when we got him down to the [landing zone] . . . Helicopters were now coming in to pick up wounded, drop off ammunition, things like that. The anti-aircraft fire was so heavy, I believe there were sixteen helicopters shot down around Hill 875, which is quite a bit.

So I started back up the hill [to] get back with my unit and there's another sergeant. Well I've got to—he hands me ammunition, machine gun ammunition and M-79 grenade ammunition. He says, "Take this up with you and then help bring more wounded down. You're with us now." So, okay, I've got to work with him. So I carry ammunition up the hill, and then I'm helping carrying other wounded down and back and forth and back and forth . . .

[It] was starting to get dark. I said, "To hell with this. I'm going to go back, find my position that we started from, where my rucksack was. I'm going to get some food, some water and the like and then . . . I'm going to find my unit and join them for the night." So I started walking around and it was getting a little dusk, not real dusk. I was trying to figure out which way the line went. I come to this one position and there were three guys there; one guy was sitting on top of the position, and I clearly remember to this day, he was eating a C-ration can and it was turkey loaf, which wasn't one of the great favorites, but it wasn't one of the most horrible things either. There were two other guys standing in front of the bunker. I asked them, I said, "It looks like the line has changed a bit. Which way does the perimeter go now?" They pointed in one of the directions. So I started to walk. I took about two steps and I was in between the two guys that were standing in front of the bunker facing the guy sitting on the bunker. I heard what sounded like a far distant explosion. All of a sudden it was like Babe Ruth had stepped up behind me with a baseball bat and hit one of his greatest homers. I felt the impact. I knew instantly what had happened. I had been hit. I was picked up off the ground.

The ground was sloped, thrown forward. When things happen like this, car accidents, things like that, things kind of go in slow motion, they say. I remember flying forward towards this big mahogany tree about, oh, I don't know, three-and-a-half, four feet in diameter. I was going face first. I consciously in mid-air turned my body to the right and slammed into the tree—is that right?—yeah, into the tree with my shoulder. Then the rest of my body came forward, slammed into the tree and I fell off to the left, bounced off to the left, I believe. The next thing I knew I was on my stomach. Wherever my helmet or my weapon went, I have no idea . . .

The panic suddenly went to elation as I realized, great, I've been wounded, I'm getting the hell off this hill. I'm even going to sleep in a real bed tonight. Of course, I had to worry about getting off the hill first, but I turned off to my right, and the guy that had been standing there was laying on his back and he was dead. He had taken severe wounds in the chest and . . . the face and the head. I looked off to the left and that man was laying on his face. There was an awful lot of blood from around his head that I could see. I just knew he was dead. I made a slight twist to the back, and here's that guy sitting on the bunker. He's got a spoonful of turkey loaf and it's halfway to his mouth and he's frozen. He's just looking at me and I said, "I'm hit, man." . . .

The medic said, "Where are you hit?" I said, "In the back." He looked and he said, "I don't see anything." All of a sudden my heart dropped down and I thought, oh, God, that was only concussion that hit me. Well, then he takes the bottom of [my shirt] and he lifts it up and he says, "Oh, shit." Then all of a sudden I'm thinking he's seeing this thing going ba-boom, ba-boom, ba-boom, ba-boom in this big hole in my back. He says, "Well, you got a huge chunk of shrapnel. It went in at an angle and it's under the skin, but there's no bleeding and it hasn't penetrated inside." Well, great, then I became elated again.

7
THE TET OFFENSIVE

IN THE EARLY MORNING of January 30, 1968, communist troops launched surprise attacks against dozens of cities and towns throughout South Vietnam. Hanoi's goal was to inspire a popular insurrection that would topple the Saigon government. As it turned out, U.S. and South Vietnamese forces quickly repulsed the offensive. Yet in one crucial respect, the assault was a major success for the communists. Many Americans, including key political leaders, concluded that the war was hopelessly stalemated and urged a negotiated peace.

The offensive sprang from complex rivalries in Hanoi during 1967. Some North Vietnamese leaders were increasingly anxious about losses suffered by communist forces. But other Hanoi leaders, including communist Secretary General Le Duan, insisted that the moment was ripe to mount a "general offensive and general uprising." The hawks prevailed, and planning began for a bold assault that would bring the fighting for the first time into South Vietnam's urban areas.

Americans were shocked by the offensive, which flew in the face of assurances by the Johnson administration and the U.S. military that the war was going well. American commanders insisted that the U.S.–South Vietnamese counteroffensive inflicted devastating losses on Viet Cong and North Vietnamese forces. But the offensive changed the tenor of debate within the United States, and few Americans were open to the idea that the offensive had been a huge failure for Hanoi.

In the White House, President Johnson called for a reappraisal of American policy and concluded a few days later that the United States must change direction. On March 31, 1968, Johnson declared that he would not seek reelection, ended most bombing of North Vietnam, and called for negotiations to end the war.

Johnson's announcements and the opening of talks in Paris on May 13 suggested that the United States might soon seek a way to end the war, but in fact little changed. Some of the most intense fighting of the war took place in the year following the offensive. Defiant in the face of his critics, Johnson refused to back away from the basic goal that the United States had pursued since 1954: a secure and independent South Vietnam. In Paris, neither side budged from the bargaining positions they had long maintained.

Meanwhile antiwar activism continued to grow in the United States. In the winter and spring of 1968, two presidential aspirants running on antiwar platforms, Senator Eugene McCarthy of Minnesota and Senator Robert F. Kennedy of New York, made strong showings in the Democratic primaries. In August, Chicago witnessed brutal street battles between police and protesters during the Democratic National Convention. Some observers feared that social order was disintegrating in the United States.

DOCUMENT 7.1

American Optimism

Speech by General William Westmoreland at the National Press Club, Washington, D.C., November 21, 1967

As the war dragged on into late 1967, U.S. leaders sought to project optimism. Among the most striking expressions of this tone was a speech delivered by General William Westmoreland, the commander of U.S. forces in Vietnam, at the National Press Club during a trip to Washington in November. Westmoreland asserted that U.S. forces were methodically implementing a four-stage approach to the war. In Phase I, he explained, American combat forces had prevented the collapse of South Vietnam. In Phase II, starting in mid-1966, Americans had taken the offensive against the communists and turned the tide of the war. In the following excerpt, Westmoreland lays out his vision of Phase III, which he asserts would begin at the start of 1968, and the final Phase IV.

The war in Vietnam eludes any precise numerical system of measurement or any easy portrayal of progress on battle maps. The war is unique and complicated in origin, in diversity of form, and in its diffusion throughout Vietnam. It is a war which probably could not have occurred in this pattern in any other country in these times. But, if we had not met it squarely, it well could have been the precedent for countless future wars of a similar nature.

But we have confronted this challenge. We have found it to be like no other war we have fought before. There are no moving front lines—just a changing picture of small actions scattered over the country. Only a few of these actions are reported in detail. Even the trained observer is drawn to the unusual and the spectacular and finds his attention shifting to another action before the significance or impact of the first can be analyzed.

I have been observing the war in South Vietnam at close hand for almost four years . . . I am absolutely certain that whereas in 1965 the enemy was winning, today he is certainly losing. There are indications that the Viet Cong and even Hanoi may know this . . .

It is significant that the enemy has not won a major battle in more than a year. In general, he can fight his large forces only at the edges of his sanctuaries . . . His Viet Cong military units can no longer fill their ranks from the South, but must depend increasingly on replacements from North Vietnam. His guerrilla force is declining at a steady rate. Morale problems are developing within his ranks . . .

With 1968, a new phase is now starting. We have reached an important point when the end begins to come into view. What is this third phase we are about to enter?

In Phase III, in 1968, we intend to do the following:

- Help the Vietnamese Armed Forces to continue improving their effectiveness.
- Decrease our advisers in training centers and other places where the professional competence of Vietnamese officers makes this possible.
- Increase our advisory effort with the younger brothers of the Vietnamese Army—the Regional Forces and Popular Forces.
- Destroy North Vietnamese forays while we assist the Vietnamese to reorganize for territorial security.
- Provide the new military equipment to revitalize the Vietnamese Army and prepare it to take on an ever-increasing share of the war.
- Continue pressure on the North to prevent rebuilding and to make aggression more costly.
- Turn a major share of front line DMZ defense over to the Vietnamese Army.
- Install an anti-infiltration system.
- Increase U.S. support in the rich and populated Delta.
- Help the Government of Vietnam single out and destroy the communist shadow government.
- Continue to isolate the guerrilla from the people.
- Help the new Vietnamese government to respond to popular aspirations and to reduce and eliminate corruption.
- Help the Vietnamese strengthen their police forces to enhance law and order.

■ Open more roads and canals.

■ Continue to improve the Vietnamese economy and standard of living.

Now for phase IV—the final phase. That period will see the conclusions of our plan to weaken the enemy and strengthen our friends until we become superfluous. The object will be to show the world that guerrilla warfare and invasion do not pay as a new means of communist aggression.

I see phase IV happening as follows:

■ Infiltration will slow.

■ The communist infrastructure will be cut up and near collapse.

■ The Vietnamese government will prove its stability, and the Vietnamese Army will show that it can handle Viet Cong.

■ The Regional Forces and Popular Forces will reach a higher level of professional performance.

■ US units can begin to phase down as the Vietnamese Army is modernized and develops its capacity to the fullest.

■ The military physical assets, bases, and ports will be progressively turned over to the Vietnamese.

■ The Vietnamese will take charge of the final mopping up of the Viet Cong (which will probably last several years). The US, at the same time, will continue the developmental help envisaged by the President for the community of Southeast Asia.

You may ask how long phase III will take, before we reach the final phase. We have already entered parts of phase III. Looking back on Phases I and II, we can conclude that we have come a long way.

I see progress as I travel all over Vietnam.

I see it in the attitudes of the Vietnamese.

I see it in the open roads and canals.

I see it in the new crops and the new purchasing power of the farmer.

I see it in the increased willingness of the Vietnamese Army to fight North Vietnamese units and in the victories they are winning.

DOCUMENT 7.2

An Image of Chaos

Associated Press Photo by Photographer Hong Seong-Chan, January 31, 1968

In political terms, the offensive paid considerable dividends for Hanoi. The display of military power and bravado by the communists contradicted assurances by U.S. leaders that the war was going well and reinforced doubts among many Americans that the United States could prevail in Vietnam at a reasonable cost. Striking images from the battle fronts did much to reinforce such pessimism. Among the most remarkable—and widely published— images was this photo taken in the first hours of the offensive on the grounds of the U.S. embassy in Saigon, the epicenter of American authority in the country. The image shows three U.S. military policemen taking shelter behind a wall near the bodies of two other U.S. soldiers killed earlier in the fighting. After blowing a hole in the wall of the embassy compound, NLF commandos occupied part of the grounds for about six hours before they were killed or captured.

DOCUMENT 7.3

U.S. Intelligence Assesses the Damage
Central Intelligence Agency Report, "The Tet Offensive—A Plus or a Minus?"
February 12, 1968

In the first days after the Tet Offensive began, the U.S. command and intelligence services struggled to assess the impact on the military and political situation in South Vietnam. Most reports offered a mixed appraisal, noting major setbacks but also reasons for optimism. A perceptive example is the following report completed by the CIA on February 12, 1968. CIA Director Richard Helms immediately sent the document to the White House, where National Security Adviser Walt Rostow passed it to President Johnson along with a covering memorandum judging the paper "an extremely well balanced assessment."

The Year of the Monkey had an inauspicious beginning for the people of South Vietnam as the VC/NVA forces violated the sacred Tet holidays and launched virtually simultaneous attacks against 36 province capitals, five of the six autonomous cities, and numerous other population centers throughout the country. Their objectives have been clearly spelled out in captured documents—to destroy or subvert the GVN/allied forces, eliminate the GVN governmental structure, create a general uprising among the people, and establish a revolutionary government dominated by the National Liberation Front. In what appears to be an almost incredible miscalculation of their own military capabilities and the degree of support they could command from the people, the Communists failed to achieve these stated objectives. It has cost them dearly in manpower—in 12 days some 31,000 killed, 5,700 detained, probably another 10,000 dead from wounds, and unknown number dead from air and artillery strikes—a total probably amounting to more than half of the forces used in this attack. Nevertheless, the enemy's well-planned, coordinated series of attacks was an impressive display of strength which has given him a major psychological victory abroad, dealt a serious blow to the pacification program, and created problems that will tax the energies and resources of the government for many months to come.

The enemy's military strategy consisted of a two-phase offensive. Wherever possible, the first phase assaults were conducted by VC local forces. Psychologically, this was more appropriate than using NVA units, given the enemy's objective of winning the support of the people. NVA forces were used in I and II Corps where VC forces were inadequate, but throughout the country most VC/NVA main forces were withheld for the second phase when they would move in to capitalize on the expected chaos and general uprising.

The passive reaction of the population, the fierceness of Free World and ARVN counteroffensives after the initial surprise and confusion, and the effectiveness of massive air and artillery fire obviously forced cancellation of the commitment of VC/NVA main forces. It is estimated that slightly less than half of the enemy's main force maneuver units outside of those in the DMZ, but well over half of his local force units, participated in the attacks. Thus, he still has substantial uncommitted forces available for a new "second phase" attack . . .

Although the enemy has been seriously weakened, he is not on the verge of desperation. He has over half of his main forces basically intact with more men and matériel en route or available from NVN. He has taken substantial losses in the past and shown an amazing degree of resiliency. On the other hand, his logistics and recruitment problems will be greatly increased with such heavy losses from the local and guerrilla forces who provide manpower for support and combat . . .

It is not yet possible to make a firm assessment of the damage which has been caused to the pacification program, but it probably has been extensive. The pacified areas did not at least initially appear to have been a priority target, probably because most of the VC guerrillas were drawn into local force units for the city battles or were engaged in interdicting LOC's. However, GVN forces providing security for the pacified areas and the [Revolutionary Development] teams were in many cases withdrawn to assist in the defense of urban areas, leaving the VC free to penetrate previously secured hamlets and conduct propaganda, recruit, acquire food, eliminate the GVN administration, and occasionally terrorize the population. The impact of the VC presence was especially severe in the larger hamlets which generally are located close to the population centers and were on the VC route of entry. This activity was responsible for part of the large refugee flow into the cities . . .

There has naturally been a mixed reaction from the people to the Communist onslaught—initially, it was one of shock at the strength of the attack, and anger at its perfidy. However, even those skeptics who would not previously acknowledge that the large electoral turnouts, the inability of the VC to get a response to calls for a general strike, and the almost totally conscript nature of the VC forces were proof that the VC lacked popular support, can hardly deny it now. Despite the creation of a revolutionary administration, supposedly untainted by association with the NLF, no significant element of the population or of the armed forces defected. The refusal of the people to respond to the VC call for an uprising, and in fact often to render assistance to the government forces, was the key to the failure of the VC plan, and is one of the most encouraging aspects of the whole affair.

There are negative factors, of course—the people now have a greater respect for the capabilities of the VC, and this will probably result in some cases in a more cautious attitude toward open support for the government. There is criticism over the government's lack of preparedness, charges of excessive property damage and civilian casualties, and looting by the counterreaction forces, and a persistent belief that somehow the U.S. was in collusion with the VC. However, the population is universally angry at the VC for violating both a sacred holiday and their own truce, and the blame for all of the ills is generally placed on the VC. There was left no doubt in the minds of the people as to the superiority of the government forces and as to who won this engagement. On balance, we feel that in the contest for the hearts and minds of the people, the VC have so far suffered a severe loss. In common danger, there was a tendency to unite behind the government. With a residue of ill will toward the VC which will not be easily erased, the task of nation-building, at least in those areas still under government control, should become a little easier. Much will depend, however, on the skill and alacrity with which the government handles the severe social and economic problems it faces . . .

We are not sanguine about future political problems. The schisms which divide this society are deeply rooted, and will inevitably arise again as the first flush of unity begins to fade. Demands will be made for the removal of officials, both national and local, who proved unequal to the task in a crisis, and this will be certain to restore the endemic factional infighting. The military, some of the Catholics, and those favoring a rough, directed system will fault the government for not being tough enough, while others will be concerned over even the temporary sacrifice of democratic processes and the continued preeminent role of the military.

The crisis has ignited a spark of unity, but to sustain it will require a successful relief and recovery operation, and a sublimation of personal and partisan political interests which this society has never before demonstrated.

The Communists can be credited with having maintained excellent security for such a comprehensive plan, but they are guilty of a massive intelligence failure. Documents captured over the past four months and interrogations of the prisoners involved in the recent attacks indicate quite clearly that the VC did intend to take and hold the cities, did expect a general uprising, and did plan to install a revolutionary government, as evidenced by the presence of a standby VC administrative structure in the major cities. It may seem incredible that VC expectations should have been so divorced from reality, but there are three factors which probably explain this. First, the Communists are and always have been victims of their doctrine, and in the present case the articles of faith were: "The longer we fight, the stronger we become;" and, "The more viciously the enemy fights, the closer he is to collapse;" and "The people support us and when the urban people have the chance to rise up, our victory will be assured." Second, the leaders have been consistently and greatly misinformed by lower cadres. Given the doctrinal bias alluded to above and the Oriental penchant for telling people what they want to hear, the reports going upward have so misinterpreted the facts that the leaders could not base their decisions on reality. Third, the need for a significant victory after two years of drought may have introduced a lack of prudence. By any rational standard, North Vietnam has been losing too much in order to gain too little. For too long, VC strength and support has been dwindling. The entire nature of the war, the entire environment of the struggle, changed with the massive U.S. involvement. The Tet assault must have been part of an expected VC plan to inflict heavy physical and psychological damage in hope of gaining, if not all their objectives, something which could be construed as a victory.

DOCUMENT 7.4

"Mired in Stalemate"
Commentary by Walter Cronkite, CBS News, February 27, 1968

Just like U.S. political leaders and military commanders, American journalists struggled in February and March 1968 to understand the implications of the Tet Offensive. CBS television decided to send the anchorman of its evening news program, Walter Cronkite, to Vietnam in mid-February to assess the situation in person. Upon his return to New York, Cronkite delivered the following commentary at the end of a special report about the war. Many historians and former policymakers argue that Cronkite's words marked a turning point in the war. Cronkite had generally supported the U.S. effort in Vietnam in earlier years, and polls rated him "the most trusted man in America." His gloomy appraisal of the fighting therefore left a deep impression on the nation. Among those allegedly affected was President Johnson, who supposedly said to his press secretary, George Christian, "If I've lost Cronkite, I've lost Middle America." Others doubt Johnson paid any attention and downplay the significance of Cronkite's editorial.

Tonight, back in more familiar surroundings in New York, we'd like to sum up our findings in Vietnam, an analysis that must be speculative, personal, subjective. Who won and who lost in the great Tet offensive against the cities? I'm not sure. The Vietcong did not win by a knockout, but neither did we. The referees of history may make it a draw. Another standoff may be coming in the big battles expected south of the Demilitarized Zone. Khesanh could well fall, with a terrible loss in American lives, prestige and morale, and this is a tragedy of our stubbornness there; but the bastion no longer is a key to the rest of the northern regions, and it is doubtful that the American forces can be defeated across the breadth of the DMZ with any substantial loss of ground. Another standoff.

On the political front, past performance gives no confidence that the Vietnamese government can cope with its problems, now compounded by the attack on the cities. It may not fall, it may hold on, but it probably won't show the dynamic qualities demanded of this young nation. Another standoff.

We have been too often disappointed by the optimism of the American leaders, both in Vietnam and Washington, to have faith any longer in the silver linings they find in the darkest clouds. They may be right, that Hanoi's winter-spring offensive has been forced by the Communist realization that they could not win the longer war of attrition, and that the Communists hope that any success in the offensive will improve their position for eventual negotiations. It would improve their position, and it would also require our realization, that we should have had all along, that any negotiations must be that—negotiations, not the dictation of peace terms.

For it seems now more certain than ever that the bloody experience of Vietnam is to end in a stalemate. This summer's almost certain standoff will either end in real give-and-take negotiations or terrible escalation; and for every means we have to escalate, the enemy can match us, and that applies to invasion of the North, the use of nuclear weapons, or the mere commitment of one hundred, or two hundred, or three hundred thousand more American troops to the battle. And with each escalation, the world comes closer to the brink of cosmic disaster.

To say that we are closer to victory today is to believe, in the face of the evidence, the optimists who have been wrong in the past. To suggest we are on the edge of defeat is to yield to unreasonable pessimism. To say that we are mired in stalemate seems the only realistic, yet unsatisfactory, conclusion. On the off chance that military and political analysts are right, in the next few months we must test the enemy's intentions, in case this is indeed his last big gasp before negotiations.

But it is increasingly clear to this reporter that the only rational way out then will be to negotiate, not as victors, but as an honorable people who lived up to their pledge to defend democracy, and did the best they could.

This is Walter Cronkite. Good night.

DOCUMENT 7.5

Weighing Westmoreland's Request for More Troops

Notes of a Meeting between President Johnson, Secretary of Defense Clark Clifford, and Other Senior Aides, March 4, 1968

On the battlefield, American and South Vietnamese forces quickly repulsed the communist offensive and, in fact, inflicted severe losses on the Viet Cong and North Vietnamese. General William Westmoreland hoped to build on this progress and asked President Johnson to send another 205,000 American troops. Alarmed by the prospect of further escalation, Johnson referred the request to a committee of senior advisers chaired by the new secretary of defense, Clark M. Clifford. On March 4, the committee recommended that the president reject Westmoreland's request and send only 22,000 troops, enough to meet short-term U.S. needs. The following document summarizes the discussion when Johnson met with Clifford and other key aides to discuss the committee's proposal. Participants included National Security Adviser Walt W. Rostow and Secretary of State Dean Rusk.

The President: As I told you last week, I wanted you to return today with your recommendations in response to General Westmoreland's request. Among the things I asked you to study were the following questions:

1. What particular forces are you recommending that we dispatch immediately? How do we get these forces?
2. How soon could we formulate what we want from the South Vietnamese?
3. What difficulties do you foresee with your recommendations, both with the Congress and financially? . . .

As I understand it, Clark Clifford, Secretary Rusk, and Rostow and others have been meeting on these questions in conjunction with the Joint Chiefs of Staff.

Walt Rostow: That is correct.

Clark Clifford: . . . The subject is a very profound one, and I consider it advisable to outline the difficulty we face and the central problem which your advisers see you facing.

As you know, from time to time, the military leaders in the field ask for additional forces. We have, in the past, met these requests until we are now at the point where we have agreed to supply up to 525,000 men to General Westmoreland.

He now has asked for 205,000 additional troops. There are three questions:

1. Should the President send 205,000?
2. Should the President not send any more?
3. Should the President approve a figure somewhere in between and send an alternative number?

Your senior advisers have conferred on this matter at very great length. There is a deep-seated concern by your advisers. *There is a concern that if we say, yes, and step up with the addition of 205,000 more men that we might continue down the road as we have been without accomplishing our purpose—which is for a viable South Vietnam which can live in peace.*

We are not convinced that our present policy will bring us to that objective . . .

For a while, we thought and had the feeling that we understood the strength of the Viet Cong and the North Vietnamese. You will remember the rather optimistic reports of General Westmoreland and Ambassador Bunker last year.

Frankly, it came as a shock that the Vietcong-North Vietnamese had the strength of force and skill to mount the Tet offensive—as they did. They struck 34 cities, made strong inroads in Saigon and in Hue. There have been very definite effects felt in the countryside.

At this stage, it is clear that this new request by General Westmoreland brings the President to a clearly defined watershed:

1. Do you continue to go down that same road of "more troops, more guns, more planes, more ships"?
2. Do you go on killing more Viet Cong and more North Vietnamese and killing more Vietcong and more North Vietnamese?

There are grave doubts that we have made the type of progress we had hoped to have made by this time. As we build up our forces, they build up theirs. We continue to fight at a higher level of intensity.

Even were we to meet this full request of 205,000 men, and the pattern continues as it has, it is likely that by March [Westmoreland] may want another 200,000 to 300,000 men with no end in sight.

The country we are trying to save is being subjected to enormous damage. Perhaps the country we are trying to save is relying on the United States too much. When we look ahead, we may find that we may actually be denigrating their ability to take over their own country rather than contributing to their ability to do it.

We recommend in this paper that you meet the requirement for only those forces that may be needed to deal with any exigencies of the next 3–4 months. March-April-May could be an important period.

We recommend an immediate decision to deploy to Vietnam an estimated total of 22,000 additional personnel. We would agree to get them to General Westmoreland right away. It would be valuable for the general to know they are coming so he can make plans accordingly.

This is as far as we are willing to go. We would go ahead, however, and call up a sufficient number of men. If later the President decides Westmoreland needs additional reinforcements, you will have men to meet that contingency.

The President: Westmoreland is asking for 200,000 men, and you are recommending 20,000 or so?

Clark Clifford: The strategic reserves in the United States are deeply depleted. They must be built up . . . We do not know what might happen anywhere around the world, but to face any emergency we will need to strengthen the reserve.

Out of this buildup you can meet additional requests from Westmoreland in the event you decide he needs more than the 22,000 later. The first increment will meet his needs for the next three to four months.

Westmoreland must not have realized it, but it would have taken much longer than he had anticipated to provide the men and units he originally requested anyway. We could not meet that schedule . . .

We also feel strongly that there should be a comprehensive study of the strategic guidance to be given General Westmoreland in the future.

We are not sure the present strategy is the right strategy—that of being spread out all over the country with a seek and destroy policy.

We are not convinced that this is the right way, that it is the right long-term course to take. We are not sure under the circumstances which exist that a conventional military victory, as commonly defined, can be had.

After this study is made—if there is no clear resolution in the actions of the next 3–4 months except long drawn-out procedure—we may want to change the strategic guidance given Westmoreland. Perhaps we should not be trying to protect all of the countryside, and instead concentrate on the cities and important areas in the country.

There will be considerably higher casualties if we follow the Westmoreland plan. It just follows that if we increase our troop commitment by 200,000 men, there will be significantly higher casualties.

We may want to consider using our men as a "shield" behind which the government of South Vietnam could strengthen itself and permit the ARVN to be strengthened. Under the present situation, there is a good deal of talk about what the ARVN "will do" but when the crunch is on, when the crunch comes, they look to us for more. When they got into the Tet offensive, Thieu's statement wasn't what more they could do but that "it is time for more U.S. troops." There is no easy answer to this.

If we continue with our present policy of adding more troops and increasing our commitment, this policy may lead us into Laos and Cambodia.

The reserve forces in North Vietnam are a cause for concern as well. They have a very substantial population from which to draw. They have no trouble whatever organizing, equipping, and training their forces.

We seem to have a sinkhole. We put in more—they match it. We put in more—they match it.

The South Vietnamese are not doing all they should do.

The Soviets and the Chinese have agreed to keep the North Vietnamese well armed and well supplied.

The Vietcong are now better armed than the ARVN. They have:

▪ better rifles

▪ better training

▪ more sophisticated weapons (mortars, artillery, rockets).

I see more and more fighting with more and more casualties on the U.S. side and no end in sight to the action.

I want to give a whole new look at the whole situation. There is strong unanimity on this. If it were possible, we would want to look at the situation without sending more troops to him. But we should send the 22,000—that is, until a new policy decision is reached . . .

We can no longer rely just on the field commander. He can want troops and want troops and want troops. We must look at the overall impact on us, including the situation here in the United States. We must look at our economic stability, our other problems in the world, our other problems at home; we must consider whether or not this thing is [tying] us down so that we cannot do some of the other things we should be doing; and finally, we must consider the effects of our actions on the rest of the world—are we setting an example in Vietnam through which other nations would rather not go if they are faced with a similar threat?

It is out of caution and for protection that we recommend these additional forces. *Now the time has come to decide where do we go from here.*

I can assure the President that we can reexamine this situation with complete protection to our present position . . .

We should tell the South Vietnamese that the General has asked for 200,000 more troops, but we are giving only 25,000. We should let them know that you are delaying your decision until you know what the GVN will do about:

▪ removal of the poor unit commanders

▪ meaningful steps to eliminate corruption

▪ meeting their own leadership responsibilities

▪ not only saying they will do something, but meaning it as well . . .

We should consider changing our concept from one of protecting real estate to protecting people. We need to see if these people are really going to take care of themselves eventually. I am not sure we can ever find our way out if we continue to shovel men into Vietnam . . .

Secretary Rusk: Mr. President, without a doubt, this will be one of the most serious decisions you will have made since becoming President. This has implications for all of our society.

First, on the review of strategic guidance: we want the Vietnamese to do their full share and be able to survive when we leave. This was one of the things that saved us in Korea. The question is whether substantial additional troops would eventually increase or decrease South Vietnamese strength . . .

We must also consider what would happen to our NATO troop policies. To reduce NATO troops is a serious matter indeed.

We have also got to think of what this troop increase would mean in terms of increased taxes, the balance of payments picture, inflation, gold, and the general economic picture.

We should study moving away from the *geographic* approach of Vietnam strategy to a *demographic* approach.

On the negotiation front, I wish we had a formula to bring about a peaceful settlement soon. We do not . . . *[T]he negotiation track is quite bleak at the current time.*

DOCUMENT 7.6
A Communist Appraisal of the Offensive
Sixth Resolution of the Central Office of South Vietnam (COSVN), March 1968

Just like the Americans and the South Vietnamese, the Vietnamese communists struggled in the first weeks after Tet to assess how the offensive had changed the military and political situation. The Central Office of South Vietnam, the highest decision-making body below the seventeenth parallel, issued the following appraisal in March 1968. The document largely mimicked a resolution adopted by the Communist Party in Hanoi on the eve of the offensive two months earlier, but it also updated that statement of party goals by noting the problems that had arisen during weeks of heavy fighting since the start of what the communists called the "General Offensive and General Uprising."

In this phase of General Offensive and General Uprising, after a month of continuous offensives and simultaneous uprisings conducted on all battlefronts in the South, we have recorded great and unprecedented victories in all fields, inflicting on the enemy heavier losses than those he had suffered in any previous period . . .

We attacked all U.S.-puppet nerve centers, occupied and exerted our control for a definite period and at varying degrees over almost all towns, cities and municipalities in the South, and destroyed and disintegrated an important part of puppet installations at all levels, seriously damaging the puppet administrative machinery.

We liberated additional wide areas in the countryside containing a population of 1.5 million inhabitants, consolidated and widened our rear areas, shifted immense resources of manpower and material . . . to the support of the front-line and of victory; encircled and isolated the enemy, and reduced the enemy's reserves of human and material resources, driving him into a very difficult economic and financial situation.

We have quantitatively and qualitatively improved our armed forces and political forces which have become outstandingly mature during the struggle in the past month . . .

We have won great successes but still have many deficiencies and weak points:

1. In the military field—From the beginning, we have not been able to annihilate much of the enemy's live force and much of the reactionary clique. Our armed forces have not fulfilled their role as "lever" and have not created favorable conditions for motivating the masses to arise in towns and cities.
2. In the political field—Organized popular forces were not broad and strong enough. We have not had specific plans for motivating the masses to the extent that they would indulge in violent armed uprisings in coordination with and supporting the military offensives.
3. The puppet troop proselyting failed to create a military revolt movement in which the troops would arise and return to the people's side. The enemy troop proselyting task to be carried out in coordination with the armed struggle and political struggle has not been performed, and inadequate attention had been paid to this in particular.
4. There has not been enough consciousness about specific plans for the widening and development of liberated rural areas and the appropriate mobilization of manpower, material resources and the great capabilities of the masses to support the front line.
5. The building of real strength and particularly the replenishment of troops and development of political forces of the infrastructure has been slow and has not met the requirements of continuous offensives and uprisings of the new phase.
6. In providing leadership and guidance to various echelons, we failed to give them a profound and thorough understanding of the Party's policy, line and strategic determination so that they have a correct and full realization of this phase of General Offensive and General Uprising. The implementation of our policies has not been sharply and closely conducted. We lacked concreteness, our plans were simple, our coordination poor, control and prodding were absent, reporting and requests for instruction were much delayed . . .

Although the enemy is suffering heavy defeat and is in a passive and confused situation, he still has strength and is very stubborn. In his death throes he will resort to more murderous and savage actions. He will massacre the people, thrust out to break the encirclement and create many new difficulties for us. The struggle between the enemy and us will become fiercer, particularly in areas adjoining the towns and cities. Therefore, we must be extremely vigilant, urgently and actively exploit our past successes, overcome all difficulties and hardships with determination to secure final victory and be ready to fight vigorously should the war be prolonged and widened.

However, it must be clearly realized that this will be but the enemy's convulsions before death, his reaction from a weak, not a strong position. The situation will continue to develop in a way favorable to us and detrimental to the enemy with the possibility of sudden developments which we must be ready to take advantage of in order to secure final victory.

DOCUMENT 7.7

Confrontation in Chicago

Testimony by Rennie Davis before the House Un-American Activities Committee, December 3, 1968

The 1968 Democratic National Convention in Chicago was the site of one of the most violent and divisive protests of the Vietnam era. In the months leading up to the event, antiwar groups announced plans to demonstrate against U.S. policy in Vietnam, but Chicago Mayor Richard Daley refused to grant permits that would have allowed protesters to gather legally. Daley put all 12,000 city police on twelve-hour shifts and called in 6,000 National Guardsmen. No more than 10,000 protesters took part in any single demonstration during the convention, but it was enough to produce mayhem in the streets. Images of policemen clubbing demonstrators captivated the nation, leading some commentators to suggest that the country was nearing a state of civic collapse. A few months later, the House Committee on Un-American Activities, long a conservative bastion, subpoenaed key antiwar leaders to testify about their activities. The following selections are drawn from the testimony of Rennard "Rennie" Davis, a leader of the National Mobilization Committee to End the War in Vietnam. Participants in the hearing included Representatives Richard H. Ichord (Democrat of Missouri), John M. Ashbrook (Republican of Ohio), Albert W. Watson (Republican of South Carolina), and Frank Conley, the committee's lead council. The excerpts begin with Conley questioning Davis about whether activists went to Chicago with "militant" intentions. At the time of his testimony, Davis, along with seven other men, was the subject of a grand jury investigation considering criminal charges. Davis and four others were later convicted of crossing state lines with intent to riot and sentenced to five years in prison, but the convictions were overturned on appeal.

Mr. CONLEY. What does the word "militancy" mean to you?

Mr. DAVIS. It means when people feel the democratic process has broken down . . . —in every conceivable way they have been working to try to end this terrible war in Vietnam—that they have to do what they can to undercut, to prevent this authority from continuing in the way that it has.

Essentially, the movement of the last 8 years has been a movement that tries to bring about a change in the consciousness of both the people who run this country and the general population. I think that we have demonstrated our moralism and nonviolence and our willingness to go to jail for our convictions, our refusal to go into the draft, our nonviolent sit-ins, where we subject ourselves to all kinds of abuse in an effort to try to make this country face up to what it is doing, not only in the black and poor communities of the Nation, but all over the world.

I think that militancy is an appropriate term for a movement that is angry, that wants change, that is trying to reach more and more people to understand what we are doing to human lives all over the world. I think militancy is a word that is appropriate to young people and black people and concerned Americans facing the kinds of opposition, the kinds of oppression, and the kinds of war policies that this Government stands for.

Mr. WATSON. Whose blood did you plan to shed in Chicago?

Mr. DAVIS. We didn't plan to shed anybody's blood. The plan was announced months ago, and we were seeking permits so we could have a legal, peaceful assembly, and that right to assemble was being crushed by the officials of Chicago.

We felt that this kind of blatant disregard of the Constitution and the military buildup that was occurring in Chicago could only mean that Chicago officials were interested in a police riot and the destruction of any possibility or opportunity to have a peaceful assembly. As we know, that is exactly what happened.

Mr. WATSON. You have nothing but contempt for this committee, for the President, Secretary Rusk, and everything else?

Mr. DAVIS. No, not everything else. I don't have contempt for—

Mr. WATSON. Love-ins—

Mr. DAVIS. I don't have contempt for American soldiers. I don't have contempt for black people, for poor people, for welfare mothers, for university people trying to open up democratic channels. I don't have contempt for people trying to earn a living. I don't have contempt for humanity and decency. People believe in democratic processes and want to bring the democratic values and processes into this society. There are many things, Mr. Watson, for which I do not have contempt.

Mr. WATSON. In other words, those things for which you and your organization stand for, you have no contempt for. I think we can be in accord with this: So far as what happened in Chicago, your part in it, you absolutely did nothing wrong, said nothing wrong, the whole blame is to be placed at the feet of Mayor Daley and the police department?

Mr. DAVIS. The whole blame is to be placed on a society or a government that is increasingly out of touch with the young people in this country and with what the real interests of this country are.

Chicago is a kind of watershed event, I think. In August of 1963, . . . some 250,000 people marched for jobs and justice in the city. Exactly 5 years later, another demonstration that was trying to mount its concern about peace in Vietnam was clubbed and brutally suppressed by police in a general military environment that had been created by officials of Chicago.

During those 5 years we dropped more bombs in Vietnam than we did in World War II. We spent three times as much in riot control as was spent on poverty. We saw scores of cities go up in smoke out of rebellion to the conditions in those communities. We saw thousands of young people face prison rather than fight in a war they considered unjust.

I think Chicago really has to be seen in the context of a society or a government that increasingly resorts to military and police force rather than consensus for insuring its policies.

Well, at the same time more and more American citizens are joining in a movement to create some kind of a new basis, just basis, humane basis on which this country can operate.

Mr. ICHORD. If I may interrupt, Mr. Watson, at that point, do you feel they have a democratic society in North Vietnam?

Mr. DAVIS. I was not in North Vietnam [in order] to say very much about them. What I would say is that the American people are deluded if they believe there is a small group of people at the top that terrorize . . . to resist American aggression against them.

My general impression was in the countryside and cities—the Vietnamese people are united in trying to stop the bombing and the aggression [against] that country and that, in general, they feel that their own interests for freedom and independence . . . [are] consistent with a struggle that has been going on for 25 years in that country and consistent with the positions of the recognized leaders of that country. But that to me is an irrelevant question, [we should ask] whether or not we have any business being there. We have no right deciding the fate and destinies of a country 25,000 miles away, and that is why I say American forces should be withdrawn from there . . .

Mr. ASHBROOK. Talking about the North Vietnamese interests, I gather . . . the North Vietnamese feel they gained great benefit from what transpired in Chicago, the efforts of the National Mobilization Committee, the response to the police, the general Chicago situation. Would it be your impression that this Chicago fiasco, whoever is at fault, did help the Vietnamese?

Mr. DAVIS. I think Chicago as well as other peace demonstrations help to convey to Vietnam, but to the people around the world, that there is a significant section of the American people who would like to see us return to some of the democratic ideals for which our Revolution stood . . . [T]o give hope to other nations, I think, is beautiful.

Mr. ASHBROOK. Getting back to the GIs with whom you supposedly identify, the GI about whom you express great concern. Isn't it difficult to get across to the GI that he is your friend, when the enemy he is fighting in Vietnam is gaining great heart and encouragement from your work in Chicago? How can you identify with a GI or how are you going to get through the communication barrier when he hears broadcasts from Hanoi as to what great work, in effect, you are doing in Chicago?

Mr. DAVIS. I think the way that we get through to the GI [is to point out our] work to rebuild this country, to make this country something other than the people's policeman of the world.

Mr. ASHBROOK. Do we do it through a peaceful process?

Mr. DAVIS. It depends on you. This committee, this Congress, and this Government generally is so unresponsive to what people are saying in this country, particularly the young, that it becomes more and more difficult for us to find any channel through which we can operate.

As I said, that demonstration in August of 1963 was ignored. We petitioned the Government. We met with President Kennedy, and 5 years later the two Kennedys were assassinated. The spiritual leader of the civil rights movement, Dr. King, was assassinated, and the horrors both abroad and at home had been [wreaked] on people by the Johnson administration.

I think in some ways that the best thing would be for you to get off of the committee and join us in the streets of this country trying to figure out the answer to this problem.

Mr. ASHBROOK. Thank you for your advice.

Mr. WATSON. One final question. You state the Government and the American people—the old fuddy-duddys as I and others—are unresponsive to the young. You made that statement.

Mr. DAVIS. There are some young people that are growing up like you.

Mr. WATSON. Do you speak for all young Americans?

Mr. DAVIS. No; I speak for myself.

Mr. WATSON. You speak for a small fraction of them. Most young Americans are responsible citizens. They want to help bring a better America and not help bring about an anarchy, as you and your associates wish. And the record should show you represent only a small fraction of America.

Mr. DAVIS. Mr. Watson, you had better watch out.

Mr. ICHORD. What are you going to do?

Mr. DAVIS. If you have children—

Mr. WATSON. I have three children. I assure you I will teach them responsibility and not irresponsibility.

Mr. DAVIS. And you keep that up, Mr. Watson, and right in your own house there will be trouble. Young people are not going to be whiplashed into an unjust society. The hope that we have is that the young people at least have the advantage of opening their eyes and seeing what this country is doing. We do not claim to speak for or represent all young people in the United States, but we do say that there are many people who more and more understand that it is people like you that are destroying America and that the hope of America is in the people who will stand up to people like you and make it right.

8
NEW DEPARTURES

AS A CANDIDATE FOR president and then after his election in November 1968, Richard Nixon promised to end the fighting in Vietnam, but he insisted that the United States could not simply abandon the war. Doing so, he feared, would damage the nation's credibility and invite new communist aggression around the world. The administration therefore insisted on a peace agreement that preserved an independent South Vietnamese nation, the same goal Americans had pursued for many years. Nixon and his top foreign policy aide, Henry Kissinger, expressed confidence that various military and diplomatic innovations would enable them to achieve this elusive goal. In time, however, they ran up against the same problems that had bedeviled their predecessors.

Nixon and Kissinger undertook four new approaches to the war in 1969. First, they began to withdraw U.S. forces from South Vietnam, hoping that lower American casualties would weaken antiwar sentiment and thereby buy them time to achieve an "honorable" peace. Second, they increased support for the South Vietnamese army. More robust local forces could, they believed, offset declining American troop strength and preserve South Vietnamese independence. Third, they authorized bold military operations—most notably aerial and ground attacks on communist bases in Cambodia—that the Johnson administration had prohibited. Finally, they sought improved relations with the Soviet Union and China in the expectation that the communist powers would in turn press Hanoi to make peace on American terms.

None of these measures achieved decisive results, and the negotiations sputtered on with no breakthroughs. Although U.S. forces dwindled to 334,600 at the end of 1970, 156,800 at the end of 1971, and just 24,200 a year later, the administration still faced strong pressure to end the war. Expansion of the fighting into Cambodia, in fact, stirred an unprecedented explosion of antiwar activity in 1970. The South Vietnamese army, meanwhile, continued to perform poorly even as it grew into the fourth largest military force in the world. Diplomatic overtures to Moscow and Beijing, while helping to ease overall Cold War tensions, did little to alter Hanoi's behavior.

Unquestionably, communist forces suffered major setbacks in 1968 and 1969, yet the Hanoi government continued to calculate that time was on its side and refused to concede anything in the Paris talks. North Vietnamese forces pulled back into a defensive posture in 1970 and 1971 to recover and await better opportunities.

Increasingly frustrated and desperate to end the war, Nixon and especially Kissinger began to consider that the best the United States could hope for was a satisfactory span of time between a U.S. withdrawal and the ultimate collapse of South Vietnam—long enough, that is, to avoid the taint of direct responsibility for the defeat of a longstanding ally. Washington took a step in that direction in 1971 by conceding that North Vietnamese forces could remain in the South following a cease-fire.

DOCUMENT 8.1

NLF Struggles

Reminiscence by Trinh Duc, a Communist Official in Long Khanh Province, 1968–1969, Published in 1986

The Vietcong suffered devastating losses during and after the Tet Offensive, not least because NLF operatives took the lead in the effort to encourage popular uprisings in the cities and towns of South Vietnam. The following statement comes from a communist functionary named Trinh Duc, who had served in the anti-French resistance before 1954 and then remained in the South following the Geneva agreements. After ten grueling years in South Vietnamese prisons, Trinh Duc rejoined the revolutionary movement in 1964 and was sent to Long Khanh province, about 50 miles northeast of Saigon, as a village official. At the time of the Tet Offensive, his responsibilities included maintaining the communist political apparatus and supplying local military forces. Trinh Duc's reflections were published in 1986 as part of a scholarly project to collect the reminiscences of communist soldiers and officials.

The Tet Offensive brought on the worst time of the war. Long Khanh was not a key area, and my villages certainly weren't, so the offensive didn't have as much immediate effect on us as it had elsewhere. But we still were prepared for it. The slogan was "Each One Ready to Die to Save the Country!" We knew about the "General Uprising," and I firmly believed we'd win. But afterwards the effects were terrible.

First of all, casualties were very, very high, and the spirit of the soldiers dropped to a low point. Secondly, afterwards the enemy changed over to what we called the "two-pincer strategy." They began to reoccupy posts they had abandoned before—they mostly let the ARVN do that. Then they began to send out guerrilla forces to ambush us in the jungle. That was the second pincer. After a while there was no-where to turn. I would send units out on supply missions and they would disappear. People would be killed while they were cooking or going for water. Sometimes I could find out what happened to them, sometimes I couldn't.

During the period 1968–70, I was ambushed eleven times and wounded twice. It seemed the enemy had learned a lot about how to fight in the jungle . . .

Early in 1970 I was ambushed along with eight others in a jungle clearing. The nine of us were walking single file across a vegetable field that the villagers had carved out of the jungle, on our way from one hamlet to another. It was a cloudy night. The moon was partially covered over and no one could see much. I knew I should have taken the line around the clearing, keeping to the jungle, but I was in too much of a hurry. Toward the middle of the clearing there was a clump of banana trees. Just as I pulled even with them, I realized there were some shapes in the trees. They saw me at exactly the same instant . . .

Just at that moment claymore mines fired off on the path behind me, huge explosions. The instant they stopped I crawled back along the path right over where they had gone off. As I crawled I felt some of the bodies, then squirmed off at a right angle toward the jungle. Firing was going on all around. At least two bul-lets hit my backpack before I got to the tree line. I had to leave the bodies there in the field. I kept thinking how demoralizing it would be for the peasants when they came out in the morning.

So many were killed in 1969 and 1970. There was no way we could stand up to the Americans. Every time they came in force we ran from them. Then when they turned back, we'd follow them. We practically lived on top of them, so they couldn't hit us with artillery and air strikes. During those years I had to reorganize my unit three times. Twice, the entire unit was killed. Each time I reorganized, the num-bers were smaller. It was almost impossible to get new recruits . . .

There's no doubt that 1969 was the worst year we faced, at least the worst year I faced. There was no food, no future—nothing bright. But 1969 was also the time I was happiest. I destroyed several American tanks from the "Flying Horses" tank battalion that was stationed in Suoi Ram. I did it with pressure mines that our bombmakers made from unexploded American bombs. Each mine had seven kilos [15 pounds] of TNT. I was given an award as a champion tank killer.

The year 1969 was also the period when the true heroism of the peasants showed itself. Although we were isolated from the villagers, many of them risked their lives to get food to us. They devised all sorts of ingenious ways to get rice through the government checkpoints. Their feeling for us was one of the things that gave me courage to go on.

Another thing was the conviction that the Americans couldn't last. In 1969 they began to pull out some of their troops. We believed that eventually they would have to withdraw altogether. We knew that even though we faced tremendous difficulties, so did they. They had terrible problems, especially at home. We didn't think their government could stand it in the long run. That gave me heart.

One of the things that demoralized a lot of guerrillas were the B-52 attacks. The fear these attacks caused was terrible. People pissed and shat in their pants. You would see them come out of their bunkers shaking so badly it looked as if they had gone crazy. The B-52s always came in groups of three. They dropped two different kinds of bombs. We called one *bomb dia*, "lake bomb," and the other *bomb bi*, "gravel bomb." Lake bombs were so powerful they blew gigantic ten-meter-deep craters in the ground, like a small lake. The other kind, *bomb bi*, was filled with steel ball bearings. *Bomb bi* hits would mow down the jungle. They'd leave a swath clear enough to drive a jeep through . . .

Toward the end of 1970 things began to get better. We started gaining more control. I could feel the optimism starting to return. One of the ways you could tell this was that the peasants felt more comfortable about contacting us and giving us support. They didn't have to be heroes to do that anymore, especially after 1971.

DOCUMENT 8.2

The Struggle for "Hearts and Minds"

Reminiscence by Nguyen Cong Luan, Major in the South Vietnamese Army, of an Armed Propaganda Unit Operation in 1969, Published in 2012

Following the Tet Offensive, the war was punctuated by major operations involving tens of thousands of soldiers on each side and capturing headlines around the world—the invasion of Cambodia in 1970, the incursion into Laos in 1971, the Easter Offensive and the South Vietnamese–U.S. counter-attack in 1972. Yet the grassroots struggle for the loyalty of South Vietnam's farmers and villagers continued. In the following excerpt from his memoir, Army Major Nguyen Cong Luan recalls his experiences in 1969 as a high-ranking officer in South Vietnamese programs to encourage defections by communists to the government's side and to build good will for the Saigon regime in the countryside. He begins by describing the objectives and activities of the South Vietnamese "Armed Propaganda Unit" that he commanded in the Saigon area.

My armed propaganda company consisted of many ex-communist soldiers who were born and brought up near Sai Gon and served the local communist units in the areas for years. The appearance of those ex-VCs proved to the peasants that, contrary to communist propaganda, defectors were well treated and were serving just like any other ARVN soldier. The peasants' sympathy would bring us valuable information that had never been expected previously.

A company of the 199th [U.S. Light Infantry Brigade], an ARVN Medical/Civic Action team and a platoon of our armed propaganda troops started the first operation of this kind in early 1969 in the villages near Cho Dem, only a few miles from the 199th [headquarters] at Binh Dien, the southern boundary of Sai Gon . . .

When we approached the village, young women ran away in panic out of the hamlet upon seeing the Americans, and we knew why. The old women told us that they saw the GIs for the first time and were scared to death. They said, "In the hamlet three kilometers from here, five women died after being raped by several dozen American black soldiers." The young women only returned to their homes after our troops stopped them and assured them of their safety. We knew that story was nothing more than a VC propaganda trick to evoke images of abuses by French soldiers two decades earlier. We sent several trucks with Vietnamese soldiers to the hamlet. There we conducted an operation with a MEDCAP team, inviting women from a nearby hamlet as well. The women were given health examinations and medicines and some gifts that included toys for their kids.

When my men asked the women from the nearby hamlet about the alleged "rapes," they gave the same story about the "five women." But they said the incident had happened "here" and added that the American troops had never been to their hamlet. The women from both hamlets shared their stories and changed their opinion about the GIs. Their pale faces turned pink with smiles as if light bulbs had just turned on.

One of my men remarked: "The truth can't reach a place three kilometers away. How could it reach newsrooms in New York City 20,000 [kilometers] from here?"

In a nearby village, there was a respectable eighty-four-year-old man who drew our attention. He welcomed us to his home every time we came to see him, but he never let us take his picture. His face was so beautiful, expressing the classic facial features of an aging Vietnamese. He said he didn't want his pictures to be displayed by American officers in their living rooms to show their American friends how barbarous the Vietnamese were and to justify why they could kill them without remorse. We knew that at his age, there was no easy way to shake his conviction. But we visited him about every two weeks. He kept calling us "Americans' puppets" and praised Ho Chi Minh without fear of being arrested. The Sai Gon regime never arrested senior citizens who just talked against the government.

He was angry about an air strike that had destroyed a small pagoda 500 yards from his home during the Tet Offensive while "there was no VC in it." We took pains to explain to him that it must have been a mistake. He kept dismissing our explanation until an officer showed him a photomap and asked him to pick out his house and the pagoda sites from the map. He accepted our argument when he couldn't tell a house from a temple on the aerial photo.

One morning about two months later when I was walking on the dirt road in front of his home, he called me in. It was the first time he had invited anyone in my group to come in with such a friendly manner . . .

Unexpectedly, the old gentleman asked me, "Major, you always tell me that you in the Republic Army are not American puppets. Could you prove that by telling the two American soldiers there to climb up my coconut tree and pick two coconuts for our refreshment?"

I stepped out and talked to the two GIs guarding the road leading to their company command post. It was not a problem to have the GIs do such a nonmilitary task, but climbing was difficult for the two GIs. If only they had been Hawaiian natives! Seeing the two Americans failing to get more than two yards up the coconut tree, the old man laughed and asked me to thank the two GIs for their effort. Then he called his ten-year-old grandson. The slim boy reached the treetop, climbing with the ease of a monkey, and brought down four large coconuts to his grandpa.

The old man became more pleasant and friendly. "Major, now I believe in what you say." . . .

However, he complained forcefully about the spreading corruption in the government and the unscrupulous use of firepower by some units that resulted in the death of innocent victims and destruction of their homes. He told us that his eldest son had been killed by our troops in an operation a long time ago, and that a VC death squad executed the second son a few years later, leaving him his grandson, who picked the coconuts. Neither of his sons had been collaborating with either side.

His change in political attitude proved to be very helpful. Many of his villagers, who held him in high regard, became friendlier. Some secretly gave us valuable information concerning VC activities. A few others persuaded VC soldiers to defect to our side. One of the villagers disclosed to us the local cell of the *kinh tai* (economic-financial) network after we agreed that we would not kill or arrest the VC *kinh tai* cell leader, who was his relative. *Kinh tai* was the most important branch that procured money and material support for local VC activities.

We passed all such information on to the local military and police officials and to the 199th Brigade. I heard later that the information was processed successfully with extreme care for the safety of the tip providers, especially ones who disclosed information related to the *kinh tai*. As a rule, the VC "security" branch listed villagers as well as their defectors who disclosed to our intelligence agencies information on communist *kinh tai* networks as "number one traitors" to be executed. Those who provided destructive military information only came in the second line of the list. The Communist Party gave *kinh tai* the supreme authority and called it the Party's "main artery." . . .

It took my men nearly three months to win the sympathy of just one octogenarian. But his influence carried his opinion to other villagers. That's what we were looking for after several previous failures.

DOCUMENT 8.3

Kissinger's Pessimism
Memorandum from National Security Adviser Henry Kissinger to President Nixon, "Our Present Course on Vietnam," September 10, 1969

The Nixon administration hoped to achieve "peace with honor" in Vietnam through a variety of military, political, and diplomatic innovations. Nixon began withdrawing American forces, initiated the secret bombing of Cambodia, and intensified U.S. negotiations with the Soviet Union within his first few months in office. But none of these steps brought appreciable results. On September 10, Kissinger sent the president the following gloomy assessment of the situation and prospects for the future.

I have become deeply concerned about our present course on Vietnam. This memorandum is to inform you of the reasons for my concern. It does not discuss alternative courses of action, but is provided for your background consideration . . .

While time acts against both us and our enemy, it runs more quickly against our strategy than against theirs. This pessimistic view is based on my view of Hanoi's strategy and the probable success of the various elements of our own.

I. U.S. Strategy

In effect, we are attempting to solve the problem of Vietnam on three highly interrelated fronts: (1) within the U.S., (2) in Vietnam, and (3) through diplomacy. To achieve our basic goals through diplomacy, we must be reasonably successful on *both* of the other two fronts.

a. U.S.

The pressure of public opinion on you to resolve the war quickly will increase—and I believe increase greatly—during the coming months. While polls may show that large numbers of Americans now are satisfied with the Administration's handling of the war, the elements of an evaporation of this support are clearly present. The plans for student demonstrations in October are well known, and while many Americans will oppose the students' activities, they will also be reminded of their own opposition to the continuation of the war. As mentioned below, I do not believe that "Vietnamization" can significantly reduce the pressures for an end to the war, and may, in fact, increase them after a certain point. Particularly significant is the clear opposition of many "moderate" leaders of opinion, particularly in the press and in the East (e.g., *Life* Magazine). The result of the recrudescence of intense public concern must be to polarize public opinion. You will then be somewhat in the same position as was President Johnson, although the substance of your position will be different. You will be caught between the Hawks and the Doves.

The effect of these public pressures on the U.S. Government will be to accentuate the internal divisiveness that has already become apparent to the public and Hanoi. Statements by government officials which attempt to assuage the Hawks or Doves will serve to confuse Hanoi but also to confirm it in its course of waiting us out.

b. Vietnam

Three elements on the Vietnam front must be considered—(1) our efforts to "win the war" through military operations and pacification, (2) "Vietnamization," and (3) the political position of the GVN.

(1) I do not believe that with our current plans we can win the war within two years, although our success or failure in hurting the enemy remains very important.

(2) "Vietnamization" must be considered both with regard to its prospects for allowing us to turn the war over to the Vietnamese, and with regard to its effect on Hanoi and U.S. public opinion. I am not optimistic about the ability of the South Vietnamese armed forces to assume a larger part of the burden than current MACV plans allow. These plans, however, call for a thirty-month period in which to turn the burden of the war over to the GVN. I do not believe we have this much time.

In addition, "Vietnamization" will run into increasingly serious problems as we proceed down its path.

■ Withdrawal of U.S. troops will become like salted peanuts to the American public: The more U.S. troops come home, the more will be demanded. This could eventually result, in effect, in demands for unilateral withdrawal—perhaps within a year.

■ The more troops are withdrawn, the more Hanoi will be encouraged—they are the last people we will be able to fool about the ability of the South Vietnamese to take over from us. They have the option of attacking GVN forces to embarrass us throughout the process or of waiting until we have largely withdrawn before doing so (probably after a period of higher infiltration).

■ Each U.S. soldier that is withdrawn will be relatively more important to the effort in the south, as he will represent a higher percentage of U.S. forces than did his predecessor. (We need not, of course, continue to withdraw combat troops but can emphasize support troops in the next increments withdrawn. Sooner or later, however, we must be getting at the guts of our operations there.)

■ It will become harder and harder to maintain the morale of those who remain, not to speak of their mothers.

■ "Vietnamization" may not lead to reduction in U.S. casualties until its final stages, as our casualty rate may be unrelated to the total number of American troops in South Vietnam. To kill about 150 U.S. soldiers a week, the enemy needs to attack only a small portion of our forces.

■ "Vietnamization" depends on broadening the GVN, and Thieu's new government is not significantly broader than the old . . . The best way to broaden the GVN would be to create the impression that the Saigon government is winning or at least permanent. The more uncertainty there is about the outcome of the war, the less the prospect for "Vietnamization."

(3) We face a dilemma with the GVN: The present GVN cannot go much farther towards a political settlement without seriously endangering its own existence; but at the same time, it has not gone far enough to make such a settlement likely.

Thieu's failure to "broaden" his government is disturbing, but not because he failed to include a greater variety of Saigon's Tea House politicians. It is disturbing because these politicians clearly do not believe that Thieu and his government represent much hope for future power, and because the new government does not offer much of a bridge to neutralist figures who could play a role in a future settlement. This is not to mention his general failure to build up political strength in non-Catholic villages. In addition, as U.S. troops are withdrawn, Thieu becomes more dependent on the political support of the South Vietnamese military.

c. Diplomatic Front

There is not therefore enough of a prospect of progress in Vietnam to persuade Hanoi to make real concessions in Paris. Their intransigence is also based on their estimate of growing U.S. domestic opposition to our Vietnam policies. It looks as though they are prepared to try to wait us out.

II. Hanoi's Strategy

There is no doubt that the enemy has been hurt by allied military actions in the South, and is not capable of maintaining the initiative on a sustained basis there. Statistics on enemy-initiated activities, as well as some of Giap's recent statements, indicate a conscious decision by Hanoi to settle down to a strategy of "protracted warfare." This apparently consists of small unit actions with "high point" flurries of activity, and emphasis on inflicting U.S. casualties (particularly through rocket and mortar attacks). This pattern of actions seems clearly to indicate a low-cost strategy aimed at producing a psychological, rather than military, defeat for the U.S.

This view of their strategy is supported by our estimates of enemy infiltration. They *could* infiltrate more men, according to intelligence estimates, despite growing domestic difficulties. The only logical reason for their not having done so is that more men were not needed in the pipeline—at least for a few months—to support a lower-cost strategy of protracted warfare. It seems most unlikely that they are attempting to "signal" to us a desire for a de facto mutual withdrawal, although this cannot be discounted . . .

Hanoi's adoption of a strategy designed to wait us out fits both with its doctrine of how to fight a revolutionary war and with its expectations about increasingly significant problems for the U.S.

III. Conclusion

In brief, I do not believe we can make enough evident progress in Vietnam to hold the line within the U.S. (and the U.S. Government), and Hanoi has adopted a strategy which it should be able to maintain for some time—barring some break like Sino-Soviet hostilities. Hence my growing concern.

An Appeal to the "Silent Majority"
Nationally Televised Speech by President Richard Nixon, November 3, 1969

When he took office in January 1969, President Nixon hoped that U.S. troop withdrawals would ease political pressure on the White House while Vietnamization, the bombing of Cambodia, and intensified diplomacy with Moscow would lead to North Vietnamese concessions at the bargaining table in Paris. By the fall, however, Nixon's hopes had been dashed. Hanoi remained steadfast in its negotiating position, and dissent against the war within the United States surged anew as expectations of a breakthrough to end the war faded. On October 15, as many as two million Americans took part in nationwide demonstrations known as the Moratorium to End the War in Vietnam. Anxious to contain popular discontent and buy more time for his policies, Nixon delivered a nationally televised speech on November 3 to describe his plans for Vietnam.

[T] he question facing us today is: Now that we are in the war, what is the best way to end it?

In January I could only conclude that the precipitate withdrawal of American forces from Vietnam would be a disaster not only for South Vietnam but for the United States and for the cause of peace.

For the South Vietnamese, our precipitate withdrawal would inevitably allow the Communists to repeat the massacres which followed their takeover in the North 15 years before.

They then murdered more than 50,000 people and hundreds of thousands more died in slave labor camps.

We saw a prelude of what would happen in South Vietnam when the Communists entered the city of Hue last year. During their brief rule there, there was a bloody reign of terror in which 3,000 civilians were clubbed, shot to death, and buried in mass graves . . .

A nation cannot remain great if it betrays its allies and lets down its friends. Our defeat and humiliation in South Vietnam without question would promote recklessness in the councils of those great powers who have not yet abandoned their goals of world conquest . . .

We have adopted a plan which we have worked out in cooperation with the South Vietnamese for the complete withdrawal of all U.S. combat ground forces, and their replacement by South Vietnamese forces on an orderly scheduled timetable. This withdrawal will be made from strength and not from weakness.

As South Vietnamese forces become stronger, the rate of American withdrawal can become greater . . .

I recognize that some of my fellow citizens disagree with the plan for peace I have chosen. Honest and patriotic Americans have reached different conclusions as to how peace should be achieved . . .

For almost 200 years, the policy of this Nation has been made under our Constitution by those leaders in the Congress and the White House elected by all of the people. If a vocal minority, however fervent its cause, prevails over reason and the will of the majority, this Nation has no future as a free society.

And now I would like to address a word, if I may, to the young people of this Nation who are particularly concerned, and I understand why they are concerned, about this war.

I respect your idealism.

I share your concern for peace. I want peace as much as you do. There are powerful personal reasons I want to end this war. This week I will have to sign 83 letters to mothers, fathers, wives, and loved ones of men who have given their lives for America in Vietnam. It is very little satisfaction to me that this is only one-third as many letters as I signed the first week in office. There is nothing I want more than to see the day come when I do not have to write any of those letters.

I want to end the war to save the lives of those brave young men in Vietnam.

But I want to end it in a way which will increase the chance that their younger brothers and their sons will not have to fight in some future Vietnam someplace in the world.

And I want to end the war for another reason. I want to end it so that the energy and dedication of you, our young people, now too often directed into bitter hatred against those responsible for the war, can be turned to the great challenges of peace, a better life for all Americans, a better life for all people on this earth . . .

Two hundred years ago this Nation was weak and poor. But even then, America was the hope of millions in the world. Today we have become the strongest and richest nation in the world. And the wheel of destiny has turned so that any hope the world has for the survival of peace and freedom will be determined by whether the American people have the moral stamina and the courage to meet the challenge of free world leadership.

Let historians not record that when America was the most powerful nation in the world we passed on the other side of the road and allowed the last hopes for peace and freedom of millions of people to be suffocated by the forces of totalitarianism.

And so tonight—to you, the great silent majority of my fellow Americans—I ask for your support.

I pledged in my campaign for the Presidency to end the war in a way that we could win the peace. I have initiated a plan of action which will enable me to keep that pledge.

The more support I can have from the American people, the sooner that pledge can be redeemed; for the more divided we are at home, the less likely the enemy is to negotiate at Paris.

Let us be united for peace. Let us also be united against defeat. Because let us understand: North Vietnam cannot defeat or humiliate the United States. Only Americans can do that.

DOCUMENT 8.5

The My Lai Massacre
Photo by Army Photographer Ron Haeberle, Published by *Life* Magazine, December 1, 1969

Criticism of the war intensified in late 1969 when *Life* magazine published shocking photos of a massacre carried out by U.S. troops in South Vietnam. The images, taken by Army photographer Ron Haeberle, helped generate pressure for an official investigation into the killings. That investigation and legal proceedings against several U.S. soldiers captured headlines over the next two years, stirring fierce debate over the conduct of the war and the culpability of the American personnel involved. The military initially covered up the massacre, which took place on March 16, 1968, in the hamlets of My Lai and My Khe on Vietnam's central coast. But the full horror eventually became known: despite encountering no armed resistance, American soldiers engaged in four hours of rape and murder that killed somewhere between 347 and 504 Vietnamese, mostly women, children, and old men. The photo above was part of the *Life* exposé.

DOCUMENT 8.6
Veterans Against the War
Testimony by Navy Lieutenant John F. Kerry before the Senate Committee on
Foreign Relations, April 22, 1971

The explosion of antiwar activism that followed the U.S. invasion of Cambodia
in April 1970 subsided later that year, and the Republican Party fared well in
midterm elections in November. Yet the Nixon administration faced a steady
drumbeat of criticism over the war as the fighting dragged into 1971 with no
end in sight. Revelations about the My Lai massacre suggested that the nation
had lost its moral compass, and the poor performance of South Vietnamese
soldiers during a major operation in Laos revealed that Vietnamization, a
cornerstone of U.S. policy, was not working. Against this backdrop, the Senate
Foreign Relations Committee held a new round of hearings critical of the war.
On April 22, highly decorated Navy veteran John F. Kerry gave testimony on
behalf of Vietnam Veterans Against the War, an organization established in
1967. The testimony launched the career of a man who would eventually
become a U.S. Senator from Massachusetts in 1984, the Democratic presidential nominee in 2004, and Secretary of State in 2012. But it also drew attention at the time as an expression of views held by a small but eloquent group
of veterans.

I would like to say for the record, and also for the men behind me who are also
wearing the uniforms and their medals, that my sitting here is really symbolic.
I am not here as John Kerry. I am here as one member of the group of 1000, which
is a small representation of a much larger group of veterans in this country, and
were it possible for all of them to sit at this table, they would be here and have the
same kind of testimony . . .

I would like to talk, representing all those veterans, and say that several months
ago in Detroit, we had an investigation at which over one hundred fifty honor-
ably discharged and many very highly decorated veterans testified to war crimes
committed in Southeast Asia, not isolated incidents, but crimes committed on
a day-to-day basis with the full awareness of officers at all levels of command.

It is impossible to describe to you exactly what did happen in Detroit, the emotions in the room, the feelings of the men who were reliving their experiences
in Vietnam, but they did. They relived the absolute horror of what this country,
in a sense, made them do.

They told stories that at times they had personally raped, cut off ears, cut off
heads, taped wires from portable telephones to human genitals and turned up the
power, cut off limbs, blown up bodies, randomly shot at civilians, razed villages in
fashion reminiscent of Genghis Khan, shot cattle and dogs for fun, poisoned food
stocks, and generally ravaged the countryside of South Vietnam in addition to the

normal ravage of war, and the normal and very particular ravaging which is done by the applied bombing power of this country . . .

I would like to talk to you a little bit about what the result is of the feelings these men carry with them after coming back from Vietnam. The country doesn't know it yet, but it has created a monster, a monster in the form of millions of men who have been taught to deal and to trade in violence, and who are given the chance to die for the biggest nothing in history; men who have returned with a sense of anger and a sense of betrayal which no one has yet grasped . . .

In 1970 at West Point, Vice President Agnew said, "Some glamorize the criminal misfits of society while our best men die in Asian rice paddies to preserve the freedom which most of those misfits abuse," and this was used as a rallying point for our effort in Vietnam.

But for us, as boys in Asia whom the country was supposed to support, his statement is a terrible distortion from which we can only draw a very deep sense of revulsion. Hence the anger of some of the men who are here in Washington today. It is a distortion because we in no way consider ourselves the best men of this country, because those he calls misfits were standing up for us in a way that nobody else in this country dared to, because so many who have died would have returned to this country to join the misfits in their efforts to ask for an immediate withdrawal from South Vietnam, because so many of those best men have returned as quadriplegics and amputees, and they lie forgotten in Veterans Administration Hospitals in this country which fly the flag which so many have chosen as their own personal symbol. And we cannot consider ourselves America's best men when we are ashamed of and hated what we were called on to do in Southeast Asia.

In our opinion, and from our experience, there is nothing in South Vietnam, nothing which could happen that realistically threatens the United States of America. And to attempt to justify the loss of one American life in Vietnam, Cambodia, or Laos by linking such loss to the preservation of freedom, which those misfits supposedly abuse, is to us the height of criminal hypocrisy, and it is that kind of hypocrisy which we feel has torn this country apart.

We found that not only was [the war in Vietnam] a civil war, an effort by a people who had for years been seeking their liberation from any colonial influence whatsoever, but also we found that the Vietnamese whom we had enthusiastically molded after our own image were hard put to take up the fight against the threat we were supposedly saving them from.

We found most people didn't even know the difference between communism and democracy. They only wanted to work in rice paddies without helicopters strafing them and bombs with napalm burning their villages and tearing their country apart. They wanted everything to do with the war, particularly with this foreign presence of the United States of America, to leave them alone in peace, and they practiced the art of survival by siding with whichever military force was present at a particular time, be it Vietcong, North Vietnamese, or American . . .

We rationalized destroying villages in order to save them. We saw America lose her sense of morality as she accepted very coolly a My Lai and refused to give up the image of American soldiers who hand out chocolate bars and chewing gum. We learned the meaning of free fire zones, shooting anything that moves, and we watched while America placed a cheapness on the lives of Orientals.

We watched the U.S. falsification of body counts, in fact the glorification of body counts. We listened while month after month we were told the back of the enemy was about to break. We fought using weapons against "Oriental human beings," with quotation marks around that. We fought using weapons against those people which I do not believe this country would dream of using were we fighting in the European theater, or let us say a non-third-world people theater, and so we watched while men charged up hills because a general said that hill has to be taken, and after losing one platoon or two platoons, they marched away to leave the hill for the reoccupation by the North Vietnamese because we watched pride allow the most unimportant battles to be blown into extravaganzas, because we couldn't lose, and we couldn't retreat, and because it didn't matter how many American bodies were lost to prove that point . . .

Each day to facilitate the process by which the United States washes her hands of Vietnam someone has to give up his life so that the United States doesn't have to admit something that the entire world already knows, so that we can't say that we have made a mistake. Someone has to die so that President Nixon won't be, and these are his words, "the first president to lose a war."

We are asking Americans to think about that because: how do you ask a man to be the last man to die in Vietnam? How do you ask a man to be the last man to die for a mistake? . . .

We are asking here in Washington for some action, action from the Congress of the United States of America, which has the power to raise and maintain armies, and which, by the Constitution also has the power to declare war . . .

We are here in Washington also to say that the problem of this war is not just a question of war and diplomacy. It is part and parcel of everything that we are trying as human beings to communicate to people in this country, the question of racism, which is rampant in the military, and so many other questions also, the use of weapons, the hypocrisy in our taking umbrage in the Geneva Conventions and using that as justification for a continuation of this war, when we are more guilty than any other body of violations of those Geneva Conventions, in the use of free fire zones, harassment interdiction fire, search and destroy missions, the bombings, the torture of prisoners, the killing of prisoners, accepted policy by many units in South Vietnam . . .

We wish that a merciful God could wipe away our own memories of that service as easily as this administration has wiped their memories of us. But all that they have done and all that they can do by this denial is to make more clear than ever our own determination to undertake one last mission, to search out and destroy the last vestige of this barbaric war, to pacify our own hearts, to conquer the hate and the fear that have driven this country these last 10 years and more. And so when, in 30 years from now, our brothers go down the street without a leg, without an arm, or a face, and small boys ask why, we will be able to say, "Vietnam" and not mean a desert, not a filthy obscene memory, but mean instead the place where America finally turned and where soldiers like us helped it in the turning.

DOCUMENT 8.7

"Decent Interval"?

Notes of a Conversation between U.S. National Security Adviser Henry Kissinger and Chinese Premier Zhou Enlai, July 9, 1971

The Nixon administration grew frustrated as its military and diplomatic innovations failed to achieve major breakthroughs in Vietnam or in the negotiations in Paris. In 1971, Washington revised its negotiating position, agreeing that North Vietnamese forces could remain in the South following a ceasefire. Many historians argue that National Security Adviser Henry Kissinger, if not the president, also lost hope that it would be possible to preserve an independent South Vietnam over the long term. Some suggest, in fact, that Kissinger accepted the idea of what he termed a "decent interval." According to this logic, the United States should aim for a peace deal that would preserve an independent South Vietnam only long enough to protect American credibility from accusations that Washington had blatantly betrayed its ally. One piece of evidence that Kissinger was thinking in these terms is the following memorandum of a conversation between Kissinger and Chinese Premier Zhou Enlai during Kissinger's trip to Beijing in the summer of 1971.

Dr. Kissinger: . . . I can assure you that we want to end the war in Vietnam through negotiations, and that we are prepared to set a date for the withdrawal of all our forces from Vietnam and Indochina as you suggested before.

But we want a settlement that is consistent with our honor and our self-respect, and if we cannot get this, then the war will continue, with the consequences which you yourself have described, and which may again, despite our interests, interrupt the improvement in our relations.

The actions in Cambodia and Laos and other actions that would happen if the war continues will never be directed against the People's Republic of China, but they will have unfortunate consequences for our relations which we would very much like to avoid.

One of the difficulties, in our judgment, which I want to mention frankly, is that we look at the problem from the perspective of world peace, but the North Vietnamese and the NLF have only one foreign policy problem, and that is Indochina.

I know Hanoi is very suspicious, and they are afraid to lose at the conference table what they have fought for on the battlefield. And sometimes I am frank to say that I have the impression that they are more afraid of being deceived than of being defeated. They think that they were deceived in 1954. But I want to say that we are realists. We know that after a peace is made we will be 10,000 miles away, and they will still be there . . .

There are two obstacles now to a rapid settlement . . . The two are the following:

- One, North Vietnam in effect demands that we overthrow the present government in Saigon as a condition of making peace.

- Secondly, they refuse to agree to a ceasefire throughout Indochina while we withdraw.

With respect to the political solution, they claim that the present government is a phantom government supported only by American forces. If this is true, then the removal of our forces should bring about the conditions which they are speaking of and which they desire.

Moreover, they are unrealistic. The longer the war goes on, the longer we will strengthen the Saigon Government; and the more we withdraw our forces, the less we can meet demands they make of us. They threaten us with the continuation of the war which will make it impossible to fulfill their demands even if we wanted to, and we don't want to . . .

I would like to tell the Prime Minister, on behalf of President Nixon, as solemnly as I can, that first of all, we are prepared to withdraw completely from Indochina and to give a fixed date, if there is a ceasefire and release of our prisoners. Secondly, we will permit the political solution of South Vietnam to evolve and to leave it to the Vietnamese alone.

We recognize that a solution must reflect the will of the South Vietnamese people and allow them to determine their future without interference. We will not re-enter Vietnam and will abide by the political process.

But what we need is what I told the Prime Minister [about the U.S. position] with relation to Taiwan. The military settlement must be separated in time from the political issues. It is that which is holding up a solution.

On July 12, after I leave here, I shall see Mr. Le Duc Tho in Paris, and I shall make another proposal to him along the lines I have outlined to you . . .

PM Chou: . . . [O]ur attitude toward the Vietnam question and toward a solution of the question of Indochina is composed of the following two points:

The first point is that all foreign troops of the United States and the troops of other countries which followed the United States into Indochina should be withdrawn.

The second point is that the peoples of the three countries of Indochina should be left alone to decide their own respective fates.

Dr. Kissinger: We agree with both points.

PM Chou: You must know that for all this time we have truly supported them, but we have not sent one single soldier to fight.

As to what political system the people choose for themselves, it is for them to decide. So long as no foreign force interferes in that area, then the issue is solved.

Dr. Kissinger: Let me give you the personal impression from the other side of the Pacific, from one who has seen Le Duc Tho five times and Xuan Thuy nine times.

I agree the Vietnamese are heroic people. The same qualities which make the Vietnamese such great fighters make it hard for them to make peace. The single-mindedness with which the Vietnamese people fight may deprive them of the perspective to make peace. If some of their friends, and you may not want to reply to this, can help with their perspective so that they understand that some political evolution is necessary, then we could end the war rapidly. If the war continues it will not be in the interest of the people of Indochina, or peace, but only perhaps for outside peoples. It would only disturb our relationship.

The two principles you mentioned, we are prepared to accept them . . .

. . . President Nixon has two objectives:

First of all, he is dedicated to ending the war, and he has already withdrawn over 300,000 troops.

Secondly, he is also dedicated not to sign a peace which will undermine our basic principles in the world. I frankly believe that this would not be in your interest. If we are to have a permanent relationship, it is in your interest that we are a reliable country.

We must look at it from the point of view of a great country, not in terms of a local problem. Therefore, we may need to continue if we do not get reasonable terms, such as I have mentioned, which I have presented and will propose again Monday to the North Vietnamese. The war may have to continue, no matter what the newspapers say. But to continue is not in the interests of the peace of the world. There's no sense in continuing the war . . .

[W]e are not children, and history will not stop on the day a peace agreement is signed. If local forces develop again, and are not helped from forces outside, we are not likely to again come 10,000 miles. We are not proposing a treaty to stop history . . .

Our position is not to maintain any particular government in South Vietnam. We are prepared to undertake specific obligations restricting the support we can give to the government after a peace settlement and defining the relationship we can maintain with it after a peace settlement.

What we cannot do is to participate in the overthrow of people with whom we have been allied, whatever the origin of the alliance.

If the government is as unpopular as you seem to think, then the quicker our forces are withdrawn the quicker it will be overthrown. And if it is overthrown after we withdraw, we will not intervene.

9
PEACE AND WAR

A PEACE AGREEMENT BEGAN to take shape in 1972 following one more explosion of violence: the communist Easter Offensive and the intense U.S.–South Vietnamese counterattack. With utmost solemnity, U.S., North Vietnamese, and South Vietnamese leaders signed the Paris agreements on January 27, 1973, but the treaty was hardly the end of conflict in Vietnam. Within weeks, North and South Vietnamese forces had resumed combat. The fighting would stop only on April 30, 1975, when communist forces captured Saigon and definitively ended thirty years of fighting over Vietnam's postcolonial political order.

The major U.S. concession in 1971—that North Vietnamese troops could remain in the South following a cease-fire—sparked intense negotiations in Paris, but a deal remained elusive. Washington continued to insist that the South Vietnamese regime of Nguyen Van Thieu must remain in office after the fighting ended, while Hanoi insisted that Thieu must be removed. Although Moscow and Beijing pressed North Vietnam to concede the point, Hanoi leaders remained adamant. And so the war continued.

In the spring of 1972, Le Duan and his allies abandoned the defensive posture they had held over the previous two years and launched a major new military campaign, known in the West as the Easter Offensive. Communist forces, relying on sophisticated equipment supplied by the Soviets and Chinese, advanced quickly. Yet South Vietnamese resistance and especially intensive U.S. bombing brought communist progress to a halt in the middle of the year. It was clear that the United States, despite its dwindling ground force, could still play a major role in Vietnam.

Far from ending the war, the Easter Offensive and the successful U.S.–South Vietnamese response demonstrated that the fighting had entered a new, even costlier period of stalemate. For the first time since talks had opened in 1969, both sides decided that their interests lay in making a deal. Following the Easter Offensive, Hanoi conceded that the South Vietnamese regime could remain in place alongside a new tripartite body designed to oversee eventual elections for a new government. Following a final U.S. bombing campaign against North Vietnam at the end of 1972 intended mostly to demonstrate Washington's ongoing commitment to defend South Vietnam, the two sides struck a deal on January 23, 1973.

Provisions of the Paris accords affecting the United States were quickly implemented. Washington withdrew the last of its soldiers from the South, and North Vietnam released all 591 American prisoners of war. It required little imagination, however, to see that the peace would not hold. Both North and South Vietnamese forces quickly violated the cease-fire, leading to major fighting by the end of 1973. Nixon pledged to defend South Vietnam, but his promises carried less weight as the Watergate scandal eroded his authority and ultimately forced him from office in August 1974. Exhausted by the war and hostile to Nixon's priorities, Congress forbade further U.S. military operations in Southeast Asia and reduced funding for the South Vietnamese army. Hurt by those cuts but also suffering from the same basic shortcomings that had plagued it since 1954, the South Vietnamese state collapsed in the face of a major Northern offensive in the first months of 1975.

DOCUMENT 9.1

Chinese Pressure for a Deal
Meeting between Chinese Premier Zhou Enlai and North Vietnamese Chief Negotiator Le Duc Tho, July 12, 1972

The Nixon administration hoped that its bold decision to reopen relations with communist China, culminating in President Nixon's trip to Beijing in February 1972, would pay dividends in Vietnam. More specifically, Americans hoped that Chinese leaders would be so eager for improved relations with Washington that they would apply pressure on Hanoi to make peace on terms acceptable to the United States. By the middle of 1972, the U.S. approach was finally paying some dividends. In the following summary of a conversation held in Beijing, Chinese Premier Zhou Enlai makes clear to the top North Vietnamese negotiator, Le Duc Tho, that Beijing wished to see Hanoi back down on the key remaining sticking point in the Paris talks: the status of the South Vietnamese regime under General Nguyen Van Thieu. The North Vietnamese insisted that Thieu must leave office as part of any peace deal, while the Americans demanded that Thieu remain. Later in 1972, after taking stock of North Vietnam's failure to end the war through the Easter Offensive, the Hanoi government accepted the Chinese view, dropping the demand for Thieu's resignation.

Zhou Enlai: On the one hand, it is necessary to prepare for fighting. On the other hand, you have to negotiate. China has some experience with that. We also conducted fighting and negotiating with Jiang Jieshi. During the Korean War, we fought one year and negotiated two years. Therefore, your tactic of fighting and negotiating, that you have been conducting since 1968, is correct.

At first, when you initiated negotiations, some of our comrades thought that you had chosen the wrong moment. I even said to comrades Le Duan and Pham Van Dong that you had to choose the moment to start negotiations when you were in an advantageous position. Yet, comrade Mao said that it was correct to have negotiations at that time and that you were also prepared to fight. Only you would know when the right moment for negotiations was. And your decision was correct, thus showing that comrade Mao was more farsighted than we were.

We do not recognize Nguyen Van Thieu as he is a puppet of the US. Yet we can recognize him as a representative of one of the three forces in the coalition government. The coalition government will negotiate the basic principles for it to observe and control the situation after the US withdrawal of troops. The US will see that Thieu is sharing power in that government, and therefore, find it easier to accept a political solution. In case negotiations among the three forces fail, we will fight again. Similar situations can be found in Kashmir and the Middle East.

Le Duc Tho: But we still think of a government without Thieu.

Zhou Enlai: We are asking the US to remove Thieu. However, if we hint that Thieu can be accepted, the US will be surprised because they do not expect that. Of course, Thieu cannot be a representative of a government. But in negotiations, surprise is necessary.

In the pro-American force, Thieu is a chieftain. He is the one that sells out his country. Yet, he plays a decisive role in his party. We, therefore, cannot solve anything if we only talk with other figures in his party rather than him. Of course how to solve this problem is your job. However, as comrades, we would like to refer to our experience: In the civil war, no result would be gained if we insisted on talking with Jiang's ministers but not with Jiang himself. In the Korean War, we talked with Eisenhower. At the Geneva Conference, because [French Prime Minister Georges] Bidault was stubborn, siding with the US, talks did not continue. When [Bidault's successor as Prime Minister in 1954, Pierre] Mendes-France came to power and was interested in negotiations, the problem was solved. That means we have to talk with the chieftains. Again, our talks with the US did not proceed until the visit by Nixon to China. [North Korean Prime Minister] Comrade Kim Il Sung is also trying to talk directly with [South Korean President] Park Chung Hee. We do the same in our relations with Japan. These are historical facts. The CCP Politburo has discussed this matter, but it is up to you to decide.

May I put it another way: you can talk directly with Thieu and his deputy, thus showing that you are generous to him when he is disgraced. Since Thieu is still the representative of the Right faction, and there is not yet anyone to replace him, the US can be assured that their people are in power. The NLF should also name its representative, who may be Mr. Nguyen Huu Tho or Mr. Huynh Tan Phat, and the neutralist faction should also do the same. However, the real struggle will be between the NLF and the Right faction.

Le Duc Tho: We are asking Thieu to resign. If he does not, we will not talk with the Saigon government.

Zhou Enlai: If he does, who will replace him?

Le Duc Tho: We are ready to talk with anyone.

Zhou Enlai: That also means Thieu's policy without him.

Le Duc Tho: But they have to compromise.

Zhou Enlai: On general elections?

Le Duc Tho: We have not mentioned general elections. If they agree on a tripartite government and recognize the power of this government, then we agree to hold general elections.

Zhou Enlai: General elections will be very dangerous, maybe more dangerous than Thieu being the representative of the Right faction, not to mention international supervision and control of the elections.

Le Duc Tho: We hold that a tripartite government must be established. One of the duties of this government is to hold elections. And free elections require realization of democratic rights . . .

Zhou Enlai: Chairman Mao has also spent much time talking with me on the question of a tripartite government. He told me to talk with you on this issue. We also have experience on this issue. A coalition government could be established, but we later had to resume fighting. The question is to play for time with a view to letting North Vietnam recover, thus getting stronger while the enemy is getting weaker.

DOCUMENT 9.2

Coercing Saigon to Accept a Deal

Notes of a Meeting in Paris between National Security Adviser Henry Kissinger and Nguyen Phu Duc, Special Assistant to the South Vietnamese President, November 24, 1972

U.S. and North Vietnamese negotiators reached a tentative deal on October 8, 1972. The keys to the agreement were a major concession that Washington had already offered (North Vietnamese troops could remain in the South after a cease-fire) and a new one offered by Hanoi (South Vietnamese President Nguyen Van Thieu could remain in office). Kissinger announced that "peace is at hand." But the deal quickly unraveled because of opposition from South Vietnam. President Thieu objected especially to the provision allowing Northern soldiers to remain in the South. Nixon and Kissinger were infuriated that their allies in Saigon were scuttling a complex deal years in the making. With U.S.–South Vietnamese tensions running high and the agreement hanging in the balance, Kissinger met with senior South Vietnamese officials on November 24 in Paris. Kissinger opened the meeting by reading a letter he had received from Nixon threatening to cut off U.S. aid for South Vietnam if Saigon did not accept the deal. Participants in the meeting included Thieu's special assistant, Nguyen Phu Duc, as well as U.S. Deputy National Security Adviser Alexander Haig and William Sullivan, deputy assistant secretary of state. Nixon did not follow through on his threat to cut off U.S. aid, and, in a gesture of solidarity with Saigon, ordered intensive bombing of North Vietnam at the end of December. But Saigon understood American impatience and swallowed its doubts in January, when a peace deal—essentially the same agreement that had fallen apart in the fall—was signed.

Dr. Kissinger: . . . I . . . want to read you a message I have received from the President, of which I will give you a copy:

"November 24, 1972

"I have checked today as to the attitude of the leading Democrats and Republicans who support us in the Senate on Vietnam. In preparing them for the consultation which must take place once agreement is reached we have informed them of the key elements of the October 8 agreement: the return of our POWs, a ceasefire, and a formula under which Thieu remains in power and all South Vietnamese have an opportunity to participate in a free election to determine what government they want for the future. The result of this check indicates that they were not only unanimous but vehement in stating their conclusions that if Saigon is the only roadblock for reaching agreement on this basis they will personally lead the fight when the new Congress reconvenes on January 3 to cut off all military and economic assistance to Saigon. My evaluation is that the date of the cut-off would be February 1. They further believe that under such circumstances we have no choice but to go it alone and to make a separate deal with North Vietnam for the return of our POWs and for our withdrawal.

"These are men who have loyally supported us on November 3, Cambodia, and Laos, and May 8. They have great affection for the South Vietnamese people and great respect for President Thieu personally, but they point out that the votes in the Senate this past year for appropriations for support of the effort in Vietnam have been won only by great effort and by very small margins. They also point out that this time the House cannot save appropriations because the Senate would block any House move to restore funds which, incidentally, in view of the makeup of the new House, is highly unlikely, by simply letting the appropriations bill die in conference.

"This message, unless you have strong feelings otherwise, should be immediately passed on through the South Vietnamese negotiators to Thieu. Tell him the fat is in the fire. It is time to fish or cut bait. We do not want to go it alone. I personally want to stand by Thieu and the South Vietnamese Government but as I have told him in three separate messages, what really counts is not the agreement but my determination to take massive action against North Vietnam in the event they break the agreement. The North Vietnamese troops in the South mean absolutely nothing in that eventuality. If they had no forces there at all and I refused to order air retaliation on the North when infiltration started to begin, the war would be resumed and the outcome would be very much in doubt.

"You must tell Thieu that I feel we have now reached the crossroads. [Either] he trusts me and signs what I have determined is the best agreement we can get or we have to go it alone and end our own involvement in the war on the best terms we can get. I do not give him this very tough option by personal desire, but because of the political reality in the United States it is not possible for me, even with the massive mandate I personally received in the election, to get the support from a hostile Congress to continue the war when the North Vietnamese on October 8 offered an agreement which was far better than both the House and the Senate by resolution and directive to the President during this last session indicated they thought we ought to accept.

"Tell Thieu that I cannot keep the lid on his strong supporters in the House and Senate much longer. They are terribly disturbed by what they read and hear out of Saigon. It is time for us to decide to go forward together or to go our separate ways. If we go separate ways, all that we fought for, for so many years, will be lost. If, on the other hand, he will join us in going forward together on the course I have laid out we can, over the long pull, win a very significant victory.

"The third option of our trying to continue to go forward together on the basis of continuing the war is simply not open. The door has been slammed shut hard and fast by the longtime supporters of the hard line in Vietnam in the House and Senate who control the purse strings."

This is all I have to tell you. I will see Le Duc Tho at 10 o'clock in the morning and seek a postponement of one week. If he refuses a negotiation, we have no choice but to go our own way. If he accepts a negotiation you have one week for consultations.

If you wish to get in touch with me before 10 o'clock, you are free to do so . . .

Mr. Duc: Did you give [Le Duc Tho] our November 19 proposal about withdrawal of North Vietnamese troops and demobilization in two phases? What was his reaction?

Dr. Kissinger: I told him. He said there were no North Vietnamese in the South and the only forces are southerners or the sons of southerners who regrouped in the North. I told you yesterday this was an absurdity. I told him today that it was a lie, which we went along with only because it has the advantage of not claiming any North Vietnamese right to keep forces in the South. It is the principal subject we have discussed. Out of twenty hours of conversation with him we have spent almost sixteen on this . . .

If the provisions on Laos and Cambodia and the DMZ are maintained they cannot maintain their forces in the South. If these provisions are not kept, adding an additional provision that is not maintained won't help . . .

They tell us that they have given up their demand for the immediate resignation of President Thieu and the installation of a coalition government, and stripped their political demands to nothing.

Mr. Duc: You say the agreement is a surrender for them, but there are a number of obligations for the United States and South Vietnam, but what obligations are there for North Vietnam?

Dr. Kissinger: The ceasefire, respect for the DMZ, Laos and Cambodia, and a political process. In all other negotiations they have constantly demanded the resignation of Thieu and a coalition government. As a result of this agreement, the legitimacy of the GVN is established, the possibility of unlimited American aid is legally maintained for the postwar period, and the possibility of strong American action to defend the agreement is preserved. I told President Thieu that we should treat this as a joint victory. You have managed to turn it from a victory into a setback.

If the President—who has supported you all alone, all along—has lost his patience as this letter indicates, imagine how the others are . . .

Mr. Duc: Whatever the decision President Nixon has to take, we remain grateful for all your help, particularly Vietnamization, which has succeeded. But for us to accept an agreement that does not explicitly deal with the North Vietnamese troops, our Government could not explain to the people.

Dr. Kissinger: I will ask him for one week. If he accepts you have a deadline. If he refuses, the negotiations are at an end and the consequences described in the President's letter will take place . . .

We have to look at it from our point of view. For four years, by maneuvering and manipulation, we have managed to keep the Congress from passing resolutions requiring United States withdrawal in exchange for our POWs. This was my nightmare. On October 8 I thought that their acceptance of our proposal plus your enthusiastic support would make the American people so proud of what we had achieved that they would enable us to support your government. Imagine now the attitude of a Mid-westerner who reads every day that we are accused of betrayal. If it is portrayed as a worthless agreement, how can the American people support it?

What is your protection? Your protection is our unity. Your protection is our enthusiastic support. You won't be able to wave a document at them, whatever is in it. The North Vietnamese fear is whether the B-52s may come again; if we convince them of this, the agreement will be kept. If we can't convince them of this, all your 69 changes mean nothing.

We think we are watching a suicide. You are losing your public support. Why did we want an agreement in October, in November and now? The election meant nothing. If we got it now it would be our success. If it happens next March, every liberal newspaper in the country would think it had brought it about.

It has to be an agreement that you say is a success.

If we had wanted to sell you out, we had more opportunities for this. We have fought for four years and sent you another billion dollars of aid.

Mr. Duc: We never said it was a sell-out.

Dr. Kissinger: That is the impression you are giving in America.

Mr. Duc: You say the best guarantee is not a scrap of paper but your willingness to retaliate. I am not arguing with this. But if there is no provision about the North Vietnamese troops, on what basis could you retaliate?

Dr. Kissinger: In the agreement there are the following provisions: respect for the DMZ, respect for Laos and Cambodia, a ceasefire, a ban on the introduction of military personnel into South Vietnam, and military equipment on a replacement basis. In addition, there is the unilateral statement we gave you yesterday in which we announce that we do not recognize any right of North Vietnam to keep troops in the South. And in his speech announcing the agreement, the President would say that if there is any violation we would respond violently.

I must tell you, the next thing our opponents will do is try to undermine any remaining obligation of ours to you. The more we disagree, the easier it is for them . . .

General Haig: Mutual confidence between us is the key and this has broken down.

Mr. Duc: No, we still maintain confidence in you.

Dr. Kissinger: Not actively.

Mr. Duc: The disagreement is because Vietnam is an important problem for you but a vital matter for us . . .

Dr. Kissinger: Let me make a more fundamental point. We have no more time for debate. We do not believe you can start another round of discussions. There is no more time for working groups and memoranda. The President will tell you the same. Hopefully Le Duc Tho will agree to another meeting. Hopefully, we can bluff him with a threat of air attacks—which we did. By the latest by next Thursday, we will have a common position or we will go alone . . .

The choice isn't between this agreement and the continuation of the war. It is between this agreement and a Congressional cut-off of aid. We don't like it. Your choice is to join with us or destroy yourselves. These are facts. I tried to tell you this in Saigon. General Haig tried to tell you this in Saigon.

General Haig: One other thing is not understood. At present Hanoi is licked, defeated.

Mr. Duc: Militarily, not politically.

Dr. Kissinger: Militarily and politically, because the cadres know what they fought for. When I first told Le Duc Tho our proposal for a ceasefire some years ago, he laughed: "Did we fight for twenty years to stop fighting? We have fought to bring about a political solution. The objective of war is victory." Yet now he is pushing for a ceasefire without a political settlement. His cadre knows what this means. The fruit of ten years of revolutionary war is a ceasefire with your government still there.

They are pleading with us for economic aid. Do they think they can get economic aid from us if they are fighting our ally?

Mr. Duc: Economic aid is not a sufficient incentive . . .

DOCUMENT 9.3

A Plea for Continued American Support

Letter from South Vietnamese President Nguyen Van Thieu to U.S. President Gerald R. Ford, September 19, 1974

When the Paris agreement was signed in January 1973, President Richard Nixon assured President Nguyen Van Thieu that the United States remained strongly dedicated to the defense of South Vietnam even though American troops were going home. As new fighting between North and South Vietnamese forces intensified over the ensuring months, however, it became clear that Nixon's assurances, essentially personal promises from one leader to another, had little meaning in Washington. The Watergate scandal badly undermined Nixon's power and then led to his resignation in August 1974. Meanwhile, the U.S. Congress grew increasingly hostile to proposals for new military and economic aid for South Vietnam, which many Americans perceived as a corrupt and wasteful dictatorship on which the United States had already spent far too much. The widening gap between South Vietnamese expectations and U.S. intentions poisoned relations between Saigon and Washington as North Vietnamese forces gained ground. In the following letter dated September 19, 1974, President Thieu appealed to President Gerald R. Ford to live up to what South Vietnamese leaders regarded as ironclad promises.

About a month ago, I wrote to Your Excellency about the situation facing the Republic of Viet-Nam as the Communist side spurned all negotiations and stepped up their armed attacks in complete disregard of the Paris Agreement.

Since then, the situation has become even more serious. In fact, the prospects for the resumption of the talks between the two South Vietnamese parties are bleaker than ever, while the Communist generalized offensive continues unabated. Now the leaders of the Hanoi regime openly declare their active support for movements aimed at overthrowing the legal Government of the Republic of Viet-Nam while they intensify their infiltrations and military action, thus baring their plans for a forcible conquest of the whole South Viet-Nam.

I think that the main cause for the increasingly defiant and bellicose attitude of the Communists resides in their believing that the United States is now wavering in its dedication to our common goal, namely a South Viet-Nam capable of defending itself and of deciding its own future. The utterly inadequate amount of military and economic aid to the Republic of Viet-Nam which has been voted by the U.S. Congress might have induced the Communists to make such speculations.

This can in turn lead to very dangerous miscalculations on the part of the Communists, as they might be tempted to launch an allout offensive to complete their forcible conquest of South Viet-Nam.

Therefore, it is essential that the United States unmistakably demonstrates once again its attachment to a serious implementation of the Paris Agreement and its support for the Government of the Republic of Viet-Nam, if peace is to be restored in South Viet-Nam and South East Asia.

In this respect, I am most appreciative of your efforts made on September 12th to persuade leaders of Congress to restore the cuts in aid funds. I sincerely hope that Your Excellency will succeed in bringing the amounts of military and economic assistance up to the levels required by the new realities of the situation and the need for South Viet-Nam to achieve an economic takeoff.

The Government of the Republic of Viet-Nam had signed the Paris Agreement in good faith, under the double assurance that, on the one hand, Russia and Red China will exercise a restraining influence upon Hanoi and that, on the other hand, all necessary military equipments and economic assistance will be provided by the United States to the Republic of Viet-Nam to maintain its capabilities of selfdefense and to develop its national economy.

The first assumption turned out to be an empty promise, as Russia and Red China continue to give North Vietnam all the ingredients to pursue an aggressive war in South Viet-Nam.

But I am convinced that thanks to your generous efforts, the second assumption will be borne out.

Our valiant soldiers by enduring daily sacrifices in the battlefields have proved beyond doubt our will to resist Communist aggression. If would be unfortunate indeed if sufficient means could not be supplied to them because of the lack of resolve and misconception on the part of our allies.

Besides providing us with an adequate amount of military and economic assistance, the United States can also show its support for the just cause of the Republic of Viet-Nam by solemnly restating our common goals. In this regard, I hope that some time in the near future, we can meet together to discuss about ways and means to achieve a genuine peace in South Viet-Nam.

DOCUMENT 9.4

The Final Offensive

Reminiscence of Events in January to March 1975 by North Vietnamese Major General Tran Cong Man, Published in 1990

How boldly should North Vietnam seek to overrun the South? This question weighed heavily on North Vietnamese leaders in late 1974 and early 1975. Communist forces had tried three times—in 1964, 1968, and 1972—to achieve a total military victory, and each time they had failed. Now the situation was different because American combat forces had been withdrawn. But the United States might intervene again to save South Vietnam, and South Vietnamese forces might put up stiff resistance. In the passage below, Major General Tran Cong Man of the North Vietnamese Army recalls the crucial battles that resolved Hanoi's uncertainties and sealed Saigon's fate. Communist forces first captured Phuoc Long province in January and then overran the strategically important city of Ban Me Thuot in March, leading the Saigon government to withdraw South Vietnamese forces from the Central Highlands.

Phuoc Long province was liberated in early 1975. The attack on Phuoc Long left us with two possible results after its liberation. Either it would be retaken or it would be forever in our hands. And it was the first experiment by our Army to see what the situation was in the South.

In order to regain Phuoc Long the South Vietnamese government would have to have intensive military aid from the American government. But we were not afraid that would happen, because the attack took place after the Watergate business and there were clear signs that the American public was fed up with the war and the American Congress was becoming dispassionate toward the South Vietnamese.

If you want to win a war, you have to understand the other side, their government. Maybe the planners in Hanoi could not get the finer details of how the Americans operated, but the general patterns we saw and understood, so we had a pretty good idea of how Americans behaved and what we could expect from them.

The morale of the South Vietnamese soldiers was attached to the air power of the American government, and when that decreased, so did their morale. The common soldiers were tired of the war; going on with fighting when the war didn't go anywhere. But the war meant something for the officers in the South Vietnamese Army and their morale was higher, because they knew that if the war should end, their careers would be over.

The Phuoc Long attack was a carefully calculated experiment. We wanted to test the American and the South Vietnamese governments. If we struck Quang Tri, for example, or Danang, that would be too far away and we could not test their response. If we struck Saigon that would be too close. So Phuoc Long was just about the right distance from Saigon, we felt. And, of course, there was no response. That was what we wanted to find out—would they respond or were they ready to let go? They were ready to let go . . .

In the attack in Ban Me Thuot we surprised the South Vietnamese. On the other hand, the South Vietnamese troops surprised us, too, because they became so disorganized so quickly. We did not expect that to happen. We thought that after the attack on Ban Me Thuot the South Vietnamese troops would draw the line there and fight back. We had expected a very intense and long battle with the South around Ban Me Thuot. But the way Mr. Thieu responded to the attack was not even within our imagination.

In fact, his response created a great question in our minds as to whether or not this was a trap, a brilliant tactic to lure us in . . . But when Thieu withdrew his troops from Pleiku, we realized suddenly that there was no trap, and there was no plan, and the South was not up to fighting anymore. That is when we decided to chase them as fast as we could.

In the beginning, in the 1970s, the American government had used B-52s to fight us, and we were wary of that; but in 1975 that was not an issue anymore because the Americans were not successful in 1972 in bombing us out of South Vietnam, so we knew that there was only the remotest chance that the Americans would try that again.

After we had liberated the central area of Vietnam, there was some diplomatic work between the U.S. government and Hanoi in order to slow down the movement of Northern troops.

But this was not done directly between us, but between a number of other countries and intermediaries. The Americans were asking us to slow down our armies in order to give the Americans time to complete the withdrawal from Saigon. They warned us that if we did not do that, they would intervene again in Vietnam and make the offensive a very costly one for us. That is what we were told.

But we didn't take that seriously any more. It was just a meaningless threat in 1975, and we knew it. The Americans were not coming back again.

So despite the warnings there was no slowdown of movement. On the contrary, we quickened our steps so we would not have to fight during the monsoon season. We wanted to be in Saigon before the rain started. If there had been any moment when it seemed that there was a slowdown, it was due only to the need for a tactical deployment of our troops.

I wasn't in the few privileged to know about this, but it was my opinion that the offensive was managed exclusively by us and there was absolutely no outside planning with the Russians or the Chinese.

After the Paris Agreement there was a diminishing in arms supplies from other socialist countries. But for China it was different, because prior to the Paris Agreement, China and the U.S. had the Shanghai Agreement [resulting from the U.S.–Chinese summit in 1972], and judging by the announcement it was clear that China would not support us and did not really want to have an end to the war in Vietnam. China wasn't really that pleased or happy about the war finally being resolved or about our Great Spring Victory.

The high-ranking officers in South Vietnam were trying to get an agreement to end the war. When they saw that they were going to lose, they suddenly decided that they wanted a coalition government. But we ordered our troops to press on and end the war with a complete victory as soon as possible. We were not interested in any coalition government in Saigon. It was too late.

A Last-Minute Appeal

Statement by Secretary of State Henry Kissinger to the Senate Appropriations
Committee, April 15, 1975

In the spring of 1975, North Vietnamese forces overran much of South Vietnam,
including, in late March, the major cities of Da Nang and Hue. Heavy fighting
erupted on April 9 at Xuan Loc, a city considered the last line of defense for
the capital, Saigon. With the very existence of South Vietnam in jeopardy,
the Ford administration asked Congress for an additional $722 million in
emergency military aid to help Saigon's forces make a last stand. In the document below, Secretary of State Henry Kissinger appeals to the Senate Foreign
Relations Committee to approve the request. Kissinger knew he faced a difficult task. Congress had steadily cut U.S. military support for South Vietnam
over the previous two years and showed little enthusiasm for new spending
on what increasingly appeared a lost cause. Some historians believe Kissinger
sincerely hoped to rescue South Vietnam; others believe he was mainly trying
to shift the blame onto Congress for Saigon's inevitable collapse. In any case,
Congress rejected the request, approving only smaller funds for humanitarian
purposes.

While North Viet-Nam had available several reserve divisions which it could
commit to battle at times and places of its choosing, the South had no strategic reserves. Its forces were stretched thin, defending lines of communication
and population centers throughout the country.

While North Viet-Nam, by early this year, had accumulated in South Viet-Nam
enough ammunition for two years of intensive combat, South Vietnamese commanders had to ration ammunition as their stocks declined and were not replenished.

While North Viet-Nam had enough fuel in the South to operate its tanks and
armored vehicles for at least 18 months, South Viet-Nam faced stringent shortages.

In sum, while Hanoi was strengthening its army in the South, the combat effectiveness of South Viet-Nam's army gradually grew weaker. While Hanoi built up its
reserve divisions and accumulated ammunition, fuel, and other military supplies,
U.S. aid levels to Viet-Nam were cut—first by half in 1973 and then by another third
in 1974. This coincided with a worldwide inflation and a fourfold increase in fuel
prices. As a result almost all of our military aid had to be devoted to ammunition and
fuel. Very little was available for spare parts, and none for new equipment.

These imbalances became painfully evident when the offensive broke full force,
and they contributed to the tragedy which unfolded. Moreover, the steady diminu-
tion in the resources available to the Army of South Viet-Nam unquestionably
affected the morale of its officers and men. South Vietnamese units in the northern and central provinces knew full well that they faced an enemy superior both in

numbers and in firepower. They knew that reinforcements and resupply would not be forthcoming. When the fighting began they also knew, as they had begun to suspect, that the United States would not respond. I would suggest that all of these factors added significantly to the sense of helplessness, despair, and, eventually, panic which we witnessed in late March and early April . . .

Neither the United States nor South Viet-Nam entered into the Paris agreement with the expectation that Hanoi would abide by it in every respect. We did believe, however, that the agreement was sufficiently equitable to both sides that its major provisions could be accepted and acted upon by Hanoi and that the contest could be shifted thereby from a military to a political track. However, our two governments also recognized that, since the agreement manifestly was not self-enforcing, Hanoi's adherence depended heavily on maintaining a military parity in South Viet-Nam. So long as North Viet-Nam confronted a strong South Vietnamese army and so long as the possibility existed of U.S. intervention to offset the strategic advantages of the North, Hanoi could be expected to forgo major military action. Both of those essential conditions were dissipated over the past two years. Hanoi attained a clear military superiority, and it became increasingly convinced that U.S. intervention could be ruled out. It therefore returned to a military course, with the results we have seen.

The present situation in Viet-Nam is ominous. North Viet-Nam's combat forces far outnumber those of the South, and they are better armed. Perhaps more important, they enjoy a psychological momentum which can be as decisive as armaments in battle. South Viet-Nam must reorganize and reequip its forces, and it must restore the morale of its army and its people. These tasks will be difficult, and they can be performed only by the South Vietnamese. However, a successful defense will also require resources—arms, fuel, ammunition, and medical supplies—and these can come only from the United States . . .

The objectives of the United States in this immensely difficult situation remain as they were when the Paris agreement was signed—to end the military conflict and establish conditions which will allow a fair political solution to be achieved. We believe that despite the tragic experience to date, the Paris agreement remains a valid framework within which to proceed toward such a solution. However, today, as in 1973, battlefield conditions will affect political perceptions and the outcome of negotiations. We therefore believe that in order for a political settlement to be reached which preserves any degree of self-determination for the people of South Viet-Nam, the present military situation must be stabilized. It is for these reasons that the President has asked Congress to appropriate urgently additional funds for military assistance for Viet-Nam.

I am acutely aware of the emotions aroused in this country by our long and difficult involvement in Viet-Nam. I understand what the cost has been for this nation and why frustration and anger continue to dominate our national debate. Many will argue that we have done more than enough for the Government and the people of South Viet-Nam. I do not agree with that proposition, however, nor do I believe that to review endlessly the wisdom of our original involvement serves a useful purpose now. For despite the agony of this nation's experience in Indochina and the substantial reappraisal which has taken place concerning our proper role there, few would deny that we are still involved or that what we do—or fail to do—will still weigh heavily in the outcome. We cannot by our actions alone insure the survival of South Viet-Nam. But we can, alone, by our inaction assure its demise.

The United States has no legal obligation to the Government and people of South Viet-Nam of which the Congress is not aware. But we do have a deep moral obligation—rooted in the history of our involvement and sustained by the continuing efforts of our friends. We cannot easily set it aside. In addition to the obvious consequences for the people of Viet-Nam, our failure to act in accordance with that obligation would inevitably influence other nations' perceptions of our constancy and our determination. American credibility would not collapse, and American honor would not be destroyed. But both would be weakened, to the detriment of this nation and of the peaceful world order we have sought to build.

DOCUMENT 9.6

Declaring an End to America's War

Speech by President Gerald Ford at Tulane University, April 23, 1975

On April 22, 1975, North Vietnamese forces captured the strategically important city of Xuan Loc, east of Saigon. The path lay open for the conquest of the South Vietnamese capital and final communist triumph after thirty years of war. Desperate to stave off that outcome, the South Vietnamese regime pleaded with Washington for military aid, but Congress rejected the Ford administration's emergency request. In a speech at Tulane University in New Orleans on April 23, President Ford affirmed that nothing could, or would, be done to extend the war. Rather, Ford called on Americans to focus on the future. On April 30, North Vietnamese troops occupied Saigon and the South Vietnamese government surrendered.

Today, America can regain the sense of pride that existed before Vietnam. But it cannot be achieved by refighting a war that is finished as far as America is concerned. As I see it, the time has come to look forward to an agenda for the future, to unify, to bind up the Nation's wounds, and to restore its health and its optimistic self-confidence.

. . . In New Orleans tonight, we can begin a great national reconciliation. The first engagement must be with the problems of today, but just as importantly, the problems of the future. That is why I think it is so appropriate that I find myself tonight at a university which addresses itself to preparing young people for the challenge of tomorrow.

I ask that we stop refighting the battles and the recriminations of the past. I ask that we look now at what is right with America, at our possibilities and our potentialities for change and growth and achievement and sharing. I ask that we accept the responsibilities of leadership as a good neighbor to all peoples and the enemy of none. I ask that we strive to become, in the finest American tradition, something more tomorrow than we are today.

Instead of my addressing the image of America, I prefer to consider the reality of America. It is true that we have launched our Bicentennial celebration without having achieved human perfection, but we have attained a very remarkable self-governed society that possesses the flexibility and the dynamism to grow and undertake an entirely new agenda, an agenda for America's third century.

So, I ask you to join me in helping to write that agenda. I am as determined as a President can be to seek national rediscovery of the belief in ourselves that characterized the most creative periods in our Nation's history. The greatest challenge of creativity, as I see it, lies ahead.

We, of course, are saddened indeed by the events in Indochina. But these events, tragic as they are, portend neither the end of the world nor of America's leadership in the world.

Let me put it this way, if I might. Some tend to feel that if we do not succeed in everything everywhere, then we have succeeded in nothing anywhere. I reject categorically such polarized thinking. We can and we should help others to help themselves. But the fate of responsible men and women everywhere, in the final decision, rests in their own hands, not in ours.

America's future depends upon Americans—especially your generation, which is now equipping itself to assume the challenges of the future, to help write the agenda for America.

Earlier today, in this great community, I spoke about the need to maintain our defenses. Tonight, I would like to talk about another kind of strength, the true source of American power that transcends all of the deterrent powers for peace of our Armed Forces. I am speaking here of our belief in ourselves and our belief in our Nation.

Abraham Lincoln asked, in his own words, and I quote, "What constitutes the bulwark of our own liberty and independence?" And he answered, "It is not our frowning battlements or bristling seacoasts, our Army or our Navy. Our defense is in the spirit which prized liberty as the heritage of all men, in all lands everywhere."

It is in this spirit that we must now move beyond the discords of the past decade. It is in this spirit that I ask you to join me in writing an agenda for the future . . .

I envision a creative program that goes as far as our courage and our capacities can take us, both at home and abroad. My goal is for a cooperative world at peace, using its resources to build, not to destroy.

As President, I am determined to offer leadership to overcome our current economic problems. My goal is for jobs for all who want to work and economic opportunity for all who want to achieve.

I am determined to seek self-sufficiency in energy as an urgent national priority. My goal is to make America independent of foreign energy sources by 1985.

Of course, I will pursue interdependence with other nations and a reformed international economic system. My goal is for a world in which consuming and producing nations achieve a working balance.

I will address the humanitarian issues of hunger and famine, of health and of healing. My goal is to achieve—or to assure basic needs and an effective system to achieve this result.

I recognize the need for technology that enriches life while preserving our natural environment. My goal is to stimulate productivity, but use technology to redeem, not to destroy our environment.

I will strive for new cooperation rather than conflict in the peaceful exploration of our oceans and our space. My goal is to use resources for peaceful progress rather than war and destruction.

Let America symbolize humanity's struggle to conquer nature and master technology. The time has now come for our Government to facilitate the individual's control over his or her future—and of the future of America.

But the future requires more than Americans congratulating themselves on how much we know and how many products that we can produce. It requires new knowledge to meet new problems. We must not only be motivated to build a better America, we must know how to do it.

If we really want a humane America that will, for instance, contribute to the alleviation of the world's hunger, we must realize that good intentions do not feed people. Some problems, as anyone who served in the Congress knows, are complex. There are no easy answers. Willpower alone does not grow food.

We thought, in a well-intentioned past, that we could export our technology lock, stock, and barrel to developing nations. We did it with the best of intentions. But we are now learning that a strain of rice that grows in one place will not grow in another; that factories that produce at 100 percent in one nation produce less than half as much in a society where temperaments and work habits are somewhat different.

Yet, the world economy has become interdependent. Not only food technology but money management, natural resources and energy, research and development—all kinds of this group require an organized world society that makes the maximum effective use of the world's resources . . .

America's leadership is essential. America's resources are vast. America's opportunities are unprecedented.

As we strive together to perfect a new agenda, I put high on the list of important points the maintenance of alliances and partnerships with other people and other nations. These do provide a basis of shared values, even as we stand up with determination for what we believe. This, of course, requires a continuing commitment to peace and a determination to use our good offices wherever possible to promote better relations between nations of this world . . .

Your generation of Americans is uniquely endowed by history to give new meaning to the pride and spirit of America. The magnetism of an American society, confident of its own strength, will attract the good will and the esteem of all people wherever they might be in this globe in which we live. It will enhance our own perception of ourselves and our pride in being an American. We can, we can—and I say it with emphasis—write a new agenda for our future.

10
LESSONS AND LEGACIES

THE COMMUNIST TAKEOVER of South Vietnam in April 1975 ended three decades of fighting over Vietnam's postcolonial political and economic order. North Vietnam quickly imposed its rule on the South, and the unified nation was renamed the Socialist Republic of Vietnam the following year. The end of the fighting did not, however, mean the end of bloodshed and controversy. The aftereffects of the war would reverberate in Southeast Asia, the United States, and elsewhere around the world for decades to come.

The communist victory led to arrest, imprisonment, and sometimes execution for many South Vietnamese who had cooperated with the Saigon government or the Americans. Many other Vietnamese suffered the consequences of Hanoi's drive to collectivize agriculture and abolish private enterprise, repression that drove at least a million "boat people" to flee the country. These terrible events paled, however, in comparison to the horrors that unfolded in neighboring Cambodia. The country had been badly destabilized by the fighting in Vietnam, which helped fuel a vicious civil war from which the Khmer Rouge, a radical communist movement headed by the utopian zealot Pol Pot, emerged victorious in April 1975. Over the next four years, the Khmer Rouge murdered an estimated two million Cambodians in its drive to remake the nation. Only gradually did the brutality of the postwar years come to an end for the Indochinese nations, giving way to difficult processes of recovery and reintegration into the global community that continued in the early twenty-first century.

Americans also confronted the physical trauma of war—more than 58,000 deaths and 300,000 wounded veterans. But for most of the nation, the legacies of the war played out more in the psychological, ideological, and political realms. Many Americans drew the lesson that the United States, despite its enormous technological capabilities and material abundance, had only limited power to influence foreign societies and must pull back from international affairs in order to

173

avoid similar imbroglios in the future. Others concluded that the American defeat in Vietnam flowed not from the nation's limitations but from the failure of U.S. leaders to use the power with boldness and confidence. During the remainder of the Cold War and beyond, these two points of view clashed whenever the United States confronted decisions about whether to intervene with military force in the developing world.

If the Vietnam War played a central role in debates about foreign policy, it also occupied a central place in more fundamental debates about the nature of American society and the legacy of the 1960s. Some Americans pointed to the American defeat in Vietnam as a prime example of what could happen if the nation questioned its exceptional role in the world or strayed too far from its supposed core principles. Others viewed the war as a consequence of misplaced patriotism and excessive concentration of power in the hands of the national security establishment. Only the passing of the Vietnam generation seemed likely to diminish the role of the war as a major touchstone of American political debate.

DOCUMENT 10.1

Fleeing Vietnam
Reminiscence by Ai-Van Do of Events from 1975 to 1978, Published in 1990

The North Vietnamese conquest of the South in 1975 brought hardship for many southerners, especially those who had worked for the Saigon government or the Americans. The new government of unified Vietnam imprisoned hundreds of thousands of southerners in "reeducation camps" for varying periods of time and forced many to move to "New Economic Zones"—marginal farmlands in remote areas. Amid growing Vietnamese–Chinese tensions, the government also discriminated against Vietnam's ethnic Chinese population. In the late 1970s and early 1980s, more than a million Vietnamese fled the country, often setting out in small, rickety boats for the Philippines, Indonesia, or other destinations. These "boat people" faced storms, starvation, pirates, and other menaces, and as many as 400,000 died. Many of the survivors spent months or years in refugee camps before being resettled. The following account, written in the late 1990s by a young Vietnamese-American woman named Ai-Van Do, relates her family's experiences in the years following the communist takeover. Along with her parents, Ai-Van Do survived a fierce storm, engine troubles, and the indifference of passing ships as she struggled to reach the Philippines. The family spent one year in a refugee camp before being taken to the United States by Christian missionaries and settling in the Memphis area.

When the Communist forces [defeated] South Vietnam on April 30, 1975, they had succeeded in their domination of Vietnam. It was as if a black curtain had fallen on our country. All of former South Vietnam fell into despair. All the military and naval forces dispersed, and most of them surrendered to the Communist forces. My father also presented himself at the Communist naval headquarters to avoid trouble from the new government. My parents then left Saigon to return to my father's home town of Song Cau, with both joy and sorrow in their hearts. They were joyful because the war was over but sad about leaving Saigon, where they had had so many happy moments together. In their hearts, they knew that they might never see Saigon again. They worried about beginning a new life, not knowing how the Communists would act.

The Communists sent my father to a camp in the mountains to be "reeducated" and to do hard labor. During this time much sorrow and shame burdened my father. My mother was living with my father's family while he was away, and she was pregnant with me. After the government declared my father officially re-educated, they released him. Meanwhile my mother went to Qui Nhon City for the first of their first child.

My parents thought that because the hospital in Qui Nhon City was large, my mother would have better care there than she would in the hospital in my father's small town of Song Cau. After the delivery, she lay sick in the hospital for more than a month and was nearly paralyzed on one side of her body. Others had to attend to all her personal needs. Because new, illiterate "doctors" from the war zones and the North had replaced the hospital's former doctors, they could do nothing for her. They had neither instruction nor medicine . . .

Fortunately, my mother recovered from her illness, and we went back to Song Cau to begin our independent lives as a little family. Instead of living with my grandfather, uncles, and aunts, we built a small hut by the river's edge in my grandfather's beautiful coconut grove. It was from this place that God would later give us the opportunity to organize a successful escape. For a time in Song Cau and the rest of Vietnam, the Communists did not take over personal property. Instead, they urged everyone to increase production to create prosperity for the nation. They urged fishermen to catch more fish and farmers to cultivate idle lands in the mountainous regions. Under the "New Regime," everyone had to work hard. The slogan of the day was "Labor is the glory."

Because my parents had served under the former government, they had to work more strenuously than others. They had to prove to the Communist authorities that they had "awakened" and, thus, could feed themselves. My parents worked at two jobs during this period, fishing and farming, and they had no training for either . . .

Soon the new government became more severe and used collectivism for every type of production. The people did not own their fields, their boats, or any of the things they used to earn a living. The government ended private commerce and centralized all trades under a plan called "two-way commerce." This means that fishermen and farmers, for example, had to sell their products to the government. In return, the government would sell them needed items such as fuel, rice, clothes, meats, and medicine. However, this "two-way commerce" provided the people with too little for a productive life.

The Communists also confiscated the goods of former businesspeople. Therefore, people who still had money could not buy freely. Some of these businesspeople had hidden their goods and would sell to the people at inflated prices. In the cities, the Communists forced many businessmen, soldiers, and civil servants of the former government to leave their homes and go to New Economic Zones. There the people would break new ground and begin farming. The new government confiscated the homes the people had been forced to leave.

The Communists stripped the people of all their basic freedoms. Of course, they dealt more severely with former soldiers and former civil servants such as my parents. Typically they forced such people to perform hard labor in the harsh mountain regions for several months a year. Because of rough treatment, the people felt as though the Communists were punishing them and getting revenge. Many people died from work-related accidents or malaria. They lived as if they were snails inside their shells and did not dare go anywhere to meet anyone. Now the people understood that their hopes for peace and joy would not be realized. They began to complain and to hope for a return of the former government, as well as a return of the resisting forces still believed to be hiding in the mountains . . .

Earlier, my grandfather had given my parents a small radio. With this radio they listened secretly to the "Source of Life," a religious program broadcast in Vietnamese nightly from Manila. This Christian program, with its message of salvation and hope, brought peace to my parents after each tiring day. Believing that there was truly a God somewhere in all the bitterness and destruction eased my parents' sorrow.

One night in late March 1976 after my parents had listened to the "Source of Life," they continued to listen to the broadcast of Voice of America to hear the world news. This night they learned about a group of Vietnamese refugees who had used a fishing boat to escape from Vietnam and travel across the ocean in search of freedom. A foreign merchant ship had eventually rescued them. Later, my parents learned of others who had escaped in the same way. With this door of hope opened, my mother and father began to discuss plans for escape . . .

On the surface my father was a "good citizen." He did not refuse any labor, he attended reeducation meetings, and he talked with others about the "very good policy of socialism" and about the happiness it would bring the people in the future. However, my parents were leading double lives. Their minds were often in a dream world where they would escape to freedom . . .

Then one day my parents decided to escape on their own, with no looking back. Using my mother's meager part-time earnings as a seamstress, they saved a little money again. They still did not know how they would manage, but they were determined to succeed somehow . . .

My parents registered their fishing occupation as their legal reason to live in the coastal region, although my father continued to tend his crops as well. My mother and father developed their fishing with the purchase of more nets and other equipment and a small, old, motorized fishing boat. The boat measured 5 meters, 90 centimeters long and 1 meter, 40 centimeters wide and had a 5-horsepower motor . . .

[One night, an amateur fisherman named Thoi, who had served in the South Vietnamese Army] came to our house, his face pallid with fright, and he asked my mother to put out the light. In the dark he whispered to my father that he had just been ordered to go to a reeducation camp for an unspecified length of time. In the morning he expected my father to receive the same order. If they did not act immediately, the opportunity to escape would be lost. Thoi pleaded with my father to flee . . .

In the dark they groped about getting ready. My parents poured the water in the empty plastic containers and pulled up the floor bricks to get the six cans of fuel. My mother selected a few clothes for us. In the silence of the night, we were afraid our noise would attract the attention of the soldiers who were patrolling. My parents did not fear the departure as much as being caught during preparation.

By 1:30 in the morning, our preparation was complete. Thoi came with a small bag on his back. It was the luggage his wife had prepared for him to go to the reeducation camp. He had secretly left his parents, his wife, and his son.

. . . I was trembling all over when my mother carried me to the boat. My mother whispered: "My daughter, keep silent! If you cry, the Communists will catch us!"

Before my father started the engine, we looked at our home for the last time . . . When the boat was in deep water, we began to run at full speed. As Thoi steered the boat, my father tended the engine. We were braving the waters in a fishing boat that was probably the smallest ever to sail over the sea. We had a simple map of the world, a small compass, and three flashlights to use for plotting our course and for signaling in the night.

Our small boat struggled with many dangers crossing over more than 800 miles from Vietnam to the Philippines during eight days and nights on the sea.

DOCUMENT 10.2

A "Noble Cause"
Speech by Ronald Reagan at the Veterans of Foreign Wars Convention, Chicago, August 18, 1980

Americans of different political and temperamental stripes learned different lessons from the Vietnam War. Many drew the conclusion that the United States must steer clear of new interventions abroad since the nation lacked the power and know-how to achieve its objectives in distant, culturally alien places. Others believed that America's failure in Vietnam flowed from leaders' unwillingness to use sufficient force and concluded that the nation could achieve its goals around the world only if it used the its power with determination. The latter view gained a strong advocate with the rise of Ronald Reagan, who won the presidency in 1980. As the Republican nominee and then as president, Reagan insisted that the United States should feel no shame about the Vietnam War and must once again act with confidence on the world stage. Reagan struck these themes in a campaign speech to the national convention of the Veterans of Foreign Wars on August 18, 1980.

A merica has been sleepwalking far too long. We have to snap out of it, and with your help, that's exactly what we're going to do . . .

Clearly, world peace must be our number one priority. It is the first task of state-craft to preserve peace so that brave men need not die in battle. But it must not be peace at any price; it must not be a peace of humiliation and gradual surrender. Nor can it be the kind of peace imposed on Czechoslovakia by Soviet tanks just 12 years ago this month. And certainly it isn't the peace that came to Southeast Asia after the Paris peace accords were signed.

Peace must be such that freedom can flourish and justice prevail. Tens of thousands of boat people have shown us there is no freedom in the so-called peace in Vietnam. The hill people of Laos know poison gas, not justice, and in Cambodia there is only the peace of the grave for at least one-third of the population slaughtered by the Communists.

For too long, we have lived with the "Vietnam Syndrome." Much of that syndrome has been created by the North Vietnamese aggressors who now threaten the peaceful people of Thailand. Over and over they told us for nearly 10 years that we were the aggressors bent on imperialistic conquests. They had a plan. It was to win in the field of propaganda here in America what they could not win on the field of battle in Vietnam. As the years dragged on, we were told that peace would come if we would simply stop interfering and go home.

It is time we recognized that ours was, in truth, a noble cause. A small country newly free from colonial rule sought our help in establishing self-rule and the means of self-defense against a totalitarian neighbor bent on conquest. We dishonor the memory of 50,000 young Americans who died in that cause when we give way to feelings of guilt as if we were doing something shameful, and we have been shabby in our treatment of those who returned. They fought as well and as bravely as any Americans have ever fought in any war. They deserve our gratitude, our respect, and our continuing concern.

There is a lesson for all of us in Vietnam. If we are forced to fight, we must have the means and the determination to prevail or we will not have what it takes to secure the peace. And while we are at it, let us tell those who fought in that war that we will never again ask young men to fight and possibly die in a war our government is afraid to let them win.

Shouldn't it be obvious to even the staunchest believer in unilateral disarmament as the sure road to peace that peace was never more certain than in the years following World War II when we had a margin of safety in our military power which was so unmistakable that others would not dare to challenge us? . . .

When John F. Kennedy demanded the withdrawal of Soviet missiles from Cuba and the tension mounted in 1962, it was Nikita Khrushchev who backed down, and there was no war. It was because our strategic superiority over the Soviets was so decisive, by about a margin of 8 to 1.

But, then, in the face of such evidence that the cause of peace is best served by strength not bluster, an odd thing happened. Those responsible for our defense policy ignored the fact that some evidence of aggressive intent on the part of the Soviets was surely indicated by the placement of missiles in Cuba. We failed to heed the Soviet declaration that they would make sure they never had to back down again. No one could possibly misinterpret that declaration. It was an announcement of the Soviet intention to begin a military buildup, one which continues to this day . . .

Is it only Jimmy Carter's lack of coherent policy that is the source of our difficulty? Is it his vacillation and indecision? Or is there another, more frightening possibility—the possibility that this administration is being very consistent, that it is still guided by that same old doctrine that we have nothing to fear from the Soviets—if we just don't provoke them.

Well, World War II came about without provocation. It came because nations were weak, not strong, in the face of aggression. Those same lessons of the past surely apply today. Firmness based on a strong defense capability is not provocative. But weakness can be provocative simply because it is tempting to a nation whose imperialist ambitions are virtually unlimited.

We find ourselves increasingly in a position of dangerous isolation. Our allies are losing confidence in us, and our adversaries no longer respect us.

There is an alternative path for America which offers a more realistic hope for peace, one which takes us on the course of restoring that vital margin of safety. For thirty years since the end of World War II, our strategy has been to preserve peace through strength . . .

We must remember our heritage, who we are and what we are, and how this nation, this island of freedom, came into being. And we must make it unmistakably plain to all the world that we have no intention of compromising our principles, our beliefs or our freedom. Our reward will be world peace; there is no other way to have it . . .

DOCUMENT 10.3

The Weinberger Doctrine

Speech by Defense Secretary Caspar Weinberger at the National Press Club, Washington, D.C., November 28, 1984

After winning the presidency in 1980, Ronald Reagan reenergized American foreign policy, dramatically increased defense spending, and spoke of the communist menace in terms reminiscent of the 1950s. Yet Reagan was only partially successful in overcoming the "Vietnam syndrome"—the reluctance to use American power internationally in order to avoid similar fiascos in the future. Wariness about the use of American troops overseas became especially clear after a terrorist bombing killed 241 Marines taking part in an ill-defined peacekeeping mission in Lebanon. Among American officials who sought to reconcile the desire to use force abroad with the nation's persistent mood of caution was Defense Secretary Caspar Weinberger. On November 28, 1984, he delivered a speech laying out what became known as the "Weinberger Doctrine," an approach that generally prevailed among American policymakers for many years to come.

[T]he outcome of decisions on whether—and when—and to what degree—to use combat forces abroad has never been more important than it is today. While we do not seek to deter or settle all the world's conflicts, we must recognize that, as a major power, our responsibilities and interests are now of such scope that there are few troubled areas we can afford to ignore. So we must be prepared to deal with a range of possibilities, a spectrum of crises, from local insurgency to global conflict. We prefer, of course, to limit any conflict in its early stages, to contain and control it—but to do that our military forces must be deployed in a timely manner, and be fully supported and prepared before they are engaged, because many of those difficult decisions must be made extremely quickly.

Some on the national scene think they can always avoid making tough decisions. Some reject entirely the question of whether any force can ever be used abroad. They want to avoid grappling with a complex issue because, despite clever rhetoric disguising their purpose, these people are in fact advocating a return to post-World War I isolationism. While they may maintain in principle that military force has a role in foreign policy, they are never willing to name the circumstance or the place where it would apply.

On the other side, some theorists argue that military force can be brought to bear in any crisis. Some of these proponents of force are eager to advocate its use even in limited amounts simply because they believe that if there are American forces of any size present they will somehow solve the problem.

Neither of these two extremes offers us any lasting or satisfactory solutions. The first—undue reserve—would lead us ultimately to withdraw from international events that require free nations to defend their interests from the aggressive use of force. We would be abdicating our responsibilities as the leader of the free world—responsibilities more or less thrust upon us in the aftermath of World War II—a war incidentally that isolationism did nothing to deter. These are responsibilities we must fulfill unless we desire the Soviet Union to keep expanding its influence unchecked throughout the world. In an international system based on mutual interdependence among nations, and alliances between friends, stark isolationism quickly would lead to a far more dangerous situation for the United States: we would be without allies and faced by many hostile or indifferent nations . . .

[R]ecent history has proven that we cannot assume unilaterally the role of the world's defender. We have learned that there are limits to how much of our spirit and blood and treasure we can afford to forfeit in meeting our responsibility to keep peace and freedom. So while we may and should offer substantial amounts of economic and military assistance to our allies in their time of need, and help them maintain forces to deter attacks against them—usually we cannot substitute our troops or our will for theirs . . .

In those cases where our national interests require us to commit combat forces, we must never let there be doubt of our resolution. When it is necessary for our troops to be committed to combat, we must commit them, in sufficient numbers and we must support them, as effectively and resolutely as our strength permits. When we commit our troops to combat we must do so with the sole object of winning.

Once it is clear our troops are required, because our vital interests are at stake, then we must have the firm national resolve to commit every ounce of strength necessary to win the fight to achieve our objectives. In Grenada we did just that.

Just as clearly, there are other situations where United States combat forces should not be used. I believe the postwar period has taught us several lessons, and from them I have developed six major tests to be applied when we are weighing the use of U.S. combat forces abroad. Let me now share them with you:

(1) First, the United States should not commit forces to combat overseas unless the particular engagement or occasion is deemed vital to our national interest or that of our allies. That emphatically does not mean that we should declare beforehand, as we did with Korea in 1950, that a particular area is outside our strategic perimeter.

(2) Second, if we decide it is necessary to put combat troops into a given situation, we should do so wholeheartedly, and with the clear intention of winning. If we are unwilling to commit the forces or resources necessary to achieve our objectives, we should not commit them at all. Of course if the particular situation requires only limited force to win our objectives, then we should not hesitate to commit forces sized accordingly. When Hitler broke treaties and remilitarized the Rhineland, small combat forces then could perhaps have prevented the holocaust of World War II.

(3) Third, if we do decide to commit forces to combat overseas, we should have clearly defined political and military objectives. And we should know precisely how our forces can accomplish those clearly defined objectives. And we should have and send the forces needed to do just that . . .

(4) Fourth, the relationship between our objectives and the forces we have committed—their size, composition and disposition—must be continually reassessed and adjusted if necessary. Conditions and objectives invariably change during the course of a conflict. When they do change, then so must our combat requirements. We must continuously keep as a beacon light before us the basic questions: "Is this conflict in our national interest?" "Does our national interest require us to fight, to use force of arms?" If the answers are "yes," then we must win. If the answers are "no," then we should not be in combat.

(5) Fifth, before the U.S. commits combat forces abroad, there must be some reasonable assurance we will have the support of the American people and their elected

representatives in Congress. This support cannot be achieved unless we are candid in making clear the threats we face; the support cannot be sustained without continuing and close consultation. We cannot fight a battle with the Congress at home while asking our troops to win a war overseas or, as in the case of Vietnam, in effect asking our troops not to win, but just to be there.

(6) Finally, the commitment of U.S. forces to combat should be a last resort.

I believe that these tests can be helpful in deciding whether or not we should commit our troops to combat in the months and years ahead. The point we must all keep uppermost in our minds is that if we ever decide to commit forces to combat, we must support those forces to the fullest extent of our national will for as long as it takes to win. So we must have in mind objectives that are clearly defined and understood and supported by the widest possible number of our citizens. And those objectives must be vital to our survival as a free nation and to the fulfillment of our responsibilities as a world power. We must also be farsighted enough to sense when immediate and strong reactions to apparently small events can prevent lion-like responses that may be required later. We must never forget those isolationists in Europe who shrugged that "Danzig is not worth a war," and "Why should we fight to keep the Rhineland demilitarized?"

DOCUMENT 10.4

Fifty Years Later
Poster Issued by the Socialist Republic of Vietnam to Mark the Fiftieth Anniversary of Vietnamese Independence, 1995

The Socialist Republic of Vietnam followed a rocky road in the first twenty years after unification in 1976. The first decade brought hardship for many Vietnamese as the government collectivized industry and agriculture and punished citizens who had worked for the South Vietnamese regime or the Americans. Only in 1986 did the nation change course, embracing a series of economic reforms known as *doi moi*, or "renovation." The return of free-market incentives quickly reinvigorated the economy, which achieved some of the fastest growth rates in the world in the 1990s. Still, as in China, the communist party retained its monopoly on power and punished dissidents who spoke out against the regime. In 1995, the government marked the fiftieth anniversary of Ho Chi Minh's declaration of Vietnamese independence. The image here shows one of many celebratory posters designed for the occasion. The words say "A Glorious, Prosperous, and Magnificent Viet Nam."

DOCUMENT 10.5

Toward a New Relationship

Speech by President Bill Clinton, Vietnam National University, Hanoi, November 17, 2000

The United States and Vietnam remained hostile to one another long after the end of the war. Many Americans opposed the reopening of relations with Vietnam until Hanoi helped account for approximately 2,500 U.S. military personnel listed as "missing in action." Meanwhile, the Vietnamese government resented close American ties with China, which emerged as Vietnam's foremost enemy in the mid-1970s. Only in the 1990s, following the end of the Cold War, did Hanoi and Washington gradually overcome these tensions. Washington ended its trade embargo of Vietnam in 1994, and the two nations established full diplomatic relations the following year. In 2000, President Bill Clinton visited Vietnam, speaking warmly of the possibilities for future partnership. His speech at Vietnam National University in Hanoi, excerpted here, was a high point of his visit.

Two centuries ago, during the early days of the United States, we reached across the seas for partners in trade, and one of the first nations we encountered was Vietnam. In fact, one of our Founding Fathers, Thomas Jefferson, tried to obtain rice seed from Vietnam to grow on his farm in Virginia 200 years ago. By the time World War II arrived, the United States had become a significant consumer of exports from Vietnam. In 1945, at the moment of your country's birth, the words of Thomas Jefferson were chosen to be echoed in your own Declaration of Independence: "All men are created equal. The Creator has given us certain inviolable rights—the right to life, the right to be free, the right to achieve happiness."

Of course, all of this common history, 200 years of it, has been obscured in the last few decades by the conflict we call the Vietnam war and you call the American war. You may know that in Washington, D.C., on our National Mall, there is a stark black granite wall engraved with the name of every single American who died in Vietnam. At this solemn memorial, some American veterans also refer to the "other side of the wall," the staggering sacrifice of the Vietnamese people on both sides of that conflict, more than 3 million brave soldiers and civilians.

This shared suffering has given our countries a relationship unlike any other. Because of the conflict, America is now home to one million Americans of Vietnamese ancestry. Because of the conflict, 3 million American veterans served in Vietnam, as did many journalists, embassy personnel, aid workers, and others who are forever connected to your country.

Almost 20 years ago now, a group of American servicemen took the first step to reestablish contacts between the United States and Vietnam. They traveled back to Vietnam for the first time since the war, and as they walked through the streets of Hanoi, they were approached by Vietnamese citizens who had heard of their visit. "Are you the American soldiers?" they asked. Not sure what to expect, our veterans answered, "Yes, we are." And to their immense relief, their hosts simply said, "Welcome to Vietnam." ...

When they came here, they were determined to honor those who fought, without refighting the battles; to remember our history, but not to perpetuate it; to give young people like you in both our countries the chance to live in your tomorrows, not in our yesterdays. As Ambassador Pete Peterson has said so eloquently, "We cannot change the past. What we can change is the future."

Our new relationship gained strength as American veterans launched nonprofit organizations to work on behalf of the Vietnamese people, such as providing devices to people with war injuries to help them lead more normal lives. Vietnam's willingness to help us return the remains of our fallen servicemen to their families has been the biggest boost to improve ties ...

The desire to be reunited with a lost family member is something we all understand. It touches the hearts of Americans to know that every Sunday in Vietnam, one of your most watched television shows features families seeking viewers' help in finding loved ones they lost in the war so long ago now. And we are grateful for the Vietnamese villagers who have helped us to find our missing and, therefore, to give their families the peace of mind that comes with knowing what actually happened to their loved ones.

No two nations have ever before done the things we are doing together to find the missing from the Vietnam conflict. Teams of Americans and Vietnamese work together, sometimes in tight and dangerous places. The Vietnamese Government has offered us access to files and Government information to assist our search. And in turn, we have been able to give Vietnam almost 400,000 pages of documents that could assist in your search. On this trip, I have brought with me another 350,000 pages of documents that I hope will help Vietnamese families find out what happened to their missing loved ones.

Today I was honored to present these to your President, Tran Duc Luong. And I told him that before the year is over, America will provide another million pages of documents. We will continue to offer our help and to ask for your help as we both honor our commitment to do whatever we can for as long as it takes to achieve the fullest possible accounting of our loved ones.

Your cooperation in that mission over these last 8 years has made it possible for America to support international lending to Vietnam, to resume trade between our countries, to establish formal diplomatic relations and, this year, to sign a pivotal trade agreement.

Finally, America is coming to see Vietnam as your people have asked for years, as a country, not a war, a country with the highest literacy rate in Southeast Asia, a country whose young people just won three gold medals at the International Math Olympiad in Seoul, a country of gifted, hard-working entrepreneurs emerging from years of conflict and uncertainty to shape a bright future.

Today the United States and Vietnam open a new chapter in our relationship, at a time when people all across the world trade more, travel more, know more about and talk more with each other than ever before. Even as people take pride in their national independence, we know we are becoming more and more interdependent . . .

Over the last 15 years, Vietnam launched its policy of *doi moi,* joined APEC and ASEAN, normalized relations with the European Union and the United States, and disbanded collective farming, freeing farmers to grow what they want and earn the fruits of their own labor. The results were impressive proof of the power of your markets and the abilities of your people. You not only conquered malnutrition, you became the world's second-largest exporter of rice and achieved stronger overall economic growth . . .

The United States has great respect for your intellect and capacity. One of our Government's largest educational exchange programs is with Vietnam, and we want to do more . . .

Let me say, as important as knowledge is, the benefits of knowledge are necessarily limited by undue restrictions on its use. We Americans believe the freedom to explore, to travel, to think, to speak, to shape decisions that affect our lives enrich the lives of individuals and nations in ways that go far beyond economics.

Now, America's record is not perfect in this area. After all, it took us almost a century to banish slavery. It took us even longer to give women the right to vote. And we are still seeking to live up to the more perfect Union of our Founders' dreams and the words of our Declaration of Independence and Constitution. But along the way over these . . . 224 years we've learned some lessons. For example, we have seen that economies work better where newspapers are free to expose corruption and independent courts can ensure that contracts are honored, that competition is robust and fair, that public officials honor the rule of law.

In our experience, guaranteeing the right to religious worship and the right to political dissent does not threaten the stability of a society. Instead, it builds people's confidence in the fairness of our institutions and enables us to take it when a decision goes in a way we don't agree with. All this makes our country stronger in good times and bad. In our experience, young people are much more likely to have confidence in their future if they have a say in shaping it, in choosing their governmental leaders and having a government that is accountable to those it serves.

Now, let me say emphatically, we do not seek to impose these ideals, nor could we. Vietnam is an ancient and enduring country. You have proved to the world that you will make your own decisions. Only you can decide, for example, if you will continue to share Vietnam's talents and ideas with the world, if you will continue to open Vietnam so that you can enrich it with the insights of others. Only you can decide if you will continue to open your markets, open your society, and strengthen the rule of law. Only you can decide how to weave individual liberties and human rights into the rich and strong fabric of Vietnamese national identity.

DOCUMENT 10.6

Debating the Lessons of Vietnam
Speeches by Senator Edward M. Kennedy on January 9, 2007, and President George W. Bush on August 22, 2007

The debate over the proper lessons of the Vietnam War came to the fore whenever U.S. leaders deliberated the possibility of sending U.S. troops abroad, most notably during the crises in Central America in the 1980s, the First Gulf War and the Balkan wars of the 1990s, and the wars in Afghanistan and Iraq in the early twenty-first century. The following excerpts come from 2007, when American leaders clashed bitterly over President George W. Bush's plan to increase the number of American troops in Iraq despite persistent failure and frustration in the effort to impose peace and order in the country. In the first passage, part of a speech to the National Press Club in Washington on January 9, Democratic Senator Ted Kennedy of Massachusetts proposed legislation to block funding for the increase unless Congress explicitly approved. In the second, Bush defended the "surge" in a speech to the annual convention of the Veterans of Foreign Wars on August 22, by which time Americans were debating whether the increase was paying off.

The American people sent a clear message in November that we must change course in Iraq and begin to withdraw our troops, not escalate their presence. The way to start is by acting on the President's new plan. An escalation, whether it is called a surge or any other name, is still an escalation, and I believe it would be an immense new mistake. It would compound the original misguided decision to invade Iraq. We cannot simply speak out against an escalation of troops in Iraq. We must act to prevent it.

Our history makes clear that a new escalation in our forces will not advance our national security. It will not move Iraq toward self-government, and it will needlessly endanger our troops by injecting more of them into the middle of a civil war.

Some will disagree. Listen to this comment from a high-ranking American official: "It became clear that if we were prepared to stay the course, we could help to lay the cornerstone for a diverse and independent region. If we faltered, the forces of chaos would smell victory, and decades of strife and aggression would stretch endlessly before us. The choice was clear. We would stay the course. And we shall stay the course."

That's not President Bush speaking. It's President Lyndon Johnson, forty years ago, ordering a hundred thousand more American soldiers to Vietnam.

Here's another quotation. "The big problem is to get territory and to keep it. You can get it today, and it will be gone next week. That is the problem. You have to have enough people to clear it and enough people to preserve what you have done."

That is not President Bush on the need for more forces in Iraq. It is President Johnson in 1966 as he doubled our military presence in Vietnam.

Those comparisons from history resonate painfully in today's debate on Iraq. In Vietnam, the White House grew increasingly obsessed with victory and increasingly divorced from the will of the people and any rational policy. The Department of Defense kept assuring us that each new escalation in Vietnam would be the last. Instead, each one led only to the next . . .

Richard Nixon was elected President after telling the American people that he had a secret plan to end the war. We all know what happened, though. As President, he escalated the war into Cambodia and Laos, and it went on for six more years.

There was no military solution to that war. But we kept trying to find one anyway. In the end, 58,000 Americans died in the search for it.

Echoes of that disaster are all around us today. Iraq is George Bush's Vietnam. As with Vietnam, the only rational solution to the crisis is political, not military. Injecting more troops into a civil war is not the answer. Our men and women in uniform cannot force the Iraqi people to reconcile their differences.

The open-ended commitment of our military forces continues to enable the Iraqis to avoid taking responsibility for their own future. Tens of thousands of additional American troops will only make the Iraqis more resentful of America's occupation. It will also make the Iraqi government even more dependent on America, not less . . .

This Congress cannot escape history or its own duty. If we do not learn from the mistakes of the past, we are condemned to repeat them. We must act, and act now, before the President sends more troops to Iraq, or else it will be too late . . .

The heavy price of our flawed decisions a generation ago is memorialized on sacred ground not far from here. On a somber walk through the Vietnam Memorial, we are moved by the painful, powerful eloquence of its enduring tribute to the tens of thousands who were lost in that tragic war that America never should have fought.

Our fingers can gently trace the names etched into the stark black granite face of the memorial. We wonder what might have been if America had faced up honestly to its failed decisions before it was too late.

There are many differences between the wars we fought in the Far East and the war on terror we're fighting today. But one important similarity is at their core they're ideological struggles. The militarists of Japan and the communists in Korea and Vietnam were driven by a merciless vision for the proper ordering of humanity. They killed Americans because we stood in the way of their attempt to force their ideology on others.

Today, the names and places have changed, but the fundamental character of the struggle has not changed. Like our enemies in the past, the terrorists who wage war in Iraq and Afghanistan and other places seek to spread a political vision of their own—a harsh plan for life that crushes freedom, tolerance, and dissent.

Like our enemies in the past, they kill Americans because we stand in their way of imposing this ideology across a vital region of the world. This enemy is dangerous; this enemy is determined; and this enemy will be defeated.

We're still in the early hours of the current ideological struggle, but we do know how the others ended—and that knowledge helps guide our efforts today. The ideals and interests that led America to help the Japanese turn defeat into democracy are the same that lead us to remain engaged in Afghanistan and Iraq.

The defense strategy that refused to hand the South Koreans over to a totalitarian neighbor helped raise up an Asian Tiger that is the model for developing countries across the world, including the Middle East. The result of American sacrifice and perseverance in Asia is a freer, more prosperous and stable continent whose people want to live in peace with America, not attack America . . .

[The Vietnam War] is a complex and painful subject for many Americans. The tragedy of Vietnam is too large to be contained in one speech. So I'm going to limit myself to one argument that has particular significance today. Then as now, people argued the real problem was America's presence and that if we would just withdraw, the killing would end.

The argument that America's presence in Indochina was dangerous had a long pedigree. In 1955, long before the United States had entered the war, Graham Greene wrote a novel called *The Quiet American*. It was set in Saigon, and the main character was a young government agent named Alden Pyle. He was a symbol of American purpose and patriotism—and dangerous naivete. Another character describes Alden this way: "I never knew a man who had better motives for all the trouble he caused."

After America entered the Vietnam War, the Graham Greene argument gathered some steam. As a matter of fact, many argued that if we pulled out there would be no consequences for the Vietnamese people.

In 1972, one antiwar senator put it this way: "What earthly difference does it make to nomadic tribes or uneducated subsistence farmers in Vietnam or Cambodia or Laos, whether they have a military dictator, a royal prince or a socialist commissar in some distant capital that they've never seen and may never [have] heard of?" A columnist for The New York Times wrote in a similar vein in 1975, just as Cambodia and Vietnam were falling to the communists: "It's difficult to imagine," he said, "how their lives could be anything but better with the Americans gone." A headline on that story, dateline Phnom Penh, summed up the argument: "Indochina without Americans: For Most a Better Life."

The world would learn just how costly these misimpressions would be. In Cambodia, the Khmer Rouge began a murderous rule in which hundreds of thousands of Cambodians died by starvation and torture and execution. In Vietnam, former allies of the United States and government workers and intellectuals and businessmen were sent off to prison camps, where tens of thousands perished. Hundreds of thousands more fled the country on rickety boats, many of them going to their graves in the South China Sea.

Three decades later, there is a legitimate debate about how we got into the Vietnam War and how we left. There's no debate in my mind that the veterans from Vietnam deserve the high praise of the United States of America. Whatever your position is on that debate, one unmistakable legacy of Vietnam is that the price of America's withdrawal was paid by millions of innocent citizens whose agonies would add to our vocabulary new terms like "boat people," "re-education camps," and "killing fields."

There was another price to our withdrawal from Vietnam, and we can hear it in the words of the enemy we face in today's struggle—those who came to our soil and killed thousands of citizens on September the 11th, 2001. In an interview with a Pakistani newspaper after the 9/11 attacks, Osama bin Laden declared that "the American people had risen against their government's war in Vietnam. And they must do the same today."

His number two man, Zawahiri, has also invoked Vietnam. In a letter to al Qaeda's chief of operations in Iraq, Zawahiri pointed to "the aftermath of the collapse of the American power in Vietnam and how they ran and left their agents."

Zawahiri later returned to this theme, declaring that the Americans "know better than others that there is no hope in victory. The Vietnam specter is closing every outlet." Here at home, some can argue our withdrawal from Vietnam carried no price to American credibility—but the terrorists see it differently . . .

If we were to abandon the Iraqi people, the terrorists would be emboldened, and use their victory to gain new recruits. As we saw on September the 11th, a terrorist safe haven on the other side of the world can bring death and destruction to the streets of our own cities.

Vietnamistan

Cartoon in the *Columbia Daily Tribune*, September 24, 2009

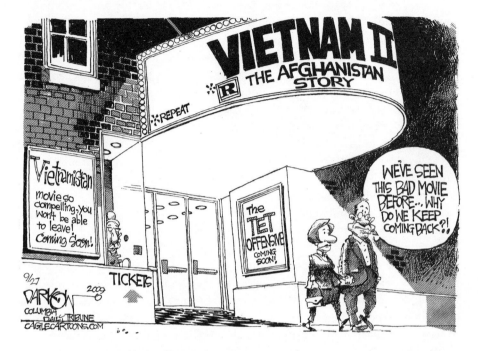

In the fall of 2009, the Obama administration undertook an intensive review of American policy toward Afghanistan, where U.S. troops had been fighting for eight years without achieving decisive results. Among the questions that generated discussion among policymakers and within the broader public was the extent to which the six-year-old effort to shore up a stable central government in Afghanistan had come to resemble the war in Vietnam. This cartoon by John Darkow appeared in the *Columbia* (Missouri) *Daily Tribune* on September 24.

CREDITS

Chapter 1: Vietnamese Nationalism and Communism

1.1. Truong Buu Lam, *Colonialism Experienced: Vietnamese Writings on Colonialism, 1900–1931* (Ann Arbor: University of Michigan Press, 2000), 109, 111, 113, 118–119. Reprinted by permission of the University of Michigan Press.

1.2. Record Group 256, Records of the American Commission to Negotiate Peace, 851G.00, National Archives and Records Administration, College Park, Maryland.

1.3. Ho Chi Minh, *Selected Writings (1920–1969)* (Hanoi: Foreign Language Publishing House, 1973), 39–41.

1.4. Duong Van Mai Elliott, *The Sacred Willow: Four Generations in the Life of a Vietnamese Family* (New York: Oxford University Press, 1999), 83–88, 91, 94, 98–99. Reprinted by permission of Oxford University Press.

1.5. State Department Central Files, 851G.00/4-545, National Archives and Records Administration, College Park, Maryland.

1.6. René J. Defourneaux Collection, Veterans History Project, Library of Congress. High-resolution image courtesy of David Marr.

1.7. Ho Chi Minh, *Selected Works*, vol. 3 (Hanoi: Foreign Languages Publishing House, 1961), 17–21.

Chapter 2: Colonial War to Cold War Crisis

2.1. Truong Chinh, *The Resistance Will Win* (Hanoi: Foreign Languages Publishing House, 1960), 111–119.

2.2. Fonds Haut-Commissariat de France en Indochine, série XIV, SLOTFOM, no. 16/ps/cab, Dépôt des Archives d'Outre Mer, Aix-en-Provence, France.

2.3. Elmer Messner Collection, RIT Archive Collections, Wallace Center, Rochester Institute of Technology, Rochester, New York. Reprinted by permission of the RIT Archive Collections.

2.4. Central Intelligence Agency Freedom of Information Act Electronic Reading Room, http://www.foia.cia.gov/sites/default/files/document_conversions/89801/DOC_0000258837.pdf.

2.5. *75 Years of the Communist Party of Viet Nam: A Selection of Documents from*

Nine Party Congresses (Hanoi: The Gioi Publishers, 2005), 147, 152–155.

2.6. *Foreign Relations of the United States, 1950–1952*, vol. 13, part 1 (Washington, D.C.: U.S. Government Printing Office, 1982), 93–98.

2.7. *Foreign Relations of the United States, 1952–1954*, vol. 13, part 1 (Washington, D.C.: U.S. Government Printing Office, 1982), 1163–1168.

Chapter 3: Between Two Storms

3.1. *Foreign Relations of the United States, 1952–1954*, vol. 13, part 2 (Washington, D.C.: U.S. Government Printing Office, 1982), 2286–2301.

3.2. Louis J. Walinsky, ed., *Agrarian Reform as Unfinished Business: The Selected Papers of Wolf Ladejinsky* (New York: Oxford University Press, 1977), 243–246, 259–260. Reprinted by permission of Oxford University Press.

3.3. Le Duan, *La Thu Vao Nam* [Letters to the South] (Hanoi: Su That, 1985). Translated by Robert K. Brigham and Le Phuong Anh. Reprinted by permission of Robert K. Brigham.

3.4. *Major Policy Speeches by President Ngo Dinh Diem*, 3d ed. (Saigon: Presidency of the Republic of Vietnam Press Office, 1957), 5–8.

3.5. Nguyen Thi Dinh, *No Other Road to Take* (Ithaca, N.Y.: Cornell University Southeast Asia Program Publications, 1976), 84–87. Translated by Duong Van Mai Elliott. Reprinted by permission of Southeast Asia Program Publications.

3.6. *Foreign Relations of the United States, 1958–1960*, vol. 1 (Washington, D.C.: U.S. Government Printing Office, 1986), 598–602.

Chapter 4: The Deepening Crisis

4.1. *Department of State Bulletin*, vol. 45, no. 1154 (August 7, 1961): 233–38.

4.2. *Foreign Relations of the United States, 1961–1963*, vol. 1 (Washington, D.C.: U.S. Government Printing Office, 1996), 607–610.

4.3. Tran Van Don, *Our Endless War: Inside Vietnam* (San Rafael, Calif.: Presidio, 1978), 82–84. Copyright © 1978 by Tran Van Don. Used by permission of Presidio Press, an imprint of Random House, a division of Random House LLC. All rights reserved.

4.4. *Foreign Relations of the United States, 1961–1963*, vol. 4 (Washington, D.C.: U.S. Government Printing Office, 1991), 18–20.

4.5. Douglas Pike Collection, Unit 02 - Military Operations, item number 2130303001, The Vietnam Center and Archive, Texas Tech University, Lubbock, Texas. This document, translated by U.S. officials from a captured Vietnamese-language document, was made available by the U.S. embassy in Saigon in 1971 as part of a series of releases entitled "Viet-Nam Documents & Research Notes."

4.6. FO 371/175501 and FO 371/175501, National Archives, Richmond, United Kingdom.

4.7. History and Public Policy Program Digital Archive, Cold War International History Project Working Paper 22, "77 Conversations," http://digitalarchive.wilsoncenter.org/document/113053.

Chapter 5: Americanization

5.1. *Foreign Relations of the United States, 1964–1968*, vol. 2 (Washington, D.C.: U.S. Government Printing Office, 1996), 174–185.

5.2. *Foreign Relations of the United States, 1964–1968*, vol. 2 (Washington, D.C.: U.S. Government Printing Office, 1996), 309–313.

5.3. *South Viet Nam National Front for Liberation: Documents* (Giai Phong Publishing House, 1968), 40–41, 43–44, 49–51.

5.4. *Public Papers of the Presidents of the United States: Lyndon B. Johnson, 1965*, vol. 1 (Washington, D.C.: U.S. Government Printing Office, 1966), 394–399.

5.5. *Washington Post*, June 15, 1965. A 1965 Herblock Cartoon, © The Herb Block Foundation.

5.6. *Foreign Relations of the United States, 1964–1968*, vol. 3 (Washington, D.C.: U.S. Government Printing Office, 1996), 190–196.

Chapter 6: The Wider War

6.1. *Human Events*, vol. 26, no. 11 (March 12, 1966), 3. Reprinted by permission of Eagle Publishing.

6.2. Reference number 09443, British Cartoon Archive, University of Kent, United Kingdom. Republished by permission of John Jensen.

6.3. Larry Berman Collection (Presidential Archives Research), folder 1, box 5, The Vietnam Center and Archive, Texas Tech University, http://www.vietnam.ttu .edu/virtualarchive/items.php?item=024 0501003.

6.4. Clayborne Carson and Kris Shepard, eds., *A Call to Conscience: The Landmark Speeches of Dr. Martin Luther King, Jr.* (New York: Warner Books, 2001), 139–160. Reprinted by arrangement with the Heirs to the Estate of Martin Luther King Jr., c/o Writers House as agent for the proprietor, New York, New York.

6.5. Rolando E. Bonachea and Nelson P. Valdes, eds., *Che: Selected Works of Ernesto Guevara* (Cambridge, Mass.: MIT Press, 1969), 170–182. © Ocean Press. www .oceanbooks.com.au/www.oceansur.com.

6.6. Central Intelligence Agency Collection, folder 191, box 14, The Vietnam Center and Archive, Texas Tech University. Accessed July 26, 2013. http://www .vietnam.ttu.edu/virtualarchive/items.php? item=04114191009.

6.7. Antoine Roy Collection, interview conducted on March 13, 2003, 158–167, The Vietnam Center and Archive, Texas Tech University, http://www.vietnam.ttu .edu/virtualarchive/items.php?item= OH0255.

Chapter 7. The Tet Offensive

7.1. *Department of State Bulletin*, vol. 57, no. 1485 (December 11, 1967), 785–788.

7.2. Associated Press photo by Hong Seong-Chan, January 31, 1968. Courtesy AP Images.

7.3. *Foreign Relations of the United States, 1964–1968*, vol. 6 (Washington, D.C.: U.S. Government Printing Office, 2002), 199–204.

7.4. *Reporting Vietnam: American Journalism, 1959–1969* (New York: Library of America, 1998), 581–582. Courtesy of CBS News Archives.

7.5. *Foreign Relations of the United States, 1964–1968*, vol. 6 (Washington, D.C.: U.S. Government Printing Office, 2002), 316–327.

7.6. Douglas Pike Collection, unit 1 – Assessment and Strategy, folder 6, box 7, The Vietnam Center and Archive, Texas Tech University, http://www.vietnam.ttu.edu/ virtualarchive/items.php?item=2120 706004.

7.7. Hearings before the Committee on Un-American Activities, House of Representatives, "Subversive Involvement in Disruption of 1968 Democratic Party National Convention," part 2, 90th Congress, second session (Washington, D.C.: U.S. Government Printing Office, 1968), 2654–2655, 2662, 2681–2685.

Chapter 8. New Departures

8.1. David Chanoff and Doan Van Toai, eds., "Vietnam": A Portrait of a People at War (London: I.B. Tauris, 1996), 107–110. Reprinted by permission of I.B. Tauris.

8.2. Nguyen Cong Luan, Nationalist in the Viet Nam Wars: Memoirs of a Victim Turned Soldier (Bloomington: Indiana University Press, 2012), 349–352. Reprinted with permission of Indiana University Press.

8.3. Foreign Relations of the United States, 1969–1976, vol. 6 (Washington D.C.: U.S. Government Printing Office, 2006), 370–374.

8.4. Public Papers of the Presidents of the United States, Richard M. Nixon, 1969 (Washington, D.C.: U.S. Government Printing Office, 1971), 901–909.

8.5. Getty Images, image no. 53372005.

8.6. Legislative Proposals Relating to the War in Southeast Asia, Hearings before the Committee on Foreign Relations, United States Senate, Ninety-Second Congress, First Session, April–May 1971 (Washington, D.C.: Government Printing Office, 1971), 180–210.

8.7. Foreign Relations of the United States, 1969–1976, vol. 17 (Washington, D.C.: U.S. Government Printing Office, 2006), 372–387.

Chapter 9: Peace and War

9.1. History and Public Policy Program Digital Archive, CWIHP Working Paper 22, "77 Conversations." 182–184, http://digitalarchive.wilsoncenter.org/document/113113.

9.2. Foreign Relations of the United States, 1969–1976, vol. 9 (Washington, D.C.: U.S. Government Printing Office, 2010), 449–460.

9.3. National Security Adviser's Presidential Correspondence with Foreign Leaders Collection, box 5, folder: Vietnam – President Nguyen Van Thieu, Gerald R. Ford Library, Ann Arbor, Michigan.

9.4. Larry Engelmann, ed., Tears Before the Rain: An Oral History of the Fall of South Vietnam (New York: Oxford University Press, 1990), 301–305. Reprinted by permission of Oxford University Press.

9.5. Department of State Bulletin, vol. 72, no. 1871 (May 5, 1975), 583–586.

9.6. Public Papers of the Presidents of the United States, Gerald R. Ford, 1975, vol. 1 (Washington, D.C.: U.S. Government Printing Office, 1977), 568–573.

Chapter 10: Lessons and Legacies

10.1. Mary Terrell Cargill and Jade Quang Huynh, eds., Voices of Vietnamese Boat People: Nineteen Narratives of Escape and Survival (Jefferson, N.C.: McFarland, 2000), 8–16. Reprinted by permission of McFarland and Company, Inc.

10.2. Ronald Reagan 1980 Presidential Campaign Papers, box 227, Ronald Reagan Presidential Library, Simi Valley, California.

10.3. National Press Club Archives, Washington, D.C.

10.4. Bridgeman Art Library, image no. XIR 200073.

10.5. *Public Papers of the Presidents, William J. Clinton, 2000–2001*, part 3 (Washington, D.C.: U.S. Government Printing Office, 2002), 2547–2551.

10.6. National Press Club Archives, Washington, D.C., and *Public Papers of the Presidents, George W. Bush, 2007*, part 2 (Washington, D.C.: U.S. Government Printing Office, 2011), 1102–1104.

10.7. Item number 69324, www.political-cartoons.com. By permission of John Darkow and Cagle Cartoons Inc. Newspaper Syndicate.

INDEX

Page numbers in bold indicate illustrations